MY LIFE IN
THE RUSSIAN THEATRE

VLADIMIR NEMIROVITCH-DANTCHENKO

[*Frontispiece*

VLADIMIR NEMIROVITCH-DANTCHENKO

MY LIFE
IN THE
RUSSIAN THEATRE

★

Translated by John Cournos

With an Introduction by Joshua Logan
A Foreword by Oliver M. Sayler and
A Chronology by Elizabeth Reynolds Hapgood

THEATRE ARTS BOOKS
NEW YORK

INTRODUCTION

He must have had a premonition I was going to write this introduction to his book. That was 35 years ago. I was an insignificant 21-year-old American student standing backstage at the Moscow Art Theatre while Russian stage-hands were dismantling the huge sets of one of the plays that were in the repertory of that season.

"Are you one of the Americans?" said a slight, dignified man with a carefully trimmed white beard, "Aren't there two of you here to learn about the Art Theatre?"

Agreeing, I turned to call Charles Leatherbee, the friend who was with me.

"Charlie," I said, "come over here. You must meet Mr.—." I stopped because I had not caught his name.

"Nemirovitch-Dantchenko," said the bearded gentleman.

I was stunned. Here before me stood the man who was the co-star of that most famous dualogue in theatrical history: the fiery 18-hour conversation that formulated the basis for the founding of the Moscow Art Theatre. We had read about this exciting meeting of two brilliant Russians in the Slavyansky Bazaar Restaurant in 1897. One was our idol Stanislavsky and the other was a man whose name we knew but whose present position was vague to us. And now here he stood.

"I have heard that you came all the way from America to see the Art Theatre and I know you have met Stanislavsky.

He and I both are responsible for it. I didn't want you to go back to America until we had met."

We were embarrassed. What he was implying was true. We had been in Moscow for weeks and had made no effort to meet Nemirovitch-Dantchenko. This was understandable because the dynamic Stanislavsky had completely absorbed our thoughts. We were there by arrangement with Stanislavsky. He would, of course, have seen to it that we met Nemirovitch-Dantchenko, but after his serious illness in 1928, Stanislavsky was no longer active in the theatre except to work with groups of actors and singers in his own home. That was why his secretary, Miss Tamantseva, was receiving us every evening before the performances as well as between acts in Stanislavsky's office at the theatre to explain the plot and dialogue of the plays we were seeing. Every afternoon we went to Stanislavsky's house (now the Stanislavsky Museum), and watched the rehearsals he was conducting.

Since it was he who had brought the Art Theatre to America in 1923 and 1924, and since he was a great actor as well as a director, it was he who left the more vivid impression on our audiences. It was his book too, *My Life In Art*, which had been read and re-read by all serious American drama students. "Stanislavsky" had become the byword, the password, to theatrical art. His name was the catalytic agent that changed any theatrical discussion into something "artistic," "worthwhile," golden.

We knew about Nemirovitch-Dantchenko and had we stopped to think in all the dizzy excitement of being in Moscow amid the gifted actors, seeing the dazzling productions, watching the thrilling rehearsals Stanislavsky was conducting—his name would have rung a very loud bell.

For the truth of the matter was that a large part of what

we were seeing, hearing, experiencing was due to this short man in a well-cut business suit, and with a carefully-trimmed square beard.

History behaves strangely with her credits. She couples the names of Chekhov and Stanislavsky while that of Nemirovitch-Dantchenko is not so familiar. Yet without him Chekhov might have stayed forever in Yalta, discouraged with the theatre and vowing never to write another play after the failure of *The Sea Gull* in St. Petersburg. Without him, too, Constantin Stanislavsky might have remained with his group of amateur actors on the fringe of the theatre and never become, as he did, its very core.

Yet slight as he was physically, Nemirovitch-Dantchenko was one of the few giants on the theatrical scene of all time.

Because of his reticence, this book will give you only a hint of the influence he had not only on the Russian theatre but also on the shape of the modern theatre in the Western world. Certainly the style of acting and direction and even of scenic production and play writing, which we take for granted today, is all influenced in part by the plays and productions of the Moscow Art Theatre. The old classical posturing and excessive intoning have been replaced by acting much closer to nature. Attitudinizing, false poetics, actors bowing after their entrance and then returning on stage after a dramatic exit to take one or more bows to the applauding public, while the play stood still, all characterized a theatre style that is now so far in the past that the oldest of us cannot remember it. And yet these were common practices all over Europe and America until they were outmoded almost in one fell swoop by the meeting of Nemirovitch-Dantchenko and Stanislavsky and the formation of their company.

Defining the exact contributions of the two men to the Art Theatre has defied many experts. Some said Stanislavsky was the "heart" and Nemirovitch-Dantchenko the "brain"; others make Stanislavsky a locomotive riding on the rails laid down by his co-director. Certainly Stanislavsky always refused to take the full credit. In thanking Gorky for a letter of praise he said that half of it must go to Nemirovitch-Dantchenko. In addition to being an "administrative genius" he was a successful playwright who shared a literary prize with Chekhov. Stanislavsky knew little about playwriting. He left the literary style entirely to his collaborator. But I wonder how many theatre lovers realize that Nemirovitch-Dantchenko was a superb director? He was a creator, an interpretive artist of the highest degree. He was greatly responsible for the actual staging and polishing of all of Chekhov's plays, of Gorky's *The Lower Depths*, most of Ibsen in translation, of Tolstoy and Dostoievsky. In 44 years he directed 47 Art Theatre plays, the last one shortly before his death. All this was in addition to his administrative duties and conferences with authors and forming a musical theatre of world renown. I did not see this last, which toured America in 1925, but I heard that *Carmencita and the Soldier*, which starred Olga Baklanova, was a milestone of originality.

During that winter of 1931 I had seen a production which was burned into my memory by the heat of its brilliance. It was *Resurrection*, a dramatization of Leo Tolstoy's novel, directed by Nemirovitch-Dantchenko. Kachalov, one of the great acting figures of the famous company, was playing the author-narrator. He appeared on the stage at the beginning of the play, talking intimately to the audience and fingering a pencil. As he talked, the curtain opened slowly behind him revealing a young nobleman sitting at a desk lost in a reverie. The setting was the richly furnished study in a great house. Behind the young man were numerous portraits of his ancestors hung in the Russian manner in such ordered profusion as almost to obscure the wall itself. The young nobleman spoke not a word, Kachalov talked for him and as he talked, he walked into the scene and crossed over to where the actor was sitting. Strong emotions were obviously absorbing the young man. Kachalov told us what they were. It did not seem to matter that one actor was giving voice to the feelings of another. There was a fusion that made one of two. Throughout the play this narrator walked through the middle of the scenes, speaking the unspoken thoughts of characters or making an author's comment. The scene continued around him as though the actors could not see him, yet he was part of the scene always. The final moments in the courtroom were brimming with emotion and enormously effective.

The pictorial effects of this production impressed me greatly. The Moscow Art Theatre has a revolving stage and allows for scenes with a depth of as much as 60 feet. Lavish stage pictures followed intimate scenes and there was a flow of feeling and thought that often became overpowering. All of these contrasting effects were achieved with a mastery that could only have been the work of a great director— Nemirovitch-Dantchenko.

A few days later I saw another of his works, a fantastic production called *Three Fat Men*. It was a Soviet propaganda play making fun of The Church, The Army and The Capitalist. The Three were represented by giant papier maché figures encasing actors who moved them and supplied the voices. It was a sort of proletariat *Alice in Won-*

derland. Although its political implications were as boring as any "message" play, the director gave a feast to the eyes and imagination that made the evening vivid and theatrical. It was Nemirovitch-Dantchenko in another mood.

I truly admired his work and hastily expressed my admiration for his staging of *Resurrection*. But there was no way to soften the fact that Stanislavsky was the chief reason for our trip to Russia. During Stalin's first Five-Year-Plan it was very extraordinary that two young Americans, just out of college, had been allowed to come to the Soviet Union, to study the production and acting technique of the Art Theatre. Until then there had been very little rapport between our two countries. Out trip was made possible by Charles R. Crane, an American philanthropist, who was Charles Leatherbee's grandfather. He had arranged for Charles to study with his friend Stanislavsky when Charles finished Harvard. Mr. Crane offered a scholarship for another student to accompany Charles on his Russian excursion. When I was chosen, I was still in my senior year at Princeton but my family allowed me to leave college and use my Princeton tuition to take advantage of this great opportunity. During that time Charles and I were part of a summer theatre group in Falmouth, Massachusetts, which called itself the University Players and was determined to become the American theatre that paralleled the Stanislavsky group. The company included Margaret Sullavan, Henry Fonda, James Stewart, Myron McCormick, Bretaigne Windust, Kent Smith, Mildred Natwick and Norris Houghton. We had all read Stanislavsky's book and marveled at the great tales of the Art Theatre. Since its director had started as ours did with a semi-amateur group of actors, we felt very close to him. I had decided to try to become a director and longed to watch the Master at work.

Seeing the Art Theatre's repertory of plays, which included some of the classics of our time, was a revelation to us. We met the great actors who were playing in the repertory. Moskvin, who had played the title role of the opening play of the Theatre in 1898, *Tsar Fyodor Ivanovitch*, was still playing in *The Cherry Orchard* in a production that had been prepared in 1904. Kachalov, Leonidov, and Chekhov's widow, Olga Knipper, were still playing.

Charles and I saw this great company when it was still in its golden age of creativity. There is no doubt that Stanislavsky contributed greatly to the acting technique and the "form" of the theatre.

But the man who was most responsible for the "content," the acquisition of the Chekhov plays and later those of Gorky and Tolstoy, was the man who introduced himself to me all those years ago and helped preserve in my memory the name of one of the greatest men of the world theatre—Nemirovitch-Dantchenko.

Joshua Logan
Burbank, California
1967

FOREWORD

Twenty years ago, America knew the Moscow Art Theatre only as a vague rumour of distant and incredible glories. Already, this extraordinary institution was nearly two decades old, but, like everything else under the wings of the Double Eagle, it remained a thing of mystery to those few who had heard about it at all.

Then began that series of revelations which were destined to make the Moscow Art Theatre the most influential single factor in the renaissance of our American Theatre—a series which reaches its climax in this volume of memoirs by the co-founder of the world's foremost stage.

It was my privilege, with 'The Russian Theatre' in 1920, to serve as prophet and interpreter. Six months after the March, 1917, Revolution, I crossed the Pacific and Siberia, determined to obtain the story of the Moscow Art Theatre before it was too late. If I had underestimated its vitality, I had not underrated its importance, for it not only survived the Soviet Revolution, but in time, with its perfected technique and organization, became the chief dramatic inspiration of the new social order, the theatre which every other stage in the Soviet Union still seeks to emulate.

For three years, sceptics doubted my report. But then came the second major revelation. Confirmed in his ambition by Feodor Chaliapin and myself, Morris Gest boldly brought the entire Moscow Art Theatre to America and led

it to the most triumphant success in the history of the
Theatre International by a campaign rivalling in brilliance
the acting of Constantin Stanislavsky and his fellow
players.

For the first time in the history of the American stage, we
saw exemplified the *possibility* and the *necessity* of the
Organized Theatre, of the Art Theatre—if our theatre were
ever to be more than mere amusement. From the acclaim
which these player artists received, our own players, great
and small, took new pride and confidence in their calling.
And, finally, the American people and the Russian people
won a new respect for each other which culminated years
later in restoration of normal diplomatic relations between
the two countries.

There were other revelatory chapters. Before returning
home, Stanislavsky completed and published here his autobiography, *My Life in Art*. And in 1925, Mr. Gest brought
to America Stanislavsky's collaborator in the founding of the
Moscow Art Theatre: Vladimir Nemirovitch-Dantchenko,
and his Musical Studio, lyric offshoot of the parent stage.

But, somehow or other, in spite of all these revelations, an
air of mystery lingered. What and who made the Moscow
Art Theatre possible?

This volume is the final and fully satisfying answer. In the
first place, it clarifies the position and function of Nemirovitch in the annals of the Moscow Art Theatre. And, in the
second, it clarifies the position and function of the Moscow
Art Theatre in the life of Russia and in the family of the
world's great theatres.

It was some years after I first met Nemirovitch-Dantchenko that I came to a full realization of the nature of his

collaboration with Stanislavsky. As I have explained in the chapter, 'A Grand Duke Incognito', in *Inside the Moscow Art Theatre*, that first meeting occurred while the bullets of the Soviet Revolution were still raking the doorways of Moscow's curved streets. Of necessity, since Stanislavsky was always the recluse, the hermit-artist, Nemirovitch was devoting his entire energy to the difficult administrative task of keeping the Art Theatre open and running.

In time, of course, I became aware of the fact—which these pages so conclusively and eloquently, though modestly, reveal—that Nemirovitch was far more than an administrator, genius that he was in that rôle. In fact, he had rivalled his great associate as a creative artist, surpassing him in literary vision and understanding. It had been he, instead of Stanislavsky, who had first believed in Chekhov and had lured him back into the theatre he had abandoned after the failure of 'The Sea Gull' in St. Petersburg.

Here, then, was a major reason, I told Nemirovitch, why he had to write his memoirs. Stanislavsky might put the actor and the trainer of actors eternally in his debt by attempting to formulate and state his 'system', as he did in *My Life in Art*. But it was only Nemirovitch—Nemirovitch, the novelist; Nemirovitch, the playwright; Nemirovitch, the critic; Nemirovitch, the suave man of the world who had tasted life's passions deeply and widely—who could recreate for posterity the three literary Titans who had fed the repertory of the Moscow Art Theatre until it was able to transmute into dramatic jewels anything that came its way: Chekhov, Gorky, Tolstoy—not to mention the dozens and scores of personalities from all walks of life who influenced the fate of the Art Theatre in one way or another.

[xv]

Only Nemirovitch, the diplomat, the brilliant extrovert, could paint the canvas of the life into which the Moscow Art Theatre was born and through which it struggled to maturity. Only Nemirovitch, the administrator, could make it clear that the Moscow Art Theatre was neither a miracle nor an accident!

For the Moscow Art Theatre is neither a miracle nor an accident. If it had been either the one or the other, it would have passed long ago into the limbo for abortive projects in the arts. Instead of holding the unassailable position to-day of the 'pattern-theatre' of the Soviet Union, instead of re-taining its pre-eminent rank among the world's great stages, it would have succumbed to the exigencies of social up-heaval.

As the following pages attest with disarming simplicity, the Moscow Art Theatre is the logical product of forces and factors which, if they ever came together at any other time or in any other place, would probably result in a comparable institution. True, the list of those forces and factors is rather formidable. They are not likely to foregather simultane-ously very often in human history. But there is nothing supernatural or adventitious about their foregathering. At the joint behest of two middle-aged men—Nemirovitch was forty, Stanislavsky thirty-six—they foregathered in Moscow in 1898. At the behest of anyone equally intelligent, equally devoted, equally able to command support, they can be made to foregather anywhere, at any time!

To begin with, there must be some leader or leaders who look upon the theatre as an art and not primarily as a busi-ness. No mere lip service, either. Passionate conviction!

Next, that leader must be practical in the sense of knowing

[xvi]

how to judge human nature and human talent. No un-balanced fanatic visionary need apply!

Then he must have potential recruits among actors and craftsmen of all kinds who are as devoted as he to the theatre as an art.

A receptive attitude toward creative talent is not enough in such a leader. If the right actors are not readily available, they must be sought with a sixth sense that reveals what they *might* become. If the right plays are not submitted, there must be vision to see a play in a writer who may never have dreamed himself a dramatist.

And finally there must be a playgoing public, too, which believes in the theatre as an art and not as mere pastime.

Oddly enough, economics, favourable or unfavourable, and social issues seem to have very little to do with the problem. The Moscow Art Theatre was born under the Tsar without a silver spoon in its mouth. It successfully survived the Russo-Japanese War and the 1905 Revolution, emerging stronger than ever. It endured through the World War, with its production schedule only slightly curtailed. And finally, it made the transition to the utterly new and strange Soviet economy with prestige and ideals unimpaired.

Is it possible that an Art Theatre, in the long run, pays better than the kind we know?

OLIVER M. SAYLER

CONTENTS

PART I

ANTON CHEKHOV

CONTENTS

PART II

BIRTH OF THE NEW THEATRE

CONTENTS

PART III

MAXIM GORKY

[xxi]

CONTENTS

PART IV

THE FIRST TOUR ABROAD

[xxii]

CONTENTS

PART V

THE TOLSTOYAN ELEMENTS IN THE ART THEATRE

ILLUSTRATIONS

[xxv]

PART I
ANTON CHEKHOV

CHAPTER ONE

·

MY biographers find that I was infatuated with Chekhov: hence the performance of 'The Sea Gull' in the
Art Theatre—a play which had had no success whatsoever
when it was presented two years before on the official stage
in St. Petersburg with a cast of superb actors.

Critics of the Art Theatre insist, however, that its history
begins only chronologically with the first performance of
'Tsar Fyodor', and that its actual beginning must be reckoned
from the time of the 'Sea Gull' production, as only from
Chekhov were the *new* theatre and its revolutionary significance clearly defined.

Finally, one of my biographers affirms that the will of my
entire life was directed toward one object: the creation of
the Art Theatre; that everything which I had sought as a
dramatist, author, journalist, stage director, theatrical pedagogue, and even amateur actor in my youth—everything
aspired toward the historical meeting with Stanislavsky,
which developed into an eighteen-hour conversation, giving
birth to the Art Theatre.

Thus, between all my labours in literature and the theatre,
my infatuation for the creative works of Chekhov and the
creation of the Art Theatre, there is established a deep inner
bond.

Now, when I turn to my recollections, I am quite ready to
believe this. I cannot recall Chekhov without associating

[3]

with his name this or that period of my personal, literary, or theatrical experiences. We lived in the same epoch, met the same people, participated in the same surrounding life, were drawn to similar ideals; it therefore becomes clear why the new colours, new rhythms, new words, which Chekhov had found for his stories found so poignant a response in me. We made use—as it were—of the same life materials and for one and the same object, which may explain why, with such infatuation, I seized upon his poetry, his lyricism, his un-anticipated truth.

Apart from that, we were similarly dissatisfied with the old theatre; I perhaps more keenly than Chekhov, because I devoted myself to the theatre more than he; he more deeply, because he suffered from it, suffered with the most painful reactions of a writer's conscience: there was incomprehensibility here, and disillusion, and repressed indignity.

That is why my recollections of Chekhov meet in me, like crossroads, with recollections of those paths which led to the birth of the Moscow Art Theatre—the *Theatre of Chekhov*.

I see three portraits of Chekhov before me, each snatched from a portion of his life.

The first: Chekhov, 'the man of great promise'. He writes an endless number of stories, some of them very short, others quite tiny, which appear chiefly in humorous periodicals and, for the most part, under the signature of 'A. Chekhonte'. How many of them had he written? Many years later, when Chekhov sold all his works and was making a selection of those to be republished in book form, I asked him, and his answer was: 'About a thousand!' These were

[4]

mostly of an anecdotal nature, superb in invention, in wit, hitting the mark, very characteristic of him.

But he is already passing to his major stories.

He loves company and would rather listen than talk. He has not the slightest self-conceit. He is regarded as 'incontrovertibly gifted', but who could have guessed that this name would find its place among the Russian classics?

The second portrait: Chekhov is already acknowledged 'among the most gifted'. His volume of tales, *Twilight*, receives the full Academy prize; he writes less, and more restrainedly; every new story from his pen is talked about; he is in demand among all editors. But the leader of the youth of the day, Mikhailovsky, does not cease to emphasize that Chekhov is a writer without ideas; and this is not without its effect and holds back loud and unanimous acclaim. On the other hand, the great Tolstoy says: 'Here's an author of whom it is pleasant to speak.'

Grigorovitch, now an old man, one of the so-called 'Coryphaeuses' of Russian literature, goes even further. When some one, in his presence, began to compare a writer of no great gifts but with 'ideas' with Chekhov, Grigorovitch said: 'He is not worthy of kissing the trail of the flea which has bitten Chekhov!' Of the story *Cold Blood* he said— almost in a whisper, it is true, as if he were saying something audacious: 'Put that story on the same shelf with Gogol!' Then he added: 'You see how far I go'.

Another Coryphaeus of Russian literature, Boborikin, said that he gave himself the pleasure of reading every day, without fail, a tale of Chekhov's.

At this period, Chekhov moves in the very midst of the metropolitan whirlpool, in the circles of artists and writers—

[5]

now in Moscow, now in St. Petersburg. He loves gatherings, witty conversations, the wings of the theatre; he travels a great deal in Russia and abroad; buoyant, he remains, as before, unassuming, and prefers to observe and to listen to others rather than do the talking himself. His fame is steadily growing.

The third portrait: Chekhov in the Art Theatre.

The second period of my recollections ends somehow abruptly with the failure of 'The Sea Gull' in St. Petersburg. It was as if this had broken his life and that here it had taken a sharp turn. Up to now there has been scarcely any mention of his disease, but, as it happens, immediately following the episode of the failure we can no longer imagine Chekhov other than as a human being gradually noticeably undermined by an invisible malady.

He writes less and less, two or three things a year; he grows stricter with himself. The most marked note in his stories is that, while remaining objective in his attitude, cultivating his enormous artistic mastery, he allows his personages to discuss life more and more, chiefly the life of the Russian intelligentsia, lost in contradictions, indulging in dreaming and inaction. From among all these discussions, with unmistakable precision, you will distinguish the thoughts of the author himself, always shrewd, well-aimed, noble, exquisitely expressed and with superb taste. Every new story by him becomes something of a literary event.

But the chief figure in this period is Chekhov the playwright, Chekhov the creator of the new theatre. He almost eclipses himself as a man of letters. His popularity grows; his image, through the theatre, attains a new charm. He becomes the most beloved of all authors; the complaint against his lack of ideas dies away; his name yields only before the great Tolstoy, still living among us and unceasing in his labours.

But even while his fame is growing, his end is approaching. His readers greet every new production not with the usual unconcern with which readers greet their favourite authors' works, but with a kind of tender gratitude, with a knowledge that here are the weakened forces of flames shortly to be extinguished.

Such are the three portraits in the course of eighteen years. Chekhov was forty-three years old when he died in 1904.

Writers' circles were often organized in Moscow; these were usually very short-lived. The leader of one of these circles was Nikolai Kitcheyev, editor of the periodical *Budilnik* (*Alarm-clock*). Always courteous, correct, and amiable, somewhat cool, and ailing, he never raised his voice and scarcely ever laughed; it was odd to think of him as the editor of a humorous journal. But he loved laughter above everything on earth, was sensible of its power, and was one of those who considered wit the greatest boon given to men. I had already known him a long time; in the years of my literary beginnings he and I jointly ran a theatrical department in the *Budilnik* under the common signature of 'Nicks and Kicks'.

It was a sufficiently variegated circle. Politically, the direction was liberal, but with quite sharp deviations to the left and to the right. At a time when some regarded 'social problems' as the chief function of creative art, others valued its form, the living image, the word. The former deliberately mixed politics with every theme; after supper they made such speeches that it was necessary to glance at the servants who waited on us, and we always wondered if there were spies among them. The others remained cool and made no effort to reply out of a feeling of comradeship.

Real 'liberals' accepted this phrase with pride. Even now I recall Goltzev at some banquet or other. He remained to the end of his life a very honest man and a journalist devoted to progress. But no sooner did he begin his after-dinner speech than he spread coldness, and the more earnest he was, the more he flushed, the duller he became. The liberal-minded young ladies, however, were pleased with his beautiful words; they and the majority of the listeners, with solemn faces, showed sympathetic appreciation of every Goltzev command, and warmly applauded when he rounded out a period. They were particularly pleased because they already shared the sentiments he expressed.

I happened to be travelling with Chekhov in a droshky; the cabby failed to turn from the rails in time, and the droshky collided with a tram and overturned; there was alarm, fright, outcries. We rose unhurt; I said: 'You see, in one instant we might have been killed.'

'It is nothing to die,' said Chekhov; 'but think, Goltzev would make a farewell speech on the grave—that would be far worse!' But this did not hinder us from treating Goltzev with respect.

Among writers, Stchedrin was their great idol—not, mind you, for his immense satirical gifts, but for his shining liberalism. At that time they had worked out the stencilled rule: at every gathering at which there are speeches and

[8]

wine, a telegram of greeting must be sent to Stchedrin. (He lived in St. Petersburg.)

Purely aesthetic problems were regarded with suspicion. 'Ah, art for art's sake? . . . "Whispers, timid breathing, the nightingales did trill"? [1] . . . I congratulate you!'

The opposing camp of writers also grew. The common-places, the *clichés*, the stereotyped thoughts had become tedious. And disgust was evoked by the fact that often behind the labels 'radiant personality', 'fighter for freedom', were hidden men without gifts, scheming fellows. . . .

The critic Mikhailovsky, who ruled over the young intellects, controlled the reins of the new creative literature. In no jesting spirit was it said that to attain success in literature it was necessary to suffer, to be sent into exile, if only for a few years. At one time a tremendous success was enjoyed by Grigory Matchtet, a writer whose entire literary talent consisted in his long, handsome beard; but he happened to have written a short story which was published immediately on his return from political exile. Yet the real living talent of a writer like Stcheglov did not attract the slightest attention. The poetical form was held in contempt. There remained only Nekrasov's 'Sow the good, the intelligent . . .', or Plestcheyev's 'Forward without fear or doubt . . . " which were quoted to satiety. Pushkin and Lermontov were forgotten.

At a gathering in a private room of a restaurant Chekhov appeared. Kitcheyev, introducing us, whispered: 'This man will go far!'

It was possible to call him handsome. A good figure;

[1] From a famous lyrical poem, considered a model of 'pure art', without ideas.

pleasantly waving chestnut-brown hair, thrown backward; a small beard and moustaches. He held himself modestly, but without visible timidity; his gestures were restrained. His voice was a low bass with a deep metallic quality; his diction was pure Russian, with a shade of pure Great Russian idiom; his intonations were flexible, even passing into a kind of sing-song, without, however, the slightest sentimentality and certainly without a shadow of artifice.

In the course of an hour it was possible to note two other marked characteristics. There was some sort of inner equilibrium, the calm of independence. There was not even the suspicion of that smile which never leaves the faces of two *vis-à-vis*, meeting on some mutually pleasing theme. You are aware of that strained amiable smile, expressing: 'Ah, how pleasant it is for me to chat with you', or, 'We have, of course, one and the same taste with you!'

But his smile—this was his second characteristic—was unique. It appeared all at once, quickly, and as quickly vanished. It was broad, frank, full-faced, and always brief. It was as if the man had quite suddenly decided that the matter wasn't worth smiling about further.

Of course, I knew his stories. He had signed his own name to many of them; and only the trifles did he sign 'Chekhonte'. He had but lately produced his first play, 'Ivanov', in Korsh's private theatre. He had written it in eight days, at one go. He had not even tried to offer it to the Imperial Theatre. A marvellous actor, Davidov, then played at Korsh's private theatre, which agreed to take the play.

It seems that the actors played 'Ivanov' fairly well. At all events, they were often and generously praised in Chekhov's family. But the success was an uneven one, and for a private theatre this is as good as a failure.

Two critics had the ear of the Moscow theatrical circles at the time: Flerov-Vassiliev, and the somewhat foppish Peter Kitcheyev, a namesake of Nikolai Kitcheyev, the editor of *Budilnik*. Peter Kitcheyev abused the play and employed all sorts of arguments to show that Chekhov could not be a poet because he was a physician. The critic Flerov, who in general deserves the most grateful remiscence, also criticized the play, but ended his criticism somewhat in this wise: 'Nevertheless, I cannot avoid the impression that the young author has real gifts.'

That, indeed, his gifts required a new and particular theatrical approach to his play was a thought that failed to enter not only the minds of the critics, but even the author's mind; the thought, in fact, was not yet born.

Before 'Ivanov' he had written two one-act jests: 'The Bear' and 'The Proposal'. They enjoyed a great success, were played everywhere and often. Chekhov said to me more than once: 'Write vaudeville pieces! You'll find them profitable.'

The charm of these jests was not alone in their comic situations, but also in that the characters were living human beings and not stage vaudeville figures, and spoke a language full of humour and typical surprises. But these jests were to be seen only on private stages.

'Ivanov' was published in a 'thick' periodical. Monthly journals, as a rule, did not publish plays; but for Chekhov —as you see—an exception was made. It is true, the fee he received was a small one; so small, in fact, that I remember Chekhov scarcely believed me when I told him that I received more than thrice as much for a play published in a weekly journal.

As it happens, it was in this same season that my new comedy, 'The Last Will', was produced in the Imperial Small Theatre. This play greatly pleased the actors. It was written, as was said in those days, in soft tones; it did not offend any one and revolutionized nothing; the chief thing about it was its excellent rôles: big scenes with temperament and effective exits.

At that time actors used to be called out in the midst of a scene. They came forward and bowed, while the other actors had to turn into dolls and wait until their colleague had finished bowing before they could resume the action.

One had to know how to write these exits. I remember the third act was indeed a series of effective exits. Muzil was called out once, and Fedotova twice, and Nikulin no less than three times. And how? By the whole theatre. Fedotova could not take offence at this, because she still had a whole scene before her with an effective curtain.

Even before the production there was quite a diverting battle for one rôle. It is pertinent to tell of it here, because the episode was typical of the theatre of the time. Within ten years something of a like problem would arise in connection with the production of 'Uncle Vanya' in the Art Theatre, and what a difference there would be in the solution of the conflict!

Muzil chose 'The Last Will' for his benefit performance. This was very flattering to the author, because Muzil, enjoying the friendship of Ostrovsky, produced every one of his new plays. The Moscow public had grown accustomed to this presentation of the *première* of the famous dramatist as a benefit performance by Muzil; and this happened to be his first such performance after Ostrovsky's death.

Then, suddenly, the first actress of the Theatre announced her intention of taking 'The Last Will' for her benefit performance. Muzil had to relinquish it to her.

There was in the play the winning rôle of the manager's wife; this rôle was assigned to Nikulina. But Fedotova, taking the play for her benefit performance, protested, and all this was equivalent to a demand—that the rôle must be given to Sadovskaya, an actress no less distinguished than Nikulina. The latter mutinied. The stage manager and the director of the Theatre were powerless to contend with the desire of Fedotova. The author helplessly shrugged his shoulders: he appreciated the equal abilities of the two actresses. At first Nikulina stormed, then she wept; she ended by taking the express-train to St. Petersburg in order to complain there to the Director of the Imperial Theatres, and, in the event of his failing to help her, to appeal to the Minister himself.

She returned with a letter to the manager. But Sadovskaya refused to surrender her rôle. Then Fedotova, in great confusion, gave up her intention of presenting the play. Little wonder the author was perturbed. But Muzil renewed his request and took the play. As far as it concerned the wife of the manager in the play (Muzil himself played the manager's part), he said to the author: 'Please allow me to settle the question. Both Nikulina and Sadovskaya are good friends of mine, and I'll somehow bring them to terms.' For several days he held feverish discussions with them. The more temperamental Nikulina won.

The Comédie Française of Paris alone could rival the excellence of the Moscow Small Theatre. The play was performed by the best actors—Fedotova, Ermolova, Nikulina, Lensky, Yuzhin, Ribakov, Muzil, all famous names—and was given before full houses. As for St. Petersburg, the play was staged there as a benefit performance for the leading actress Savina, in the presence of the Royal Family, and the author was honoured by the personal praise of Emperor Alexander III. He stood on the stage, near Savina, surrounded by his retinue, tall, robust, with a large beard and prominent bald spot. As I was approaching him, the director of the Theatres followed me, whispering: 'Don't address him first! Please don't address him first!'

I did not become acquainted with Chekhov's 'Ivanov' until it was published. At the time it appeared to me as merely a rough draft for an excellent play.

The first act, one of Chekhov's best 'nocturnes', made a deep impression on me. Apart from that, I was enraptured by the enviable boldness and lightness with which the author stripped off the pharisaic masks. But the comic figures seemed overdone, some of the scenes were a bit venturesome, the architectonics lacked harmony. It is evident that I too, at the time, did not do full justice to the forces of poetical creativeness in Chekhov. Engaged as I was in developing the stage form still controlled by the 'art of the Small Theatre', I made the same demands on Chekhov.

And this solicitude for the stage form familiar to me screened from my vision his inspired combination of simple, living, workaday truth with profound lyricism.

We did not meet often in the early days of our acquaintance; we could scarcely call ourselves 'friends'. In any case,

I do not know if Anton Pavlovitch was particularly friendly
with any one. Was this possible for him?

He was one of a large family: father, mother, four
brothers, and a sister. I am under the impression that his
relations with them differed: some he loved more, others
less. On one side were his mother, two brothers and his
sister; on the other, his father and the remaining brothers.
His brother Nikolai, a young artist, died, as it happened,
during the first years of our acquaintance. His other brother,
Ivan, I used constantly to meet at Anton Pavlovitch's place
in the village, as well as in the Crimea. Ivan, unless I am
mistaken, was the eldest. He—I felt this with particular
keenness after Anton Pavlovitch's death—reminded me
extraordinarily of him, in his voice, his intonations, and in
one of his gestures: the flourishing of a fist in the air to
accentuate his words.

I do not precisely know what the relation was between
'A. P.' and his father, but here is something he once told me.

This was when we had already been intimate for some
years, and while we were spending a winter together on the
French Riviera. We were leaving together, after an intimate
dinner given by the then celebrated professor, Maxim Kova-
levsky, who had his villa in Beaulieux. We were walking
during the 'winter spring', attired in summer overcoats, in
the midst of tropical verdure, and were speaking of youth-
fulness, youth, and childhood; and this is what I heard:
'Do you know, I could *never* forgive my father for having
beaten me as a child!'

But towards his mother he had the most tender feelings.
His solicitude reached the point where, no matter where he
went, he had to write to her every day, if only a line or two.

This did not hinder him from making an occasional jest at her piety. He would suddenly ask: '*Mamasha!* Is it true that monks wear drawers?'

'There it is again! Antosha is always saying such things!' she would say in a soft, pleasant, low voice, very quietly. And she was always so quiet, so gentle, so uncommonly gracious.

His sister, Marya Pavlovna, being the only girl in the family, enjoyed a privileged position. But her deep devotion to Anton Pavlovitch in particular was evident at the first glance. This only increased with time. Finally, she ran the whole house, dedicating her entire life to him and her mother. After her brother's death she was wholly engaged in preserving his memory; she watched over the house and all its arrangments and relics, published his letters, and so on.

Nor was Anton Pavlovitch wanting in devotion to his sister. Subsequently, to judge from the published letters, this at times even awakened the jealousy of his wife, Olga Knipper.

Anton Pavlovitch very early became the 'provider' for the whole family and, so to speak, its head. I do not remember when his father died. I met him but rarely. There has re-mained in my memory his slight figure and grey beard.

During the first years A. P. was constantly in need of money, as—with a few insignificant exceptions—all the Russian writers have been. The letters of A. P., like the letters of most writers, were at the time full of requests for money. The question of fees, how much this or that author receives, what the different publishers pay, had a leading place in conversations.

In the editor's office of *Budilnik* the talk once turned on the benefits a writer received from being paid 'by the line', and Chekhov argued that it was more profitable to write in short lines than in long periods, that it wouldn't do to imitate Gogol. He added that it was possible to receive as much for ten words as for ten solid lines.

'Just try it!' said Kitcheyev, leaning back in his chair before the editorial table and playing with a long pencil.

'And you'll pay?'

'Yes, I'll pay.'

Chekhov remained standing for half a minute or so in a concentrated attitude, then snatched the pencil from Kitcheyev's hand and wrote on the spot.

Dialogue

'Listen!'

'What?'

'Native?'

'Who?'

'You.'

'I?'

'Yes.'

'No.'

'Pity!'

'H'm!'

Incidentally, it should be said that Anton Pavlovitch was scrupulously accurate in his accounts. He could not bear to owe anybody; he was very prudent, but not miserly, and never wasteful; he conducted himself toward money as toward a great necessity, while his attitude toward wealthy folk was that their wealth was their private affair; it could not concern him in the least and could not in any wise change his conduct towards them.

When he visited Monte Carlo he gambled, but in a limited way and with restraint, never once taking great risk; for the most part he won. He never gambled in the Moscow clubs.

He gave much thought to providing for his mother and sister after his death.

When he conceived the idea of buying an estate, I asked him how could he think of bothering with it. He replied: 'Well, one won't have to think of paying house rent or buying firewood.'

Some one, in trying to write something particularly flattering about Chekhov, called him 'a champion of freedom'. Of course he appreciated freedom as the first necessity of human existence, but for him to read such a thing about himself would have been vexing in the extreme, 'but, please, what sort of champion am I?' And he would have paced the room with big steps, his hands in his pockets. 'I wouldn't shake his hand for writing such rot!' he would have added with regard to the author, straightening his pince-nez on its string in his perturbation.

Thus I picture him to myself in his last years; but in his younger years, when he did not yet wear a pince-nez, no epithet could have suited him less than 'champion'.

Eight or nine years after 'Ivanov', Treplev in 'The Sea Gull' was to say: 'We need new forms, and if they are not here, then nothing is needed.'

The dream of some kind of new theatre is never met with in Chekhov, and at no time and nowhere has he come forward as a 'champion' of new forms, neither in disputes, nor in vehement conversation, nor in any article.

[18]

More than that. Even after a year's existence of the Art Theatre, when 'The Sea Gull' had been rehabilitated, after the new forms had actually been tried, Chekhov offered his next play, 'Uncle Vanya', to the Imperial Theatre. He did not want to violate personal relations, he did not want to emphasize that he preferred the young company to the famous company of the Small Theatre. What sort of champion was this?

It is hard to say how deep was his desire to write for the theatre. In any case, for many years he gave the impression that he considered playwriting quite a secondary occupation. Was this attitude wholly sincere, or did he force himself to think so? I cannot say. I do not think any one could have known.

He did not want anyone to forget that he was, first of all, a physician, then a writer, and only last a dramatist. The last, in any case, was only incidental. As a very astute man, he clearly saw that for a play to secure production on the Imperial stage it was necessary to write in some particular way or to make the proper connections in the field of personal acquaintance. A certain writer said: 'Talent is necessary for the writing of a play, but genius for its production.' There was no incentive in Chekhov to overcome his rivals; he preferred to regard the theatre as a source of additional income.

Between Chekhov's characters and those which were brought by playwrights to the old actors there is an abyss. There is no question here of that stage lacquer which we dramatists considered so essential for covering our heroes and especially our heroines. They are simple people, speaking about the simplest things, in the simplest language, in surroundings of everyday life. None among them indulge in pathetic or lachrymose monologues, in talk of eternal ideals; none are dressed by the author in a heroic toga; on the contrary, he strips them, underlines their abominable hysteria, their petty egoism. Nevertheless, the heart widens with sympathy—not so much toward them, these people, as toward some vague dream for a better life.

And, with all this extraordinary simplicity, the final effect is astonishingly musical: this abandoned farm, this moonlit night, these sheaves of hay, this hoot of the owl, this repressed calm of Sarah, this yearning of Ivanov, this weeping violoncello of the Count.

There is no invention here. What is remarkable is that Chekhov himself did not comprehend the wealth of colours and sounds which he poured out in his scenes. He simply wanted to write a play, the most ordinary play.

And, like every dramatist, he thought of devising good rôles for the actors. He did not give the slightest thought to revolutionizing the theatre. He did not even give a thought to being more original than some one else. In a most sincere manner he wanted to meet the demands which were made on the playwright of the contemporary theatre.

He represented human beings only as he had observed them in life, and he could not dissociate them from their surroundings: from the rosy morning or the blue twilight, from sounds, odours, rain, trembling shutters, the lamp, the stove, the samovar, the piano, the harmonica, tobacco, the sisters, the in-laws, neighbours, song, drink, from everyday existence, from the million trifles which give warmth to life.

He looked at human beings with his own eyes, and not with those of Tolstoy, of Dostoievsky, of Turgenev, of

[20]

Ostrovsky; least of all did he regard them with the eyes of Goltzev, Mikhailovsky, and the journalists and publicists.

A district doctor ! Think of it; it was enough just to utter these words to bring an expression of admiration to the faces of the Russian *intelligent*,[1] the student, the college girl. Once the district doctor appears on the scene, the sympathies of the public are secure; here is the 'radiant personality', the 'common ideal', the device for the 'positive' character in the play. In my own 'Last Will' one of the principal characters is a district doctor—and, naturally, he is a good man.

Or an honest man, who boldly tells every one the truth and utters tirades about honesty, about one's duty at every step—in short, he is the heroic character in the drama. And suddenly this hero, the district doctor Lvov, in 'Ivanov', left alone, says: 'The devil knows what! As if it weren't enough that they don't pay for their visits . . . [etc.]'

There! A single line, a short phrase, and the mask is stripped off. And the further you go, the clearer it becomes that here is a type of narrow-minded, petty, 'hard-boiled', egoistical phrasemonger. He is honest, terribly honest—you can see a mile away how honest he is; in the words of the Count, he is 'bursting' with honesty, but when chivalrously he cries: 'Mister Ivanov! I proclaim in the hearing of all that you're a scoundrel . . .' then there is no longer a single member of the audience on his side. And every one thinks, 'Confound his honesty!'

Well, how could an actor flame in this rôle? How could the 'dramatic amateur' Solonin act this part in Korsh's theatre when the essence of his acting had been developed so

[1] A member of the intelligentsia. The 'g' is pronounced as in the word 'good'.

as to 'bring down the house' with such noble, passionate catchwords?

How was it possible for the chief character of the piece, Ivanov himself, with whom the author's sympathies clearly lie, to shout at his consumptive wife in the passionate final scene of the third act: 'Jewess!' and immediately afterwards: 'Know, then, that you'll soon die. The doctor told me.'

Or take Sarah's rôle: the dramatic scene is in progress, and she says: 'Let's turn somersaults on the stage'—and she a Jewess! Should not her lines be spoken with an accent? Yes, within fifteen years, when 'Ivanov' was to be produced in the Art Theatre, Knipper would act the rôle of Sarah with an effusion of Jewish intonations.

Other actors were necessary for Chekhov, a histrionic art of another kind. And something else.

Consider: among the actors of the time there were a good many with considerable gifts, with a refined taste and sensitive literary judgment. That splendid actor, Davidov, who played the rôle of Ivanov in Moscow, on returning to the St. Petersburg Imperial stage prevailed upon the management to perform 'Ivanov'.

And 'Ivanov' even scored a great success. But this success left not a trace in the theatre; because there was nothing strictly 'Chekhovian' about it—it was not the same world that had been created in Chekhov's imagination. There was nothing new in it. There were the same people the public had so often seen, the same attractive individualities of Savina, Varlamov, Dalmatov, Strapetova, and the rest, in their inspired theatrical mood. A new wig and a new mode in dress did not change the *human being*. Quite apart from this, there were the same green decorations representing the village—a garden which the public had seen yesterday in quite another play and would see to-morrow in a third play; the same diffused greenish electric illumination, which the public had grown accustomed to consider as lunar light, though there was nothing about it remotely resembling the moon. There were the same immense pavilions, which but yesterday were supposed to represent merchants' mansions, while to-day they were but the small, cosy rooms of a farmhouse.

The favourite actors had scored a success: it was so pleasant to see them again in other attire and in other make-up; and the success was also to the credit of the author, whom the public was beginning to love for his stories.

But the most important thing was lacking. Without it, all the rest had only a moderate, transient value; there was nothing of that new reflection of the life about one which Chekhov brought to the stage; in short, there was no Chekhov here.

CHAPTER TWO

During the winter we lived in Moscow or St. Petersburg, while we sought to pass the summer in the village and in journeys. It was necessary to plunge into the life of the farm and the village in order, in full measure, to appraise Chekhov the poet and Chekhov the writer of everyday reality.

I married the daughter of the famous Russian educator, Baron Korf. After his death, his estate, by the wish of his widow and daughters, was sold to peasants at half-price; there remained unsold only a farmhouse and 25 *desyatinas*[1] of land. There I passed the summer months with my wife; she and her sisters had no desire to return to the house in which Korf had died.

Abandoned farmhouses quickly go to ruin. This particular farmhouse had not been occupied for four years when I arrived, and the place was already in a state of complete neglect.

The estate was in the South, in steppe country, on the banks of a winding river, with an immense park. It was a long house and very old. During the first years, while we were putting it in repair, we occupied only half of it; in the other half, which contained a large drawing-room and reception-rooms, there were piles of winter window-frames, heaps of all kinds of seeds, lately gathered apples carefully

---

[1] A *desyatina* is 21,600 square *arshins*; roughly, 2¾ acres.

arranged, and pears and peppers. Under the rotted steps of the terrace adders made their habitation. Frogs gathered on the terrace, and when I wrote in the evening and the light of my lamp fell on the white wall, black beetles made for the lighted spots, and the frogs sprang at the wall and snapped them up.

It was possible to jump across the river anywhere within half a verst; elsewhere it was so overgrown with an abundance of tall reeds and belladonna grass as to be invisible, while along the park and farm and as far as the windmill it poured itself out in a vast reach, giving the appearance of a broad river; in the deeper parts it abounded in big eels and sheatfish weighing a *pud*.[1]

The park was in a state of neglect. It was full of hares and foxes and even of wild jumping hares—tiny hopping beasts with long tails—hedgehogs, and moles, whose subterranean ways it was possible to observe in the little mounds of earth which seemed to spring up before our eyes. Of birds there was a great number and a vast variety—from crows with their cawing, and yellow-black orioles, cuckoos, magpies, and hoopoes, to nightingales. They all vied with one another, and in the spring flaunted their enchanting trills, whistlings, warblings, quite drowning the voices of human beings.

In the evening one heard the booming sounds of a bird— the bittern, I think. It plunged its beak into the water and frightened one, as it were, with its mystery; it was indeed painful to listen to its eerie moan. If you went late in the evening into the park, you would hear the flight of the owls from tree to tree and their wild hoots.

[1] A *pud* is a trifle over 36 pounds.

All around the farm was the steppe. There were no natural forests; but here and there forests were planted. Ceaselessly by night the steppe rang with the song of the steppe crickets, field cicadas. A full moon, silence, and cicadas.

Our river was called Mokriye Yali (Wet Yali), to distinguish it from another river, Sukhiye Yali (Dry Yali), which completely dried up in the summer. Formerly rows of farmhouses stretched along these rivers; they had either fallen into ruins or passed into the hands of thriving managers, or had wholly vanished. Here was the peasants' kingdom. Between the villages, in stretches of twenty to thirty versts, was the endless steppe. The steppe is broad, beautiful, sultry, oppressively calm. Sometimes it is covered with barley, wheat and rye, or burned out, grassless, with gloomily huddled flocks of sheep.

It is fifty versts to the nearest railway station, an equal distance to the post office, one hundred and twenty to the nearest town. The neighbours are the village male or female teacher, the priest, the district chief, the doctor, the examining magistrate, the commissary of rural police, the leaseholding farmer, the shopkeeper. Practically the whole district intelligentsia had been brought up on liberal ideas: Korf's portrait hung in all the schools of the two immense districts in which he had laboured. But, long since, they had shaped a mask out of these ideas, a mask without which it was as impossible to visit people as without a necktie; the ideas themselves had long since been forgotten.

The schoolmistress was a forgotten creature, wasting love on the children; the doctor was engaged in leasing the land, and healed only with detestation of his vocation; when an old woman came to him, he would say: 'Well,

BARONESS KORF
At the time of her marriage to Nemirovitch-Dantchenko

THE COUNTRY HOME OF NEMIROVITCH-DANTCHENKO

why do you bother about getting cured? It's time you died!'

My wife and I had little inclination for receiving this company, and our whole society consisted of an old German manager and a high-school student, his adopted son.

The desolation was real. The steppe was satiated with epic poetry, but the depression and tedium were incredible. Whenever we journeyed, we greeted the first telegraph pole with joy, as on a radiant holiday.

We visited a young scholar who had received by inheritance a large estate near the village. He was a very good man, but no sooner had he received his inheritance than he became lazy; he did nothing, loved having guests, drank a great deal and liked to see others drink a great deal with him; they drank here, and sang, and raised their voices to shouts in arguing on lofty themes, and then drank again. This young man always had at his house the district intelligentsia; the Governor too stopped at his house when he went on his inspecting tours.

I was infected with a passionate desire to reproduce my observations, experiences, perplexities, to draw all these figures just as they were and as I assumed them to be. But no sooner did I begin to think of the theatre, and in particular, of the best one—the Small Theatre—than the whole novelty of my observations, their whole keenness, vanished. By what magic of the stage was it possible that in the winter the Moscow and St. Petersburg spectators should receive across the footlights my stimulation from the dark hollows of the nocturnal park or from the diurnal sultry oppressiveness over the sepulchral mound? And what could Lensky, Yuzhin, Sadovsky, Ermolova, and Fedotova find for themselves in all

[27]

these tedious, unconscionable characters of an obscure Russian province? Where was the material here for seething temperaments, for superb polished diction, for theatrical plasticity, theatrical pathos?

I return to the theatre. Why did not Chekhov find a place on the official stage? On the famous stage of the Moscow Small Theatre?

It was the 'golden age' of the Small Theatre, the bloom of its acting forces. There were even two currents here: one, comedy, drama and chiefly an Ostrovsky repertory; the second, Schiller and Hugo. Moscow was proud of its Small Theatre, even as it was proud of its University, its Tretyakov Gallery,[1] the restaurants Hermitage and Yar, and Testov's Tavern with its rolls and sucking pig.

Ostrovsky was already dead; the contemporary repertory was in the hands of five or six masters of the drama, who had learnt well the art of the Small Theatre and were capable of writing rôles for these or others of the favourite actors. At the head of the company were Fedotova and Ermolova, later—Ermolova and Fedotova. Every play was invariably written for one or the other. When they played together, many full houses were assured. If, however, neither one nor the other took part in a piece, then at best a modest success could be hoped for, but for the most part the result was—a fiasco.

These writers, whom the critics called 'juror' dramatists, held secure places. They had but to inform the stage director, Tchernevsky, when a new play would be ready and for whom the rôles were intended, and he would arrange its place in the season.

[1] A rich merchant's picture gallery, presented to the city.

MARIA ERMOLOVA

GILKERIA FEDOTOVA

Prominent Russian actresses

p. 28]

At the head of the administration were not literary men, but government officials. Prior to his appointment as chief, the manager had not the least contact with the theatres; he was an officer of the Guard, a position he had gained through his wife. The rôle of stage director was a very modest one; it had neither a creative nor a pedagogic content. Actors listened to him merely out of politeness.

If you add to all this that actors enjoyed the affection of the public and even greater trust than the authors, it is easy to understand that this was an epoch of the true kingdom of actors.

From this we perceive all the good aspects of the time, and all the bad too. Of course a play must be fitted to the theatre; of course, it must contain material for the actor's creativeness; but the understanding of stagecraft and of what was a good rôle was creatively not free, and had become stereotyped.

Here, in this comfortable, noble theatre, had been worked out its own art and its own public; they were satisfied each with the other; the artists were bright and captivating; their public held them in very high regard and spoiled them with ovations and offerings, while towards anything alien and very new it conducted itself with prejudice.

In a word, it was the old story of academic conservatism.

In literature it resulted in this situation: 'dramatist' and 'writer' were not at all one and the same thing, but were remote kinsmen. The dramatist could be the most desired personage in the Small Theatre, but among real writers he felt somewhat uncomfortable. And his plays, given before full houses, did not interest the editors of periodicals in the least. And, contrariwise, the author of short stories, which sold well, was a mere guest in the theatre. The unknown Krilov was fully at home in the theatre, while Turgenev was only an esteemed guest; because Krilov 'knew the stage', while Turgenev did not. This 'knowing the stage' was a bugbear to writers.

The time had not yet come to enter into a decisive conflict with this time-worn conception. But there was already ripening a yearning for a *literary* theatre. Soon we shall begin to speak of this with more and more emphasis.

Strange as it may seem, not even the productions of Schiller and Hugo, with the most brilliant actors in the cast, satisfied the demands of the literary theatre. These productions were sumptuous, scenic, brilliantly theatrical, impressing the audience; but for all their scenic, dramatic virtues, for all their pathos, there was little in them of what is *purely human*; hence it was difficult to believe in these heroes and their passions.

Ostrovsky was present at the then much talked-about 'Mary Stuart' of Schiller. At the summit of his fame, not far from death, he was attracted to the administration of the Small Theatre and examined the whole repertory. At the conclusion of the spectacle, those around him awaited his judgment. He shook his 'wise' head, touched—as was his habit—his beard with his left palm, and with deep breaths, producing a halting effect, he said slowly: 'How all this . . . spoils Russian actors!'

This deadly sentence spread through the entire theatre. But he was not believed—not even by the young, because they too had come from school already slaves of stereotype. The famous Russian art, proclaimed by Gogol and Stchepkin, had more and more become overgrown with conservatism and sentimentalism, and had become stationary; it was like an armoured ship, encrusted with barnacles from long rest at anchor.

It is the exceptional happiness of a human being to be constantly at his chosen work. The life of Moscow—it is superfluous to mention the provinces—seethed with human beings who did not love their work and regarded it only as a means of earning their livelihood. The physician healed, he had his office hours, and he visited his patients—for money; the court justice, the civil attorney, the official of a governmental department, the man in the banking office, served their hours without diversion, without joy; the high-school teacher, from year to year teaching one and the same subject, grew weary of imparting knowledge; as for working at it at home, there were not many who had any energy or initiative left. The manufacturer, the shopkeeper, the more thriving they were the less interested were they in any life except their stores and their goods.

The exceptions were furnished by the University with its professors and students, the theatre, the musical and artistic institutions, editors' offices—a very thin layer of the immense, inert population.

In this sense, actors are the most fortunate people: to the vocation to which they devote their whole love they are bound in all their interests. Their calling impels them to labour, the company warms up their energy; willy-nilly, the actor creates to the best of his ability. The writer, the artist, the composer, are, on the contrary, very much alone; the whole reservoir of energy is to be found wholly in them-

[31]

selves. And their very love for their work is subject to temptation.

Very shrewdly had Chekhov spoken of a writer of our own generation, Gneditch:

'This man is a real writer. There is one thing he cannot do: *not* write. Whatever conditions you surround him with, he'll take a gnawed pencil if he can't find a pen, and he'll take a piece of paper, and he'll write—a sketch, a story, a comedy, a collection of anecdotes. He married a wealthy woman, he has no need of earning a livelihood, and he goes on writing more than ever. When he's short of an original theme, then he takes to translating.'

And contrariwise about a young writer, whom I called talented:

'No. Just think, he's but twenty-five, and he's already travelled abroad and has covered half of Russia. If at his age we'd seen so much, would we have written as much? Wait and see; he'll change his writing for another occupation.'

This proved a prophecy. Thanks to connections, this literary man became a major official in St. Petersburg and thereafter wrote only reports.

Anton Pavlovitch had no permanent writing job; he neither worked for any one editorial office nor for a theatre. He was a doctor who took a pride in his profession. I cannot definitely remember how much time and attention he devoted to his medical practice while living in Moscow, but I do remember how the matter stood in his estate at Mele-khovo, where he went with his family: he very eagerly cured the peasants there. According to the registration of his pre-scriptions, stuck in separate little sheets on a nail, the number eight hundred and some odd met my eye; these covered a whole year and included all manner of illnesses. Chekhov said that a large portion consisted of women's diseases.

For all his pride in his medical diploma, his writing labours quite definitely squeezed out the healing art. No one ever so much as mentioned the latter; this fact sometimes offended Chekhov: 'But, p-p-lease, I'm a physician.'

Nor did he devote his whole time to his writing. He did not write as much and as constantly as, for example, Tolstoy; nor Gorky, while sojourning in Capri. He read a great deal, but not to excess, and almost entirely belles-lettres.

I remember his once having mentioned that he had not read Dostoievsky's *Crime and Punishment*. 'I'm saving this pleasure for my forties!' I reminded him of this when he reached forty. 'Yes, I have read it, but it hasn't impressed me very much.' It was to be seen from the way he said it that he had no desire to go into details.

He held Maupassant in very high regard—if you like, above all Frenchmen.

In any case, he had plenty of free time, which he spent in idleness.

He was not fond of lengthy explanations and disputes. This was particularly characteristic of him. He listened attentively, often out of graciousness, and frequently with interest. He himself remained silent until he had found a clear definition for his thought, which he usually expressed in a terse, well-aimed, conclusive phrase. He would give utterance to it, smile his broad fleeting smile, and again lapse into silence.

In his social relations he was gracious, simple, without the slightest mawkishness; inwardly he was, I should say, exquisite. He was not without coolness; to give an instance, when he met you and shook your hand he usually said, 'How-do-you-do?' as in passing, without waiting for an answer.

He loved imbibing in his youth; but less as he grew older.

He used to say that to drink vodka regularly at dinner was by no means necessary, but that to drink occasionally, even a great deal, was not bad. But never at any banquet or comradely evening have I seen him drinking to excess. I simply cannot imagine him intoxicated.

He had quite a success with women, I think. I say 'think', because neither he nor I liked to discuss the subject; I judge only from the rumours that reached me. Only once, for some reason, he manifested a strange and unexpected frankness, perhaps because the case was a singular one. This was long ago, before the establishment of the Art Theatre. We had not seen each other for a long time and stumbled on each other at an exhibition of pictures; we agreed to meet on the following day on the Boulevard. And almost his first words were about a woman—spoken, as it were, because of the strangeness of the thing. He had been paying court to a married woman, when suddenly, when success was imminent, it was revealed that he was making an attempt on innocence. He expressed himself thus: 'And suddenly— there's the lock!' Whether or not he had unlocked it, I did not ask; but I guessed whom he meant, and he knew what I had guessed.

The cultured Russian woman found no greater attraction in a man for her abandonment than talent. I have a notion that Chekhov could be captivating. He had no strong, prolonged bonds with any one before his marriage. But not long before it he said that no bond ever lasted beyond a year.

[34]

Two years after 'Ivanov', Chekhov wrote a new play, 'The Wood Demon'. He did not offer it to Korsh, but to Abramova's new dramatic company, which gave indications of becoming a great and earnest theatre. One of the chief actors was Solovtzov, to whom Chekhov dedicated his farce, 'The Bear'.

I dimly remember the reception given the play by the public; it could not have been a marked success, in any case. It seemed to me that the author had not quite mastered the stage form. I do remember the superb impression made on me by the dramatic scene between the two women in the second act; subsequently, in significant measure, this scene was utilized in 'Uncle Vanya'; I remember the monologue of the Forester (the wood demon). But above all I remember my personal feeling of the lack of co-ordination between the lyrical conception and the stage expression. Very good actors played the parts, but behind their speech, manner, and temperament it was impossible to recognize many familiar, living figures. The play was staged carefully, but these decorations, scene arrangements, cloth walls, swinging doors, this behind-stage din, did not for an instant remind me of nature. Everything came *from the familiar stage*, and one wished that it had come *from familiar life*.

I knew very many intelligent people who loved literature and music, but never wanted to go to the theatre. They found everything false there and often laughed at the most 'sacred' stage matters. We, from our own point of view, called them callous wretches, but this was unjust: what was to be done if theatrical illusion left them *sober*? Not they were to blame, but the theatre.

But was it possible to attain something in which the crea-

[35]

tive stimulation came not from the stage, but from life? What hindered? What was lacking? Proper staging, proper organization of the spectacle, the actor's art?

This question had only just come to birth. . . .

I wrote the comedy 'The New Undertaking'. This was an important point in my theatrical career.

I had my own problems. In the first place, the play was written more for its masculine than its feminine rôles. That meant that it contained no enticing part for Ermolova or Fedotova in Moscow, or for Savina in St. Petersburg. There was the further audacity that the love intrigue took quite a secondary place; indeed, it was scarcely existent. Finally, there was not a single external effect: no pistol shot, no fainting-spell, no hysteria, no slap in the face, indeed no *deus ex machina*—no unexpected solution.

In the soil of the peasants seams of coal are found. A neighbouring landowner leases the land for exploitation; he seeks capital and cannot find it. He is not believed, because he is for ever coming forward with one or another 'new undertaking'. Even his daughter, who is married to a rich Moscow merchant, hinders him from obtaining money.

That is all. I wanted to find an interest in the stage form itself, and with simple means to seize the spirit of comedy.

The first steps were not very much encouraged. The play was accepted for production in the Moscow Small Theatre, but somewhat coolly, without compliments. The actors rehearsed assiduously, it goes without saying, but without inspiration. The *mise en scène* and all stage directions came from me; the stage director Tchernevsky was present and, without raising an objection, merely fulfilled my wishes. This was his attitude with regard to the production:

At one of the final rehearsals, during an intermission spent in the smoking-room behind the scenes, where the actors gathered to smoke and play dominoes, Tchernevsky was moving the little bone lotto squares and saying: 'Well, we'll see: if it comes out, we'll have a success; if it doesn't, we won't!' Then, in the course of a few minutes: 'As I thought, it wouldn't come out!'

And there I stood; the majority participating in the play were also present. Tchernevsky leaned back against the divan, blinked, and went on in a hopeless tone: 'What else could you expect? Coal, coal, mines, money. . . .'

Actually, only two actors fell in love with the play and shared my perturbation—Lensky, who played the leading rôle, and Fedotova, who agreed to play and who, generally speaking, was distinguished for sensibility.

The author, no less than the actor, is never sure of success on the eve of a new production; only the arrogant have this assurance. These perturbations for the coming day, this self-distrust, is perhaps the most sacred thing in the experience of the actor, artist, or writer; in particular, of the actor and the dramatist, because on the morrow they must stand face to face with the result.

This is not alarm for one's *amour propre*, but something deeper and more moving. Suppose it should suddenly prove that I had gone astray? Suppose on the morrow all these theatrical dreams should be ridiculed? A single step to acknowledgment, and you are ready to believe in everything: in your truth, and in your powers, that you are a rich man in the best sense of spiritual wealth. And something may happen, the affair may not come off quite right; or quite clearly, in the full gleam of lights, your impotence may become revealed and you may despise yourself.

When Stanislavsky and I came to create the Art Theatre, a cautious relation to the experiences of actors lay at the basis of our mutual relations with the company. The official atmosphere, the indifference of those around the actors, were ruthlessly suppressed, as the most evil enemies of art.

Forty years have passed since 'The New Undertaking', and to this day I remember how on the day of the *première* I literally could not find a place for myself. I wandered about the streets and tormented myself with my own faintheartedness.

And suppose Tchernevsky should prove to be in the right? Suppose Sadovsky, who had rehearsed one of the best parts with languid indifference, should prove suddenly in the right? (He had displayed such indifference that I had requested the stage director to ask Sadovsky to learn his rôle.) And why had I written my play *thus*? Why had I seized upon such a difficult problem?

I reflected that I might have written a play on a more grateful theme, how I might easily have employed more familiar effects. At least, these would have guaranteed the play against failure. Should I take a journey somewhere? Avoid going that evening to the theatre? What a paradise appeared to me the life of persons remote from the arts! To sit in comfortable surroundings with friends, play whist, and jest with a care-free mind—what happiness!

But my happiness proved such as I had imagined when I was writing 'The New Undertaking': the success was a great one and a unanimous one. I could count myself as a con-

3

queror. In any case, my assurance of complete triumph still lacked one thing. What would the critics say? They still had some influence in those days. The first notices were excellent; but the best paper, *Russkiye Viedomosti*, published an article in which the critic left me, so to speak, not a leg to stand on: the play was without an idea, the characters were not sustained, and the whole thing was a piece of rank triviality.

The singular thing about it was that I myself had only lately recommended this critic to the editor of the journal. The former permanent critic of many years had died; the editor had asked me to write about the theatre. Owing to my connection with the Small Theatre, I had found this inconvenient; but I was persuaded and I wrote for them about the theatre, until I stumbled on this young critic, of whom I had great expectations.

And here he made haste to justify them!

The article created a tremendous impression on me. Again I wavered and with impatience awaited Monday, the day on which the *feuilletons* of the 'King of Critics', Flerov-Vassiliev, usually appeared.

The success with the public, which proved so friendly, was quite unexpected behind the scenes; so there too they awaited Flerov's article with keen interest.

This critic was distinguished for his independence and sound judgment. This is the sort of thing which used to happen: a play would break down, the public would hiss, the newspapers would spread the tidings; but Flerov on Monday would publish an enthusiastic article, not so much taking the play under his protection as simply sharing his impressions with the reader, and completely ignoring the play's failure.

A short time would pass and the play would suddenly gain attention, find a place in all the theatres, and then maintain its position in repertory for ten years.

This, by the way, happened with all the later plays of Ostrovsky!

And now Flerov gave a whole *feuilleton* to the praise of 'The New Undertaking'. This article—I must confess—I have preserved and have often perused. It was one of those rare instances in which the critic is in close accord with the author, because he has sensitively seized upon the innermost essence of the author's intentions and found the emotional tone and words for his paraphrase.

'The New Undertaking' was my first major success. Actually, this success developed only in St. Petersburg. There the play was given as a benefit for Varlamov, the brilliant comic actor, the idol of the metropolis. It was rehearsed and performed with interest. It was received with great *éclat*. The entire Court was present at the benefit performances for Varlamov as well as for Savina. The director of the Theatre pressed my hand more warmly than usual and conveyed the commendation of Alexander III. He said that in the first place the Emperor saw at last a real Russian comedy, and that in the second place he intended to come to the next performance with his daughter Xenia. The newspapers received the play warmly.

Furthermore, 'The New Undertaking' was awarded the Griboyedov prize, presented by the Society of Dramatists for the best play of the season. I found myself in the fore, among the leading exponents of the drama. The Imperial Theatres in Moscow and St. Petersburg organized a Theatro-Literary Committee; in Moscow the Committee invited to membership three of the most brilliant and venerable professors of literature—Tikhonravov, Storozhenko, and Veselovsky Aleksey—and myself. As a trophy for 'The New Undertaking' I remember the very flattering conversation with Tchaikovsky and his request that I write a libretto for him.

It seemed to me that all I had to do was to write more and more plays. Somewhere it was whispered that I had been called to 'continue' Ostrovsky, accept from him as my inheritance the new merchant class. The doors of the theatre were open to me. Nevertheless, I did not produce my next play until four years later.

CHAPTER THREE

Now came the beginning of a new and important journey toward the main goal: I received a proposal to teach dramatic art at the Philharmonic. This was quite a small undertaking. It could not have appeared serious to anyone, certainly not so much so that it would have a lasting influence on my activity.

There were two dramatic schools in Moscow: the Imperial, in which Lensky, Pravdin, Sadovsky and at one time Fedotova, taught; and the Philharmonic, in which the advanced courses had been formerly given by Pravdin, later by Yuzhin, while the lower courses were in the hands of the secondary actor N——. The Philharmonic's directorate was not satisfied with him, and Yuzhin recommended me for the position. This was, on his part, both perspicacious and bold. To recommend a non-actor for the position of preparing actors from among the youth implied that he saw something in me which was invisible to others. The directorate of the Philharmonic believed him.

Yuzhin told me that he was but little interested in the work; he thought that in a year or two I might count on his transferring the whole of it to me. He had faith in me as a man 'with acting potentiality', as a teacher and as a stage director.

And I had a deep faith in myself. But my pupils received me with distrust. N—— was a secondary actor, but still an

[42]

actor, while this new man—even granting he is a good playwright—what can he teach us? . . . Yuzhin found it necessary to use persuasive speech, to tell them that I was an outstanding amateur, that I directed performances, that when
my plays were produced even the actors of the Small Theatre
accepted my suggestions, and so on. For my part, I said that
I had come 'to be taught while teaching', that so far I was
only more experienced than my pupils, but that I had already
given much thought to dramatic school work,—in a word, I
began very modestly, hoping gradually to win their confidence. I was, however, soon forced to take quite another tone.

The school had a bad reputation. It had, it is true, produced several first-class actors, such as the later celebrities
Leshkovskaya and Pototzkaya. But at the same time there
was among the pupils a terrible lot of riffraff: inquisitive
girls who had come here as to an excellent exhibition; idlers
who had nowhere else to go. The majority came here to be
taught in the speediest manner possible how to act, so that
they might be given good rôles in a graduation play. The
educative aim of the school was wholly ignored. It was impossible to convince any one of the significance of voice
training, diction, plastics, dancing, fencing, cultural courses.
In short, the whole tone was extraordinarily vulgar. With
impatience the students awaited being cast in a play, produced by the oldest instructor for a private or a public performance; everything else was considered tedious and
unnecessary.

'Why did you enter the school?' I asked a pupil, who was
close to thirty years of age. 'Why, you don't want to do
anything!'

'How shall I tell you?' he answered with exceptional cynicism. 'I have the means, and it matters little what I choose to do, and here are so many women . . . *gratis*.'

The directorate of the school made no effort to discourage this attitude; evidently it had even found that this was the general tone of life behind the scenes.

The more modestly I conducted myself, the more confusion reigned in my classes. I was forced to resort to the authority granted me. Alas, how often I had to fly to it in time to come, even in the surroundings offered by the Art Theatre and in the case of human beings far nobler than this rabble. . . . Such are human beings. Once I shouted, demanded the exclusion of four or five pupils, and took the reins into my own hands. . . .

I was drawn into the courses in a degree I was ashamed to confess. Just think of it: the dramatist from whom the best theatres await plays—the writer—is giving himself up to some sort of drama school with such an expenditure of his time and strength as to give the impression that he is the youngest pupil in the school! If only there were big money in it, then there would be some justification, but such petty cash! Who would have sympathized with me? That is why, above all, I enjoyed my meetings with Lensky, who devoted himself to his courses in the Imperial School with equal zeal. We vied with each other in sharing our quests, experiments, and achievements.

It is a very absorbing business, as every one knows who has tried it, to instruct in the arts. To seize the individuality, to bring the 'spark' to life, to help it to develop; to cleanse it of obstruction, to ennoble the taste, to wrestle with bad habits, with petty self-love; to request, insist, demand; to be affectionate toward the pupil and to reprove him; ceaselessly

[44]

to keep his interest in human material alive; to feed him on
your best ideas; with joy and solicitude to follow after his
slightest progress. . . .

In all this lies the very seed of the theatre, its deepest and
most absorbing essence. . . .

It is necessary that they, these youths, should have unceasing faith in the undertaking to which they have resolved to
dedicate their lives, and that the discipline which I have imposed should be justified. . . . There are so many of them;
and each one must be given the maximum of attention; and
for some youth to be told that he has no gift for the stage
may be to murder him. . . . Is it so hard to make a mistake?
There is the case of Lensky and his examining commission
refusing Knipper! She went first there, to the Imperial
School; they did not find her interesting, so she came to the
Philharmonic. And this is, by no means, an exceptional
error. I personally, after several months of training, told
Moskvin that I doubted his capabilities. And there is Savitskaya, who on entering the school put the question to herself
thus: either the theatre or the nunnery; if she could not
become an actress, she would retire from the world altogether. Have you the right to decide whether or not she is
fitted for the stage without the most assiduous experiments
and probations? With what passionate hopes do they come
here, with what frightened anticipation do they follow at
each line the face of the instructor; what will this face reflect
—joy or hopelessness?

To offset this, with what a stream of grateful feelings
tremulous youth answers, if it has justified its expectations!

I was under obligation 'to give lessons' four times a week,
and devote two hours to each lesson. This was an absurd

[45]

condition. I was engaged daily, morning and evening, and into the late hours of the night, without any accounting; even then there was scarcely enough time.

I succeeded in putting things in order. I often used an expression I had heard somewhere: sooner would I resign from the whole affair than not have order in it.

In what precisely consisted my activities, what did I learn at these courses, and what did I teach the theatrical youth? What processes did I seek, find and develop, constantly trying them out on different individuals? Here is a theme for a separate book; these are questions dealing with a specialized technique. Eight years of this went on before the establishment of the Art Theatre. Many hundreds of young persons studied at these courses, many tens of them became good actors, and, finally, many of them attained celebrity. What a variety of themes we seized upon in our joint labours; the instruction went far beyond the bounds of first experiments in stage technique. Psychological movements, everyday features, moral questions, emotional mergings with the author, aspiration toward frankness and simplicity, the quest of vivid expression and diction, mimicry, plastics, self-assurance—but there is no recounting of all the elements which composed the hours of the stimulating school labours.

The graduation performances made the reputation of the school. The Philharmonic gave but a single performance a year, while the Imperial School gave three or four. The Small Theatre gave no performances during Lent. Lensky took advantage of this, and his whole school took possession of the theatre, while the Philharmonic had to be content with a single performance in the Small Theatre and several in its own school building. I succeeded in obtaining equal rights with the Imperial School, and Lensky and I divided the days of Lent between us. This raised the standard of my courses, and they were soon in competition with those of the official school.

These performances began to excite interest in Moscow. I was proud of some of them. This brings me to Ibsen, to whom I was attracted. The big theatres ignored him; the Small Theatre had performed his 'The Vikings at Helgeland' unsuccessfully; Korsh produced 'An Enemy of the People' and it proved a failure. If we are to add that Duse on her arrival played 'A Doll's House'—you have the whole of Ibsen. And as Duse presented the play on the basis of her own leading rôle, as is done on the stage abroad, it need only be said that in her version of the play there was little of Ibsen. I produced 'A Doll's House' with my pupils, and this was the first real Ibsen production in Moscow.

All mentors are inclined to overrate their own fosterlings; I dare say I have sinned not a little in this respect. But in one thing I was not deceived: that only through them, through the youth of the school, could the theatre be revived.

I was so absorbed in the school performances that I was ready to have my pupils produce my new play 'Gold', just as Tchaikovsky had done in producing 'Eugene Onegin' as the graduating performance of the Conservatory—but for the good of my pocket my friends in the Small Theatre, with some warmth, dissuaded me.

Some curious reminiscences are bound up with this play.

In the first place, I wanted to test the classic formula, 'unities of place, time and action'. It lured me with its monumentalism. Ibsen had so often employed this formula; the logic of the action gained from it a certain chiselled quality. And so when I actually finished the play, I went over it again: compressed it into a single scene, a single day, and so forth.

In my opinion, I spoiled the play. I overweighted it, it became more artificial, more monotonous; but I did not want to acknowledge this to myself, and thus I let it go out into the world.

But this did not hinder its success. It received the prize of the Odessa University, and was performed in Moscow and St. Petersburg with a very brilliant cast.

Again, it was the first play which enjoyed a dress rehearsal. Hitherto it had been considered that a dress rehearsal was essential only for plays of an elaborately decorative character, while in contemporary plays the authors saw the actors in their make-up and costumes only at the actual performance, perhaps five minutes before their entrance on the scene, when it was already too late to alter anything. In this respect there have been some painful surprises.

In the case of my play: 'It's an ill wind that blows no one any good.'

The play should have started in St. Petersburg. At this time Alexander III was dying in the Crimea. The rehearsals were progressing under the pressure of expectancy: it was thought the play would come to a stop in the middle of the performance, and even if not, the public would be in a gloomy state of mind—after all, it was the Imperial Theatre. The day of the *première* arrived, there was a rehearsal in the morning. About six in the evening I made my way to the theatre; crowds thronged the Nevsky Prospect, where news bulletins were displayed: the Emperor was dead.

The performance did not take place; mourning was proclaimed. The official theatres were closed for over two months. It was then that I made use of my free time to organize dress rehearsals. Thereafter they were adopted for all productions.

Between 'The Wood Demon' and 'The Sea Gull' six or seven years passed. During this time 'Uncle Vanya' appeared. Chekhov objected to its being said that this play was a re-writing of 'The Wood Demon'. Somewhere he categorically announced that 'Uncle Vanya' was a wholly independent play. Nevertheless, the basic lines and some of the scenes from 'The Wood Demon', with scarcely a change, were incorporated in 'Uncle Vanya'.

I cannot exactly remember when and how he excluded from circulation the one play and when and where he published the other. I remember seeing 'Uncle Vanya' the first time in a small collection of plays; it is possible that it made its first appearance in that form. And at the beginning 'Uncle Vanya' was performed in the provinces. I saw it on the stage in Odessa, acted by the company of the same Solovtzov of whom Chekhov was such a friend. Solovtzov himself had become a manager, and his business in the provinces was an excellent one. My sister, the actress Nemirovitch, was in his company; she played the rôle of Elena in 'Uncle Vanya'.

It was an average week-day performance, having its turn in the stock repertory. The play went successfully; but the very character of this success was, so to speak, theatrically ordinary. The public applauded, the actors were called before the curtain, but with the end of the performance came also the end of the play's life; the spectators did not bear away with them any intensely lived experience; the play did not awaken them to a new understanding of things. I repeat: there was nothing of that new reflection of life which a new poet had brought to his play.

Thus, Chekhov not only had no design on the Imperial stage, but actually ceased writing for the theatre. Nevertheless, we drew him into the interests of the theatrical life. Thus we carried on a fight in the Society of Playwrights and pulled Chekhov into it. He was cautious, he did not yield at once, but in the end he became very much interested.

The Society of Playwrights, founded by Ostrovsky, bore an official character. The whole business was conducted by the secretary, who occupied a prominent place in the office of the Governor-General. This secretary and the treasurer, also a major government official, composed the whole organization of the Society. It was necessary to wrest the power from them and to put the Society under the direction of writers, to work out new regulations, and so on. This was very complicated and difficult. The president of the Society, *doyen d'âge* of the dramatists, Shpazhinsky, successor to Ostrovsky, was a simple fiction; he was under the influence of the secretary, and was afraid that the latter would make use of the gubernatorial apparatus to work his spite on him.

The 'conspirators' usually met at my place. The new administration included Yuzhin-Sumbatov, a certain dramatist advocate, Chekhov, and myself. The militant General Meeting proved an exciting fray. We conquered. But we did not at all contemplate seizing the profitable positions of secretary and treasurer. Our problem was merely to work out a new set of regulations; we were engaged in this for a whole year, while continuing our fight.

During all this time I often met Chekhov. He showed no gift for organization, nor did he pretend to it. He was very attentive, spoke very little, and appeared, above all, to observe and make mental notes of humorous features.

He did not write any new plays and did not aspire to the Imperial stage, though he had several friends there. He used to meet Yuzhin and Lensky, leading actors in the Small Theatre, oftener than the others. With Yuzhin he was on terms of the familiar 'thou'.

Yuzhin was one of the major figures of the Russian theatrical world. Long after the November 1917 revolution there was to remain the saying that the theatrical world was supported by three whales: Yuzhin, Stanislavsky and Nemirovitch-Dantchenko.

He was a man of the broadest social interests. As the leading actor in the best company in the world, he bore the brunt of a large, strong repertory. He had been a dramatist since his student years; his plays were regarded as very theatrical: [1] they were given everywhere, and always with success. He participated in all possible theatrical, literary, and social meetings, as well as those of societies and committees. He was cultured and well read, and followed the new literature with tremendous interest. He maintained an extensive acquaintance with 'the whole of Moscow'; he was a member of all the important clubs and the creator and life-president of the popular Moscow Literary-Artistic Circle. There was not a single meeting of common interests in which Yuzhin-Sumbatov did not play a leading part. He was a real favourite of Moscow. During the summer, instead of taking

[1] This word is used throughout in such contexts in the sense of well adapted to theatrical performance.—*Translator*.

[51]

a rest, he would go to the provinces on starring tours, then to Monte Carlo to demonstrate a new system he had worked out in the winter, and from there to his home village and his estate, where his wife awaited him, there to write a play.

This man did not know what laziness was, and might have served as a model for the blacksmith who 'forged his own happiness'. He did, indeed, forge his position, mistrusting easy means and putting energy and stubborn will into his every step. In company he was inexhaustibly witty and adroit, and liked to monopolize the conversation. He was hospitable as a lord. His house was distinguished for its multitudes of gatherings, dinners, and suppers.

From our youth, it was said of me and Sumbatov: 'The devil himself has bound them with a rope!' Our friendship began in the second class of the *gymnasium*. But even there we never went together, but moved in parallel lines; it was the only *gymnasium* in town and was overcrowded; to accommodate the numbers it was necessary to divide each class into two departments; I was in one, Sumbatov in the other. While in the sixth class, though still remaining friends, we entered into a rivalry. Each department issued its own literary journal. What the themes of our disputes were I cannot remember; I only recall that my journal—I was its editor—was called *Tovarishch* (*The Comrade*), and that we exchanged shots as 'critics', 'anti-critics', etc.

We both began to act together on the stage as amateurs in our native town of Tiflis. Together we wrote a play, which had a considerable external success. We met again in the Small Theatre as playwrights. We married cousins; his wife was also born a Korf.

Sumbatov was my one real friend through life. Our

[52]

friendship never ceased, but we diverged very far in our artistic tastes. This divergence was organic; it began in youth itself. With the rise of the Art Theatre this divergence assumed a sharp tone, and we often found ourselves in belligerent attitudes. In our chief work—the theatre—we proceeded, as in the *gymnasium*, in parallel directions.

He was a romantic. He loved Hugo almost above all poets. He even received the Order of the French Academy for his rôles in 'Hernani' and 'Ruy Blas'. And his artistic taste always and in everything inclined in the direction of romantic fervour.

On this theme we once carried on a long and passionate argument, Chekhov and I taking one side and Yuzhin the other. This was in his large bright study facing the street, which after his death was named 'Yuzhinskaya'. Chekhov and Yuzhin did most of the arguing, because the dispute was concerning me. Shortly before this, my story, *The Gubernatorial Inspection*, had been published, and Chekhov had written me as follows from his estate:

Without a break, I have just read your *Gubernatorial Inspection*. In delicacy, in the purity of its finish and in all senses, this is the very best of your writings with which I am familiar. The impression is a strong one; only the end, beginning with the conversation with the writer, has a somewhat drunken aspect, whereas one desires *piano*, because it is very sad. Your knowledge of life is enormous (I have said something of the sort before). Your work is getting better and better; it is as if every year added a new story to your talent.

And before *The Gubernatorial Inspection* I had written another tale, *The Dead Tissue*, which Sumbatov liked very much. Now they were arguing which was the better. The argument developed into a general discussion and revealed two different artistic directions. Even in a novel Yuzhin preferred colourful, theatrical images; even in a play Chekhov preferred simple, living ones. Yuzhin loved the exceptional, Chekhov the ordinary. Yuzhin, a Georgian, an excellent son of his people, with an ardent temperament akin to the Spanish, loved open, sparkling effects; Chekhov, the purest of White Russians, loved the deep, secret passions, and restraint.

And the main thing that the discussion revealed was this: the art of Yuzhin rang and sparkled so that behind it you saw no life, while with Chekhov, behind life as he painted it you saw no art.

Chekhov argued a long time, a rare thing for him. Usually he expressed his opinion, and if his opponent went on trying to persuade him of his he would shake his head in silence, as much as to say: 'No, my dear fellow, I stick to my own.' But on this occasion he did not cease to look for more and more arguments.

In reality, it was the Small Theatre arguing with the new, the future, the as yet unborn theatre; with this difference, that the Art Theatre was immediately to take a militant tone, while Chekhov argued softly, with his sudden smile; he paced up and down the study with long steps, his hands in his pockets, not at all like a 'warrior' and quite without anger.

Soon the writer Trigorin was to ask in 'The Sea Gull': 'Why jostle? There's room for everybody!'

Sumbatov and I again and again urged Chekhov not to cease writing for the theatre. He listened to us and wrote 'The Sea Gull'.

Chekhov wrote the play in Melekhovo, which was situated two or three hours from Moscow by railway and then eleven versts of by-road through woods and villages. He often had visitors there from afar. Chekhov was very fond of always having cheerful, chatty people about him; but he always left them for his study when he wanted to note down a new thought or a new image which came into his mind.

There was a fine garden with a straight handsome walk, as in 'The Sea Gull', where Treplev arranges his theatre. In the evening every one played lotto—also as in 'The Sea Gull'.

During these years among Chekhov's intimate friends was the new writer, Potapenko. He had come to the fore with two tales, *The Secretary of His Excellency* and *On Actual Service*, and immediately won a name. He came from the provinces. He was very sociable, possessed an unusually pleasant, quick, sober intelligence, and infected and gladdened every one with his optimism. He wrote much and rapidly; he did not value his own writings too highly and made jests at the expense of his productions. He lived lavishly; was frank, simple, weak-willed; toward Chekhov he behaved affectionately and with complete acknowledgment of his pre-eminence. Women loved him passionately; because he loved them and—chiefly—because he knew how to love.

Many have thought that Trigorin in 'The Sea Gull' is autobiographical. And Tolstoy said as much somewhere. But I could never get away from the thought it was Potapenko, more than any one else, who served as a model for Trigorin.

Nina Zaryetchnaya gives Trigorin a medallion, on which is inscribed a phrase from some story of Trigorin's: 'If my

life ever becomes necessary to you, come and take it.'
This phrase comes from a story of Chekhov's, and it breathes
of the self-abnegation and simplicity natural to Chekhovian
maidens. This has provided the motive for associating
Trigorin with Chekhov himself. But this is a mere coin-
cidence; it is possible that Chekhov loved this strong yet
tender expression of womanly devotion and wanted to
repeat it.

More valuable for the characterization of Trigorin is his
relation to women; it does not resemble Anton Pavlovitch,
but is closer to the image of Potapenko. In general, it is, of
course, neither the one nor the other, but a combination of
the two.

'The Sea Gull' is an extraordinarily sincere production;
many details might have been taken direct from life in
Melekhovo. Even the girl who might have served as a
model for Nina Zaryetchnaya was picked out as a friend
of Anton Pavlovitch's sister. But here too the features of
similarity are accidental. There were plenty of such girls
from the provinces at the time—girls whose ambition it was
to escape from the dullness of their environment, from the
dim workaday world, to find something to which they
might 'give themselves', all of themselves; flamingly and
tenderly to sacrifice themselves to Him, the gifted man, who
had stimulated their dreams. As long as women's rights were
rudely limited, theatrical schools were full of girls like these.

CHAPTER FOUR

Anton Pavlovitch sent me the manuscript of 'The Sea Gull', then made the journey to hear my judgment.

I cannot explain why his figure has stamped itself so sharply upon my memory, as it appeared when I, in detail and at length, analysed the play. I sat at my writing-table, while he stood at the window, his back toward me, his hands as always in his pockets, never turning towards me once during at least half an hour, and not missing a single word. There was not the least doubt that he listened to me with extraordinary attention, at the same time giving the impression that with equal attention he followed something which was happening in the tiny garden outside the windows of the house; at moments he even intensified the gaze fixed on the garden and just barely turned his head. Did this arise from a desire to lighten my task of expressing myself freely, to avoid embarrassing me with eyes meeting mine? Or was it, on the contrary, an effort to preserve his own *amour propre*?

In Chekhov's house people did not generally like to reveal their souls, and all his best personages are sensitive, taciturn and restrained.

It is now difficult to say what I told Chekhov of my first impressions, and I dare not venture to re-create the interview. One of the greatest sins of 'recollections' is when the narrator confuses the time *when* something hap-

[57]

pened, and it appears to him that he had somehow foreseen it all.

My further conduct with regard to 'The Sea Gull' is sufficiently well known; and my general attitude to Chekhov's creative works has been one of intense affection. In all likelihood I gave him considerable advice on the score of the architectonics of the piece, its stage form. I was regarded as an expert on the stage, and it is plausible to think that I went to some trouble to share honestly with him my tested stage formulas. I do not suppose he needed my advice.

I can, however, easily recall one detail. In the version which I criticized the first act ended in a great surprise: in the scene between Masha and Dr. Dorn it was suddenly revealed that she was his daughter. Not a word was again said in the play concerning this circumstance. I said that one of two things must be done: either this idea must be developed, or it must be wholly rejected, all the more so if the first act was to end with this scene. According to the very nature of the theatre, the end of the first act should turn sharply in the direction in which the drama is to develop.

Chekhov said: 'But the public likes seeing a loaded gun placed before it at the end of an act!'

'Quite true,' I said, 'but it is necessary for it to go off afterwards, and not be merely removed in the intermission!' It seems to me that later Chekhov more than once repeated this rejoinder. He agreed with me. The end was changed.

When the conversation turned on the play's production, I said that it was time he gave a play to the Small Theatre. And I had already begun to discuss the possible disposition of the rôles when Chekhov suddenly handed me a letter. It was from Lensky to Chekhov.

Lensky was the leading actor of the Small Theatre; Yuzhin had only lately begun to rival him in this position. He was one of the most captivating Russian actors; in wealth of charm it is possible—later—to compare only Kachalov with him. A wonderful master of a new make-up, of interesting form, he found diversion in painting on canvas, and was something of an artist. He had at this time already grown less ardent on the subject of acting: he liked preparing a rôle and performing it two or three times; afterwards he would become bored with it. On the other hand, he devoted himself to the school, to the staging of school performances, and to the preparation of new theatrical companies.

Lensky detested the administration of the Small Theatre, and made no effort to conceal his dislike. He dreamed of the creation of new conditions in stage labours; he was preparing a whole new company composed of his pupils.

More than once in my recollections I return to Lensky. He acted in nearly all of my plays, and we were intimate in each other's homes; latterly, our school labours and our mutual dissatisfaction with the management of the Small Theatre brought us closely together. He was eight or ten years older than Chekhov and I; Chekhov valued his friendship.

The letter Chekhov showed me was in connection with 'The Sea Gull'. It appeared that Lensky had already read it, and this is what he wrote: 'You know how highly I value your talent and you know my deep affection for you. And, precisely because of this, I am impelled to speak quite frankly to you. Here is my most friendly counsel: Drop writing for the theatre. This is not at all in your line.' Such was the gist of the letter; its tone was quite categorical. It seems that Lensky even refused to criticize the play, to such a degree did he find it unfit for the stage.

I do not remember whether Chekhov allowed any one else in the Small Theatre to read it, but Fate was presently to transfer it to St. Petersburg.

Among the writing and professorial circles in Moscow Chekhov stood closer to the periodical *Russkaya Misl* (*Russian Thought*) than to any other. This did not happen suddenly; the periodical was prominently liberal, Goltzev was its editor, and for a long time it behaved cautiously towards Chekhov as toward a writer of reputation, albeit without ideas. But the public's affection for Chekhov had so widened and strengthened that finally *Russkaya Misl* had to capitulate and issue an invitation to him. Soon there developed between them the closest of bonds.

The publisher of *Russkaya Misl* was the wealthy merchant Lavrov, who excellently translated from the Polish the works of Sienkiewicz and Ozscesko. With earnest zeal he assimilated the commandments of the liberalism of the day; he learned to make speeches after supper, tried not to straggle behind his editor and friend Goltzev, and at his large isolated house in Moscow and at his summer villa arranged gatherings of friends, literary men connected with his journal, and young women; there were noisy conversations here, fine suppers, speeches, and card games. Notwithstanding the abundant drink in which the company indulged, the tone of the place never descended to vulgarity. Among other visitors there used to come the young learned historian, P. N. Miliukov, towards whom Lavrov showed real veneration. Yuzhin, Potapenko, and Chekhov were among the constant and favourite guests.

This was in Moscow. But in St. Petersburg, notwithstanding Chekhov's extensive bonds with writing circles, Suvorin took possession of him. Theirs were strange relations. Suvorin had the most popular and influential newspaper in Russia, the *Novoye Vremya* (*New Times*), which Chekhov held in contempt and to which he had no inclination to contribute. Only once, for a very short period, he yielded to persuasion and published two or three *feuilletons* there, although under a pseudonym. But he was on excellent terms with Suvorin and his household. Suvorin was positively infatuated with Chekhov's literary gifts. They maintained an extensive correspondence; they even travelled together, and during these journeys Chekhov scrupulously insisted on paying his share of the expenses.

It is very difficult to define Chekhov's exact relation to Suvorin. He was sensible of the latter's prodigious journalistic talent and his organizing gifts; apart from the newspaper, which yielded an income immense for those days, he possessed the best book-publishing firm in Russia, which issued Chekhov's books in separate form; moreover, he had his own large theatre. But Chekhov behaved as negatively toward Suvorin's theatre as toward his newspaper.

The attitude of *Russkaya Misl* toward *Novoye Vremya*, Suvorin, and his whole activity was sharply hostile; but they did not separate the man from his work. As for Chekhov, who was attached to *Russkaya Misl* during the last ten years of his life, he resolved this dilemma in his own way.

Impressed with 'The Sea Gull', Suvorin undertook to arrange the production of the play at the Imperial Theatre,

[61]

where seven years before 'Ivanov' had been staged with such success. According to accounts, what happened is this:

Levkeyeva chose the play for her benefit performance. The distribution of the rôles proved a difficult matter: Chekhov appointed Savina to the leading rôle—that of Nina Zaryetchnaya—but Savina refused it, possibly because the famous actress was already forty years old. The rôle was then given to Komisarjevskaya. This was for the best: Chekhov afterwards often recalled how well she played. In order actively to support the performance, Savina offered herself for the rôle of Masha, but later refused this also.

Chekhov arrived in St. Petersburg to be present at the rehearsals. The actors were perturbed; for a long time they could not clarify the images according to the author's conception, nor find corresponding intonations. It was evident that they were agonizingly sorting out their worn-out conventions, and that they could find none which fitted these words and scenes. There was no basis for their acting out the piece, i.e. there were no situations in which it was possible to rely on mere 'temperament' and on formulas, on individual 'tricks', with a guaranty of success. Here were the best actors of the company, who held Chekhov in tender regard as a man of letters and who exerted themselves to the utmost to please the author.

Chekhov was incapable of advising actors, even later when he came into contact with the actors of the Art Theatre. Everything appeared so comprehensible to him: 'Why, I have written it all down,' he would answer. To the stage director he said: 'They are *acting* too much.' This did not mean that the actors were *overacting*. It meant that they were acting feelings, images, words. But *how to act without acting*

[62]

anything no one could tell them, least of all the author. 'It must all be done very simply,' Chekhov said, 'just as in life. It must be done as if they spoke about it every day.' It was easy to say that!

Probably every one of these actors had played in rôles in which the actor completely merged with his part, so completely that it may be said he had wholly ceased to act; the impression thus created is usually a tremendous one. But who could have thought of attaining this in 'The Sea Gull'? How was one to utter these simplest phrases simply and yet retain the sense of the theatre and avoid desperate tedium?

There was no feeling of confidence. The actors, while showering compliments on the author, did not believe in what they did on the stage; even the stage director did not. Nevertheless, no one shouted: 'Let's put the performance off! Let us seek, rehearse, feel our way! It is impossible to show the play to the public in its present state! Finally, it is impossible with real pearls of poetry to behave as we behave with authors whose names are forgotten the moment we collect our hats near the exit!'

Routine behaviour brings only routine results. And such the undertaking remained, notwithstanding the presence of the beloved author, notwithstanding the intervention of the most influential individual in St. Petersburg—Suvorin.

The play failed miserably. It was one of the rare failures in the history of the theatre. From the very first act there was lacking any *rapport* between the public and the stage; there was no atmosphere. The most poetical lines met with laughter. Nina's magnificent soliloquy: 'Men,—lions, eagles and partridges . . .' fell on the public's ears like a tedious curiosity. As the play progressed, the auditors exchanged

[63]

glances, shrugged their shoulders, and remained mute when the curtain descended; during the interludes they hissed and exchanged spiteful words. And when, just before the conclusion, in the dramatic finale, after the shot had been fired behind the scenes—the suicide of Treplev—Dorn, in order to avoid frightening Arkadina, said: 'It's nothing, nothing! The bottle with the ether has burst!'—then the public broke into guffaws.

The poor author! Poor, poor Chekhov! During this three-to-four-hour humiliation he wandered about behind the scenes, trying to appear unconcerned. He saw people pass him, and tried awkwardly to avoid meeting their eyes, or spoke hypocritical words. It is likely that more than once he recalled Lensky's letter and his friendly counsel to drop writing for the stage, and doubtless he cursed those who had persuaded him not to do so. In such a situation did he find himself, this writer, this poet, who throughout all of Russia had already been read with such love and absorption!

Where did Anton Pavlovitch go after the performance? Usually he joined a large company at a restaurant. Chekhov was being awaited at supper at the Suvorins, where, according to accounts, there was always a big gathering of people, especially after a *première*. Chekhov appeared neither at the restaurant nor at Suvorin's; no one saw him. There is a legend that for hours on this windy autumnal night he wandered on the Embankment, that he caught cold, hastening the course of the malady which was to shorten his life.

On the following morning he left St. Petersburg without seeing a single soul. To his own family he sent this message: 'The play has fallen down with a crash. In the theatre there was a heavy atmosphere of depression, perplexity and

ANTON CHEKHOV

humiliation. The actors played abominably, stupidly. The moral: one should not write plays.'

The judgment of the play-going public is more agonizing than the judgment of the reading public in that, in the latter instance, some one may at some time read the story in question, or write a critical article, while here, at the very beginning, a thousand-voiced crowd at once flings into your face its speedy, unproven, pitiless judgment; and then for several days afterwards all the newspapers examine your labours on the basis of the recent performance.

During the last years of his life Ostrovsky never went to his *premières*, and never read criticisms.

Suvorin alone praised 'The Sea Gull'. The others wrote:

'. . . It was as if a million bees, wasps, drones filled the air of the auditorium'—'Faces burned with shame'—'From all points of view, whether of idea, literature or stage, Chekhov's play cannot even be called bad, but absolutely absurd' —'The play is impossibly bad'—'The play produced the overwhelming impression of being neither a drama nor a comedy'—'This is not a *sea gull*, but simply a *ditch*.'¹ This concerning one of the most poetical productions of Russian literature!

It chanced that during this entire month (October) I had deserted Moscow for a desolate spot in the country, in order that I might finally write my 'Worth of Life'. It was not until my return that I learned of the fate of 'The Sea Gull'. Chekhov wrote me:

'My "Sea Gull" suffered a tremendous failure at its first performance in St. Petersburg. The theatre breathed spite;

¹ This is a play on words. The word *ditch*, in Russian, means both 'wild fowl' and 'fiddle-faddle', 'nonsense', etc.—*Translator.*

[65]

the air compressed from hatred, and I, obeying the laws of physics, went flying from St. Petersburg like a bomb. You and Sumbatov, having persuaded me to write the play, are to blame.'

Then this in another letter: 'Never will I write these plays, or try to produce them, not if I live to be 700 years old.'

CHAPTER FIVE

During the same season as that of Chekhov's 'The Sea Gull' I produced 'The Worth of Life'—in Moscow in the benefit performance of Lensky, in St. Petersburg in that of Savina. In Moscow the success of the play was foreshadowed from the very first act, and developed into an ovation. A Moscow newspaper said: 'Last evening proved a double benefit—Lensky's and the author's,' while in St. Petersburg, during the numerous curtain calls, Savina asked me: 'Whose benefit is it—mine or yours?' And there were many articles praising the play.

I have not the least desire that you, reading these lines, should say, 'He's assuming modesty,' or the opposite, 'He's painting himself in glowing colours.' I am well aware that 'The Worth of Life' has some outstanding qualities. I should have been willing to introduce the first and third acts as models into my school courses: the first, for masterly exposition; the third, for guidance in stage dialogue. Apart from that I should have used as a model of particular audacity the erection of a whole act—the third at that, i.e. the culminating one for two persons—on the reading of a long letter. It is possible to point out other qualities: the capable guidance of intrigue, good rôles, etc. But that between the fates of these two plays on one and the same stage, within the course of several months, there should be such an immeasurable difference could only mean that something was profoundly wrong in the theatre itself. It was necessary that the old theatre should attain the extreme limits of its expression, where the walls are of stone, where the circle of demands is rigidly closed, where a free creative atmosphere is wholly non-existent.

This is no longer a question *of the nature of the theatre*: such a work, for all its literary pearls, is not theatrical in essence, in all its tissue; within two years you will clearly see how strong in Chekhov was the *feeling of the theatre*.

No, this is a question of *organization* of the theatre. It is necessary to reconstruct its whole life, sweep away all officialdom, beginning with the managing officials; to draw into the commonalty of interests all the creative forces, even the most trifling; to change at the root the whole order of rehearsals, the preparation of plays; to subject the public itself to the régime essential to our purpose, to take it into iron hands without its notice.

From this very winter I began to dream of a new theatre, not of a new theatre in the abstract sense, but of my *own* theatre. As a playwright I occupied an enviable position; but I was being drawn into the thick of theatrical work, and had to exert myself in order to write. While I was writing 'The Worth of Life' I had such chunks of living experience that I sometimes stood with my forehead pressed against the white wall of my room in the monastery hostel and made a vow not to write any more plays.

Why, even in the very germ of the play I was departing from the theatre. The worth of life, the question of suicide, of double suicide, naturally presupposes that the author is consumed with this tremendous moral problem, that he has been seized with the phenomenon of suicide epidemics, and

[68]

so forth. Actually, such was not the case. The author, during the summer, sat in his house in the village and said to himself that it was now absolutely necessary to write a play —necessary according to various earthly considerations. What play he himself did not yet know. It was necessary to find a theme. And one day he would put before himself the question: 'Contemporary plays usually end in suicide, but suppose I take a theme and *begin* with a suicide? A play that begins with a suicide: is it not an engaging idea?'

And then, somehow, I would put before myself this problem: 'Playwrights always write so that the third act shall be the act of conflict, the most effective act—a big ensemble scene. But suppose the most important act should be built on a duet? Yes, so that the entire act might be played, say by Ermolova and Lensky, and yet be thoroughly absorbing?'

And when the plot of the play had already been told, suicide still remained the spur for dramatic situations. It must be remembered that two acts had already taken place, yet upon the moral essence of the 'worth of life' the author had not yet begun to reflect; this problem must of itself rise above the images, the scenes, the fragments of observation, even as the mist rises above the bogs, the hillocks, and the shrubs. Then, of necessity, I was forced to pause in my labours, to drop them for a month or two, and to become wholly absorbed in the 'questions' of the worth of life.

A certain critic wrote about me that in my plays I was more a stage director than a playwright. Perhaps this was a very subtle observation.

Tell me your dreams, and I will tell you what you are. I was at this time but little consoled by dreams of an author's fame or by the conveyance of some sort of idea by means of a play. All my dreams were of a theatre, a theatre in which the actors should be endued with such a tone as I managed to endue my school pupils with, a theatre in which the plays performed would be like those produced during the year just past, like 'A Doll's House', 'The Glove' by Björnson, or Chekhov's 'The Sea Gull', or 'Soldatka' ('The Soldier's Wife') by Goslavsky (another distinguished play which failed in the theatre), or 'An Enemy of the People' by Ibsen, which failed in the hands of the superb actor Kiselevsky, or Turgenev's plays, acknowledged as unfitted for the stage. My dreams were of a theatre in which the work would proceed in quite another order, of a partnership. . . .

My dreams of the theatre, possessing me since youth, were approaching realization; they cried within me, demanded. . . .

With sorrow and intensity I thought of the young actors who had graduated from my school and were lost in inferior theatres. Where was Moskvin? While still in the second course he had created a tremendous impression in the leading rôle in 'A Doll's House'; he was really *my* actor, who had assimilated the very best I could give him of *my* theatrical art. Where was he? He was in Yaroslavl, playing little pieces in vaudeville, acquiring triteness, imbibing the insipid taste for provincial acting. Presently I would send out into the world the tremulous Roxanova and in the following year Knipper, Savitskaya, Meyerhold, Mundt . . . they would scatter among the old theatres; who among them would succeed in preserving in the professional theatrical atmosphere that which we conjointly had worked out with such an enormous and stimulating expenditure of our best strength?

[70]

Thus, in my room of the monastery hostel, 'under the tolling of bells', I crushed my desire to execute the problem I had set up for myself—the finishing of the play.

After the second performance of 'The Sea Gull' I received several letters from St. Petersburg to the effect that the play was listened to with attention, that the public was amazed that it could have proven such a failure. . . . But this could not change its fate. 'The Sea Gull' was published in *Russkaya Misl*, but not even the literary critics could rehabilitate it.

The Griboyedov prize—for the season's best play—was awarded to 'The Worth of Life'. I declared to the judges that I considered it unjust, that the prize should be given to 'The Sea Gull', and that this would be a superb glove to fling at the public and the old theatre. The judges did not agree with me; one of them, by the way, was Goltzev.

The failure of 'The Sea Gull', it goes without saying, had no effect whatsoever on Chekhov's popularity. It was taken for granted that the most gifted writers might be failures on the stage. As for the vast provinces, the event simply went by unnoticed.

Anton Pavlovitch himself, however, could not for a long time forget the blow. He became more shut in, perhaps even more gloomy. And the most terrible thing about it was that his health was shaken.

He went south. He froze in Melekhovo, he and all in the house with him. Presently he sold his books to Marx, the publisher of the widely circulated periodical *Neva*, if I am not mistaken, for 75,000 rubles. This was not bad for those days. It gave Anton Pavlovitch the possibility of moving to the Crimea, to Yalta, and to begin erecting his own villa according to his own taste. He gave himself up to the task with enthusiasm.

Throughout my life I have worked very hard. I began giving lessons when I was thirteen, and since then I have always earned my living. When I was in the eighth class of the *gymnasium*, because of the lack of teachers, I gave lessons in the evening to the younger classes. As a student I lived by lessons; then I began to write. I spent my whole life in ceaseless labour; during all these years I have worked with a kind of particular avidity, as if I were making haste to accomplish as much as possible before whole-heartedly giving myself up to the theatre alone. I wrote long and short stories, little *feuilletons*, articles; I participated in various meetings, committees, commissions; but I gave the bulk of my time to my beloved labour in the Philharmonic school.

That is why I saw very little of persons with whom I did not have the closest professional bond. Thus was it also with Chekhov. He visited Moscow less and less often. I had already had some practical conversations on the project of the theatre with Fedotov, playwright and theatrical promoter, as well as with theatre proprietors. I suggested to Korsh that he let me have his theatre for two days a week for my performances. And I worked out a plan for collecting a company of my pupils and opening in the provinces. . . . I no longer remember Chekhov among these conversations and projects. He had so definitely broken with the theatre that there was little likelihood of his taking an interest in that which gave me cause for feverish excitement.

In the summer, as always, I left for my estate, where reigned the silence of the steppe, but instead of trying to write I began to compose a long report addressed to the manager of the Imperial Theatres; I proposed in this report that the Small Theatre be reformed.

I had little idea of what was to be gained by my proposal. I have already somewhere given the impression that I was *persona gratissima* in the office of the manager, but his attitude was a purely formal one. I remember how one day, half seriously, half in jest, I suggested to him: ' If you'll let me, I'll produce "Ruslan and Liudmila",[1] quite in new style.' To which he replied: 'You should not be allowed within gunshot of the Bolshoy (Big) Theatre. Why, you'd turn everything topsy-turvy there!' In sending my memorandum, I must have foreseen that he would refuse to avail himself of a single suggestion. And so I went on thinking of my own theatre.

The longer I reflected on the matter, the more minutely the details of the project assumed shape and the clearer it became to me that I could not manage it alone; it had too many aspects, was too complex.

And now for the first time I bethought myself of Stanislavsky. For the first time during all these years of conversations and dreams I began to think of the amateur circle of the young and flourishing merchant Alekseiev-Stanislavsky, who himself put on plays and acted the leading rôles.

I knew little of Alekseiev and his affairs. Our acquaintance was, so to speak, a nodding one, but we used to meet as persons who, had we got into conversation, might have found many themes in common. I vaguely remembered that I heard about him from Fedotova, to whose house he used to come and of whose son he was a friend; that with

[1] Glinka's classical opera.

[73]

Fedotova he had acted in my play, 'The Lucky Man', in a gala performance; that I had been invited to a semi-amateur semi-scholastic exhibit of some sort of Circle, at the head of which stood Alekseiev and Komisarjevsky; that later I appeared at some inauguration, at which their Circle played Molière in the presence of the whole public which attends *premières*; it was evident that they were all interested in the Circle. The latter attracted particular attention with its production of Tolstoy's 'Fruits of Enlightenment'—the first time the famous comedy was shown in Moscow. I remember, when the play was later taken by the Small Theatre, they said there: 'But we can't play it as they can in Alekseiev's Circle.'

During later years the Circle played at the Amateurs' Club. I remembered 'Othello' and 'Uriel Acosta'; the first was shown in elegant artistic style, while the second had two superb crowd scenes. This was soon after the arrival in Moscow of the company of the Duke of Meiningen, famed for its stage-director Kronek, and the historical quality of its backgrounds and national scenes. And, immediately, Stanislavsky won the reputation of imitating the Meiningen company, a reputation which clung to him a long time.

Altogether, my general impression of the Circle was a vague one. What was it: the aspiration to create a new literary undertaking? Had this Alekseiev some serious problems in mind, or was it simply an ambitious desire to play all the remarkable rôles? He played everything—from vaudeville to tragedy. What was disturbing was that he produced all the plays for himself, and that he did not seem to be the man to play tragic rôles. The performances were prepared under strong discipline. This appealed to me; but

VLADIMIR NEMIROVITCH-DANTCHENKO AND
CONSTANTIN STANISLAVSKY
Founders of the Moscow Art Theatre

p. 74]

was it the result of a common inner fervour or of a more formal subjection to the 'master'? How much in this undertaking was due to the 'whims of the wealthy merchant', and how much to genuine creative stimulation?

I had great faith in Fedotova. Her relation to art was unusually clear and pure. And, I remember, she uttered in my presence the name of 'Kostya Alekseiev' with feelings of confidence and great sympathy.

During that summer my pupils of the oldest and second course decided to 'have practice'. They came together in a large village, and with the help of the administration of the club arranged for Sunday performances; the entrance fee was to be five to twenty kopecks for the morning performance for the peasants, and up to a ruble for the evening performance for the local intelligentsia.

I wrote to the manager of the Moscow Theatres that I would be in Moscow on June 21 and would call on him to hear his opinion on the report I sent him. I also sent a letter to Constantin Sergeievitch Alekseiev. It was a short one; in it I said I wanted to have a chat with him on a theme which might be of interest to him, and that I would be in Moscow on June 21. In reply to this I received an immediate telegram. The speed of the reply seemed significant; it occurred to me that my note had hit the mark. The telegram read: 'Will be very glad to wait you June 21 at 2 o'clock at Slavyansky Bazaar.' [1]

On the date mentioned I arrived in Moscow. I went first to see the manager of the Theatres. On his desk lay my memorandum report, marked in red pencil with exclamation and question marks. It was quite evident that he had

[1] Hotel and restaurant.

[75]

read it but 'did not approve of its contents'. We had a short conversation, lasting about half an hour. This brief interview was more than sufficient to convince me of the utter futility of our talk, and of the complete hopelessness of all my proposals. As I was leaving, I said: 'Do you know, Pavel Mikhailovitch, I'm on my way to meet Alekseiev-Stanislavsky. I'm going to propose to him to open a new theatre!'

'Alekseiev-Stanislavsky? Yes, I know him. I'd be ready to take him to manage the assembling department.'

Stanislavsky invited to take charge of the assembling department! Yet the manager ignored my words about a new theatre as though it were an idea which it was not possible to consider seriously.

I went to the Slavyansky Bazaar, where Stanislavsky was already waiting for me. We began our historic conversation at two o'clock in the afternoon, and finished it at his villa at eight o'clock the next morning.

PART II

BIRTH OF THE NEW THEATRE

CHAPTER SIX

Notwithstanding the fact that much has appeared in print about my meeting with Stanislavsky, lovers of the theatre have nevertheless retained a curiously romantic interest in it. And, actually, it was something extraordinary. Here were two theatrical visionaries, different in circumstance, temperament, and character, who had been working at a remote distance from each other, quite independently, under the stimulus of one and the same 'dominating'—as Carlyle would have called it—idea; these two men later met in an eighteen-hour discourse and immediately laid the foundation of an undertaking which was to play a tremendous part in the history of the theatre.

Moscow was celebrated for its first-class restaurants. Each had its own physiognomy. The restaurant of the hotel Slavyansky Bazaar gave the appearance, as it were, of being more sober than the others. The Hermitage was the most popular and showy. Testov's Tavern was patronized, for the most part, by merchants and the like. Although the Slavyansky Bazaar was a first-class hotel, it had an austere, modest look. It was patronized by personages from the novels of Tolstoy and the tales of Chekhov. Those honoured by benefit performances and playwrights on opening nights treated the actors to supper here, in private rooms or in large private dining-rooms.

Restaurants always played an important rôle in Moscow

life. All jubilees, celebrations, and gatherings took place in restaurants. All the most important conferences of shareholders and the many business meetings of the Art Theatre were held at the Hermitage. Mikhail Provitch Sadovsky, a member of the famous family of actors, during the final years of his life used to spend almost his entire day in this restaurant. He had his own designated place; he lunched, had his tea, and supped there; he received visitors, made appointments, and left for the theatre, only to return to his accustomed haunt. This, mind you, was in spite of the fact that he had his own house and a large family, for which he had a deep affection. The distinguished writer of *feuilletons*, Doroshevitch, like Sadovsky, constantly sat in the Hermitage, where he not only drank and conversed, but often even wrote.

One should add that Mikhail Sadovsky and Doroshevitch, as also Chaliapin, loved to talk—not merely converse, but talk—and liked to have listeners. Moreover, they talked —as did also Chaliapin—with marked originality and with scintillating wit, which always hit the mark. And, they actually attracted listeners.

At two o'clock the large handsome round hall of the ` Slavyansky Bazaar was still full of financiers, so Constantin Sergeievitch (Stanislavsky) and I engaged a private room.

Stanislavsky always presented a picturesque figure. Tall, distinguished in stature, he had an energetic bearing and his movements were plastic, though he did not give the impression of giving the slightest thought to this plasticity. As a matter of fact, this apparent beautiful casualness had cost him immense labour: according to his own words, he had spent hours and years in developing his gestures before the mirror. At thirty-three his hair was completely grey, but his heavy moustache and dense brows were black. This contrast immediately caught your eye, especially because of his immense stature.

It astonished you to find nothing specifically of the actor about him. There was no arresting feature of theatricality or of intonations borrowed from the stage, such as always so distinguished the Russian actor and so delighted persons of bad taste.

Stanislavsky was wholly new in the theatrical field, and even unique. Before everything he was an amateur, i.e. one who did not occupy any kind of position in the theatrical service and was not connected with any theatre, either as actor or director. He had not yet made a profession of the theatre, hence there was nothing that stamped him as a man of the theatre.

I was acquainted with all the well-known actors of the time. In each and every one of them, at the very first meeting, it was easy to detect the man or woman of the stage. It is true, they made no effort to conceal this, gave no thought to trying to resemble any of us, but even if they had made the effort nothing would have come of it. The necessity of maintaining all his faculties at a certain tension from day to day, both morning and night, becomes an actor's second nature. His voice is pitched with exaggerated excellence, his diction is cultivated, his gesture has a finality, or, on the contrary, gives the effect of unspoken charm, more expressive than that of a mimic; yes, his whole manner is that of a being of a special caste. The most intelligent actor, possessing the best taste, has upon him the stamp of cleverness. Moreover, the less sincerity he reveals on the stage, the

[81]

more artificial he is in life. Actors whose whole art bears a stamp can be off-stage quite unbearable; their every intonation is reminiscent of some rôle on the stage. And the public loves this—that is the horrible part of it! . . .

If somewhere within the recesses of his soul Stanislavsky harboured a desire to look like an actor, it was accomplished with great taste; he had been much abroad, and could choose models from among European actors.

A certain coquetry might have been suspected in the preservation of his moustache. It must have hindered him as an actor, and he parted with it only much later, before playing the part of Brutus in 'Julius Caesar', which means that not before 1903 did we persuade him to shave; it was indeed quite impossible to imagine Marcus Brutus with a moustache! But then the famous Salvini always wore a moustache. Quite apart from this, Stanislavsky was one of the directors of the factory of Alekseiev & Co. There they regarded the artistic endeavours of their co-director with sympathy until he began to look like a shaven actor.

How our discourse began I naturally do not remember. As I was its initiator, it is very likely that I told Stanislavsky of all my theatrical disappointments, revealed my dreams of a theatre with new problems, and proposed the creation of such a theatre by getting together a company made up of the best amateurs of his Circle and the more gifted of my pupils.

It was as if he had been waiting for just such a person as I to come and say these words, which he himself had for some time harboured in his brain! The conversation immediately gained an unusual heartiness; mutual enthusiasm developed without further hesitation. The material of our discourse

[82]

was vast. There was scarcely a spot in the old theatre that we did not attack with ruthless criticism. What a slaughter! We vied with each other in the supply of poisoned arrows. What was still more important, there was not a single spot in the whole complex theatrical organism for which we did not appear provided with a positive plan, whether by reform, reorganization, or complete revolution.

The most remarkable thing about this conversation was that we did not once disagree. In spite of the abundance of matters under discussion, in spite of the great number of details, there was nothing about which we could disagree. Our programmes either merged or complemented each other, but nowhere did they collide. In some instances he had fresher ideas, went beyond me, and lightly bore me along; in others he willingly yielded to me.

Our faith in each other grew with unrestrainable speed Apart from this, we made no special effort to please each other, as is done when, beginning a common undertaking, men above everything do a lot of bargaining with respect to their own rôles. Our whole conversation consisted in defining, agreeing upon, and affirming new laws for the theatre, and only after a formulation of these new laws did our own respective rôles emerge from it all.

Stanislavsky and I smoked a great deal (later we were both able to 'chuck' it). The private room in the Slavyansky Bazaar became unbearable; we had lunched there, partaken of coffee, and also dined there. Then Constantin Sergeievitch suggested that I journey with him to his villa and spend the night there.

It was the private villa of the family of the Alekseievs. A journey of forty minutes from one of the central stations led

[83]

through the magnificent Eastern forests of superb, ancient, gigantic firs and pines; then there were three versts by a droshky. The villa was called 'Liubimovka'. Everything in it was modest but durable, as was everything belonging to the mercantile class; the furniture, the silver-plate, the linen —everything had that 'solid' look. Besides the small two-story house there was a theatrical pavilion, where the Alekseievs once used to give their private performances. One of Constantin Sergeievitch's sisters, Anna Sergeievna, had developed into a very good amateur.

Constantin Sergeievitch was hospitable. A year later, when about five versts from Liubimovka the enthusiastic rehearsals of the future Art Theatre were already proceeding, I lived here for a couple of weeks or so. And several years later Chekhov was to spend a summer here meditating over his 'Cherry Orchard' and devoting himself to his favourite diversion: angling for fish in a stream bearing the historic name of 'Kliazma'.

The villa stood in a handsome pine grove. Apropos of this grove Constantin Sergeievitch was staging one of our famous performances—'The Blue Bird' of Maeterlinck. At one of the first dress rehearsals, when I was called to criticize (as also, when I called Stanislavsky to the first dress rehearsals of my performances), I attacked the scenery artist: 'Why, you can't tell the difference between his pine and his poplar.' Stanislavsky wanted to put in a word for the artist: 'But who's ever seen a pine? In order to see one, you have to go to the south of Italy.'

'Dear Constantin Sergeievitch! Your villa, where you spent the summer months of your childhood and youth, stands in the very midst of a pine grove.'

[84]

'Really?' He was astonished by this revelation.

And here is another instance of the same kind. He was preparing to put on 'The Blind' of Maeterlinck. There was the dress rehearsal. The moon, rising before us on the horizon, barely paused, slowly glided to the left along the horizon. I protested against such an original cosmography. But Constantin Sergeievitch was slow to see my objection, as for technical reasons it was very difficult to direct the moon according to its natural parabola.

This was very remarkable for the light it threw on the character of *régisseur* Stanislavsky. In general, he took no interest in nature. He created her only as he found her necessary in his stage imagination. To allow oneself to be captivated by nature he was inclined to call sheer sentimentality. Is it not astonishing, then, that this should not have hindered him from producing a stirring morning in 'The Cherry Orchard', wind and rain in 'Uncle Vanya', summer twilight in 'The Sea Gull', and so on?

On the way from the Slavyansky Bazaar we naturally did not cease to discuss one and the same thing.

At Liubimovka, Constantin Sergeievitch had already armed himself with writing materials. At the very first meeting he revealed one of his quite conspicuous traits of persistence, in an extreme degree: his tendency to talk a thing out to the end, even to put it down in writing—set it down as a record. All who worked with him knew this trait, whether the electrical engineer, the property man, or even the actor. He did not trust memory, either his own or any one else's. 'Write it down,' he used to say to him or to her, after a matter had been discussed to some conclusion.

'It's not necessary. I'll remember it.'

[85]

'Eh-h, no!' he would blurt out, assuming a cheerful air in order to soften his insistence. 'I don't believe you!'

'I assure you, I have a good memory.'

'I don't believe you. I don't believe you. And don't you trust your memory! Write it down! Write it down!'

Memory in the actor is an important virtue. Various stage people have various qualities of memory. Stanislavsky always had an astonishing memory for visual matters, for realistic details, for gestures. But for words he had for a very long time a poor memory. Many anecdotes were current about his faltering with words in life and on the stage. It is really remarkable that in the course of many years he even thought that this was by no means a defect in an actor. Ultimately he found his own method for memorizing. And, at the revival of 'Sorrow From Wit', for example, not only did he justify himself in the rôle of Famusov, but no one from the Chatskys, Repetilovs and Skalozubo could compare with him in clarity and facility in the use of words and rhythms.

It goes without saying that, in practice, our undertaking did not progress quite, and often not at all, according to the memorandum made at our first meeting. I have said, it will be remembered, that to the slightest question of theatrical organization we had a positive answer. But of course afterwards, in practice, we came into collision with such an endless number of unexpected things! And such shattering unexpected things! It was very good in its way that we did not know everything and had not foreseen everything. Because if we had foreseen everything, then, if you please, we would not have decided to go on with the undertaking. The important thing was that we were, in a sense, possessed. Thus

[86]

at least we seemed, one to the other, but each to himself appeared fully in his right mind. Actually, we were 'in blinkers'. We suffered no doubts, we did not question the adequacy of our powers, we might accomplish anything! Anything! We knew everything that was necessary to know, and how to accomplish things!

We went over his and my pupils, and sorted out the best of them; defined the capacities of each. As teachers, of course, we felt an affection toward our pupils and doubtless overestimated their worth. When we chanced to make comparisons of them with the actors of the Small Theatre, Stanislavsky was more decisive than I. Borne along by the freshness of his talents, his freedom from the theatrical 'stamp' (at that time this word was not yet in our vocabulary), he was still indifferent to the skill of the old actors and, failing to penetrate their 'stamp,' he underestimated their individuality. I remember, for example, there arose the question who was the more interesting—Luzhsky, the amateur from Stanislavsky's circle, with definite acting gifts, who had already performed a great deal but who had not yet created a single brilliant artistic image, or Constantin Ruibakov, a major actor in the Small Theatre, one of its 'stars'.

'Luzhsky, of course!' Stanislavsky replied without the slightest hesitation.

At this point there immediately arose an ambiguous irreconcilability, an irreconcilability with everything that was called 'the traditions of the Small Theatre'. Ruibakov grew up on these traditions; his whole artistic personality was based upon them. A pupil of Fedotova, an imitator of Samarin, he absorbed their art with all its charm and all its faults—its sentimentalism and conservatism. He absorbed it humbly, deeply, for always. And he served it brilliantly with his graceful acting talents. He was the typical bearer of 'traditions'. Incidentally, under this name the art received not only its substance, but even more often its form, congealed by repetition. These traditions barred the way to what was new and fresh, and it was against them that our dreams were directed.

It was not for us, setting sail to discover new mirages, to conquer the artistic habits of such an actor—they had become his second nature—not for us to infect him with a new faith. The main thing was: it was impossible to reconcile him to our discipline, to subject him to the dictatorial will of the director-*régisseur*.

In our very first conversation it was clear to me that the aspiration to subject human beings to measures of strict discipline was stronger in him than in me. This proved true even later, after an association of many years. Earlier it had seemed to me that I was unnecessarily strict in demanding punctuality of my pupils, and other details of behaviour consistent with the discipline to be desired between the walls of the school. I remember I had a gifted girl-pupil who had the foolish habit of turning up late at rehearsals. In order to teach her a lesson, I tried one day, in consequence of her tardiness, to put off the rehearsal; I gave up my careless pupil, so to speak, to the judgment of her comrades. The effect exceeded my expectations: they assailed her in such a way that she rushed in a sleigh in order to overtake me, and when she had caught up with me she flung herself upon her knees right there in the street and implored me to return.

As it happened, I had to use the same means many years later in the Art Theatre against two of our most remarkable artists, who were gifted and beloved, an actor and actress with the same disorganizing habit of showing up late. And again, even though there was no genuflexion in the snow, the measure proved infinitely more stern and effective than all fines or censures.

In all similar instances Stanislavsky was on my side, because, generally speaking, he went to greater excess than I. For example, he very often resorted to a proclamation of 'martial law' in order to enhance the rehearsal fervour.

In evaluating the Art Theatre, we must realize that its organization enjoyed a fame almost as great as its art. In our eighteen-hour conversation Stanislavsky and I established all the basic principles of this organization. We did not indulge in any self-satisfied flattery of dreams; we drew up a real working plan. We well knew how quickly undertakings went to pieces when human beings gave themselves up with naïve fervour to 'good intentions', while in the practical realization of them they counted on some sort of business-like secondary personages, who would suddenly appear and immediately arrange everything, yet for whom the original leaders felt even a certain measure of contempt.

The working out of a plan in all its details was not difficult, because the organized forms in the old theatre had grown decrepit to such a degree that they seemed to implore a change to new forms.

For example: the office should yield precedence to the demands of the stage. The theatre exists for that which happens on the stage, for the creativeness of the actor and author, and not for those who manage them. The office must resiliently accommodate itself to all the curves, unexpectedness, collisions, which fill the atmosphere of artistic labour. This very simple truth was in the old theatre submerged under official staffs, injunctions, procedures, protectionism, career-hunting, routine in all interrelations—so submerged, indeed, that the official form became more important than the art content. It was far easier to wound the pride of the best actor than that of the average bureaucrat. It was possible to refuse the legitimate expense of stage management or the compensation of a stage-worker, and at the same time to create a new position for a young man who had arrived from St. Petersburg with a letter of introduction from Her Highness. It was impossible to introduce the slightest reform on the stage if it necessitated some insignificant change among the desks of the office.

Another example: every play must have its own setting, i.e. its own decorations, furniture, and properties, all suited to the particular play, and costumes especially made to suit the various rôles. At present, in every theatre of the Soviet Union this is commonly accepted as the A B C of the business, but then it seemed like a revolution. The old theatre had its 'garden', its 'wood'—as the officials themselves contended, 'of the most approved verdure'; it had a reception-room with soft-lined chairs and a tall lamp in the corner with a yellow shade eminently suited for a comfortable love passage; a larger reception-room with pillars, painted of course; a middle-class room with red mahogany furniture. In the storeroom of decorations there were 'Gothic' and 'Renaissance' properties for 'classical' plays, as all costume-plays were called by the director, even though they were written by contemporary authors. They had, correspondingly, chairs with high backs, a black carved table, and a curule chair, which the director stubbornly persisted in calling the 'culture' chair. All these properties were used now in one play, now in its successor. Every actor had his own wardrobe and acquired it according to his taste. He did not even find it necessary to take counsel with the director. Actresses talked it out among themselves in order not to repeat the colour of the dresses. Of a monolithic spectacle, in which all parts were harmoniously merged, no one ever thought.

The scenery was painted by a decorator or decorator-mechanic, who received a salary. To attract artists into the theatre, the same artists who drew the public to picture exhibitions never entered the heads of the officials or of the stage-director.

We did away with the orchestra which used to play in the intermissions as something unnecessary and even harmful, a diversion affecting the unity of the emotions. It was a survival of those days when the theatre was considered as mere entertainment. On the other hand I remember that even such an actress as Ermolova said to me: 'I for one am sorry that you have done away with the orchestra. Sounds of music before the raising of the curtain always put us actors in such a good mood!'

There should be silence in the corridor during a performance. To obtain it, the light in the corridors should be dimmed, which willy-nilly has the effect of lowering the voice. The merchant Stchukin, landlord of our theatre, in which within a year we were to perform, expressed himself at the beginning as against this new order of things. 'Suppose the public should take offence!' Later, however, he himself got into our way of doing things, and never walked but on tiptoe.

It was necessary to contend with the offensive habit of the public of coming in during the actual performance. A group is gathered in the corridor and holds a conversation; the door of the auditorium is open. 'Time to go in,' says one. 'No, they haven't begun yet,' another replies, glancing through the open door and seeing that the curtain hasn't yet gone up. He, as you may know, is the sort who is used to taking his seat only after the performance has begun.

We conceived the idea of dimming the lights in the corridors just before the raising of the curtain, in order to force the public to hurry to their seats. We had not yet dared venture wholly to forbid entrance during the performance. This came only later, a full ten years later.

To such a point was the theatrical public spoiled by the servile position of the actor! He made his public more cultured, he ennobled its dreams, he accorded it the highest spiritual joy, and the public delighted in the actor; but once it entered the theatre and paid its money it seemed to think that it had a right to do as it liked and to give orders! Now there is scarcely a theatre in the Soviet Union in which it is not forbidden to enter during the performance. And yet how much struggle went on around this petty matter! I remember how one great theatregoer, who attended all first nights, altogether stopped coming to the Art Theatre when we first announced our rule not to admit anyone during the performance.

'Surely you are interested in our new productions?'

'What else is there to do? I must deny myself. I'm used to coming to the theatre when I feel like it. I might be held up by an important conversation. You want to restrict my liberty. I can't allow it!'

[92]

This was a bourgeois of the first water. But here is something that happened even in the first years of the revolution: During a performance I heard a noise in the corridor. It was revealed that some sort of imbecile, having decided that the revolution gave him the right to do as he liked, was threatening the usher because he was not allowed to enter the auditorium.

Even Meyerhold during the first year of his theatre had hung out a placard, on which it was stressed that the public was allowed not only to applaud but also to whistle and boo if the show did not please it; moreover, it was allowed to enter or go out during a performance at its own pleasure. Whether this was directed against the traditions of the Art Theatre or was a broad gesture for the gratification of a new public is of little consequence here; but it goes without saying that as an artist Meyerhold was soon convinced of the impossibility of playing in such conditions, and he reverted to the order of the Art Theatre.

Our attitude to the public was one of the important questions discussed in our conversation. In principle we wanted to establish our undertaking so that the public should not consider itself 'master' in the theatre, but feel itself happy and grateful for the privilege of entering, even if it did have to pay for it. We would meet it courteously and amiably as we would meet charming guests: we would offer it all conveniences, but at the same time would force it to submit to rules essential for the artistic unity of our spectacle.

I must mention numerous other fragments of our conversation: our announcements must be composed in a better literary style than the official ones of the Small Theatre; our curtain must be drawn to the sides rather than raised;

entrance behind the scenes must be forbidden; of actors' benefits there could not be even the slightest mention; the entire theatrical apparatus must be in such perfect order as to create the impression, even at a first performance, of the production's having been organized by experienced persons and not by amateurs; there must be no late starts, no prolonged intermissions, no accidents with lights, no catching of the curtain, no slips behind the wings, etc.

The most considerable parts of the organization were the repertory, the budget, and—the most important and most interesting—the order of rehearsals and the preparations for a production.

The most significant by far of organizational reforms consisted precisely in the way a production was prepared. It was begotten, essentially, in dramatic schools, when the final examination productions were no longer made up of fragments for showing off the pupils but consisted of complete plays; when the pedagogues no longer limited themselves to teaching their pupils to take the first steps of the stage art, but collaborated with them in a complete play. The teacher became a pedagogue stage-director. The pupil was trained to submit his individuality to the demands of the *mise en scène*, the *ensemble*, the revelation of the literary and dramatic qualities of the play. Thus both Pravdin and Yuzhin worked in the rôle of teacher. I in the Philharmonic school and Lensky in the school of the Imperial Theatres went even further. Above all, we concentrated not merely on one examination production but on several—four, even five. After this we put into the school productions ideas of a directorial, productional character, going far beyond the limits of the school programme. It was as if we had at our disposal not

[94]

merely a chance body of school youths but a complete theatrical company. In the course of the winter we gave performances on our school stages; during Lent, when for seven weeks all the play theatres were generally closed, we had the use of the stage of the Imperial Small Theatre. The performances were private, but there were people in Moscow interested in them, and the theatre was always full. In the matter of external productional effects, neither Lensky nor I, of course, had much choice: we simply made use of what properties were available in the Small Theatre. Nevertheless, even in this aspect, we often contrived to be more up-to-date than the public was accustomed to seeing us in the old theatre.

Stanislavsky had a similar method in the preparation of play production. This was of great moment in bringing us together. He, too, began with discussions of a play and then rehearsed, slowly progressing from one scene to the next, pausing on some one of them for several hours, or for several days, and arriving at the fulfilment of his conception of the scene by repeating it, or even a mere fragment of it, tens of times. What precisely he aimed at is another question; what was important was that, working along this path, we did not bind ourselves to a routine which demanded a hurried rehearsal on the stage and the play's immediate production.

Many years would pass; the Art Theatre would develop, broaden, and refine this reform, no longer under school conditions as I had done it in the Philharmonic School, and no longer in a Circle of amateurs, as Stanislavsky had tried to do it in his Society of Lovers of the Arts, but under the conditions of a large professional theatre; yet the old theatre would still continue to maintain itself and to labour as formerly.

[95]

Our organization would percolate into the other theatres with extraordinary slowness, especially in the provinces. But from the first years of the revolution, when the business of the theatre was to become one of the more considerable of Governmental businesses, when the theatre was to be given a significance hitherto unknown in the history of humanity and its spiritual culture—by then all the theatres, to the last one, to the most out-of-the-way corner of the land, were to adopt the organization of the Art Theatre as something quite natural, with no thought even of questioning it.

But in the European and American theatres to this day everything still proceeds as it did thirty-five years ago, before the creation of the Art Theatre, i.e. without preliminary discussions about the play.

The meeting of participating actors begins with the mechanical examination of rôles by means of copy-books, to make sure that they are correctly copied; the chief actors are rarely present, their rôles being substituted by the assistant *régisseur*.

The first rehearsal takes place on the stage. The actors walk about with their copy-books, with little comprehension of what the play is about, while the *régisseur* is already indicating: 'At these words you go to the table at the right, while you go to the left and sit in the armchair, and you, Kostya, retire to the rear toward the window.' Why one actor should go to the table at the right and the other to the left to sit in the armchair is not yet clear to any one but the *régisseur*; the actors obediently note down his remarks in their copy-books. And there is really no time to explain: the whole play must be gone over at each rehearsal, the entire four or five acts: the next day the *régisseur* again directs who

is to go to the table at the right and who is to sit in the armchair at the left; he next announces two days 'for the study of
the rôles'. Then the rehearsals proceed, day after day, the
whole four acts at a single rehearsal. Gradually the actors
cease glancing at their copy-books and the prompter lets up
a little, does not quite so loudly repeat the whole text. The
executors of the minor rôles, either from excessive zeal or
from a sense of humiliation, presently show that they have
mastered them. The actors in the more important rôles
struggle for some time with the necessity of uttering loudly
words as yet strange to them, of playing insufficiently
defined emotions, of exhibiting temperament without the
least apparent reason. Quite often, unceremoniously or with
courtesy, depending upon mutual relations, the *mise en scène*
ordered by the *régisseur* is changed: he has found it inconvenient for the actress to go to the window on the right,
while she finds it equally inconvenient to sit in the armchair
on the left. In truth, the latter was not inconvenient for
psychological reasons, but simply because it did not corre-
spond to the old acquired habits of the actress.

Ermolova keeps on looking into her copy-book. Once,
entering upon the rehearsal stage, she says in her low deep
voice, as if speaking to herself: 'To-day I shall try out the
third act.' This means that she has worked out her conception of it at home and now desires to verify her impression.
She is rehearsing the third act by heart, flinging out sparks
of her mighty temperament. Around her everyone is catching the infection, interest in the play is growing, the desire to
pull oneself together is awakening. During an interruption
she is being praised, the younger persons of the cast are in
raptures, they kiss her hand; she modestly pulls it away; the

[97]

play begins to move as on rails. The actors, with sincere or ostentatious affection, begin to offer advice to one another, and to create new convenient *mises en scène*. The rôle of the *régisseur* at the front, before the footlights, on a chair near the prompter's box, has come to an end; he is no longer necessary to anyone. The actors will arrange the play by themselves.

The last act is always rehearsed in a hurry; it is time to dine, in the evening a performance must be given—that is why the original conception becomes subject to reasoned or sentimental experiences, i.e. the sum of experiences associated with recent fatigue. A controlling eye is absent. As a result, some elements of the play have been preserved in their entirety; some ideas have found full expression, while others have paled or been emphasized to excess. This we shall see only at the performance, or, by a lucky chance, at the single dress rehearsal.

The conversation between Stanislavsky and me took place in 1897, while the first dress rehearsal in the history of the Russian theatre had taken place only three years before, at the time of the production of my play, 'Gold'. It happened thus: the play was being rehearsed simultaneously in Moscow and in St. Petersburg. At first it was intended for performance in St. Petersburg for the benefit of Strelskaya on October 20. The rehearsals went on under the pressure of daily bulletins from Livadya, in the Crimea, concerning the illness of Alexander III; he was dying. And on the 20th of October, when, having attired myself in a frock-coat, in expectation of being called to the footlights on the first night, I went out at seven o'clock into the Nevsky Prospect, I was immediately struck by the calm and silent crowds near the mourning bulletins on the walls. St. Petersburg was plunged into mourning—the Emperor had died. The theatres were closed for an indefinite period.

Under the pressure of the Church, the theatre in Russia was always regarded by the authorities as a sinful pastime; that is why the theatres were closed during Lent. Even shortly before the revolution a priest in Samara had refused to serve mass for the famous Komisarjevskaya because she was an actress—a creature who was beyond all hope of forgiveness in the next world. Therefore it was a sin even to pray for her.

The private theatres, if I remember rightly, were permitted to bring their mourning period to an end within six weeks. For six weeks the actors were doomed to inaction and hunger. At the State Theatres, which paid the actors yearly salaries, the mourning did not come to an end until January 2. I therefore set to work to make use of the spare time by subjecting my play to a whole series of rehearsals, and finally there was a dress rehearsal: a complete rehearsal, a full-fledged performance with the complete scenery, in full costume and make-up. Thanks to the regard the artists had for me, I succeeded in bringing this off. And the play had rôles for the four leading actresses in the company: Fedotova, Ermolova, Leshkovskaya, and Nikulina, as well as for the leading actors: Yuzhin, Lensky, Ruibakov, and Muzil.

Up to then, everything was a surprise for the author—the decorations, the costumes, the make-up. My memory has sharply preserved the feeling of horror I once experienced immediately before the *première* of one of my plays, when I saw the main character in a make-up which in no sense answered to the idea I had of his appearance. And it was

[99]

necessary to seem pleased and force a smile in order not to spoil the actor's humour just before his entrance on the stage. As for expecting an actress before the performance to don a dress only just made by a famous modiste, that was not even to be thought of!

Subsequently Stanislavsky and I were to indulge in rehearsals. We were not to be content with one dress rehearsal, but were to hold five or even six. These were complete rehearsals of the entire play. As for dress rehearsals of fragments of the play, i.e. those of the leading actors in make-up and costumes, with scenery, these we were to begin a month and a half or two months before the complete rehearsals.

And when the actors of the Art Theatre will have become partners in the undertaking, i.e. its full masters, putting into it their earnings and their salaries, then you shall see how far they have gone toward full appreciation of their artistic problems. At the very height of the season, while still playing daily to full houses, we will interrupt the performance for ten days, in order to have full freedom, without the obstacle of time, to hold a dress rehearsal of 'The Inspector General'. On another occasion we shall interrupt the performances for two weeks, in order to carry to a conclusion the staging of 'Hamlet' under the direction of Gordon Craig. The time would come when in the course of several months we should play only five evenings a week instead of seven, in order to preserve the fresh creative energies for rehearsals.

Let the clever merchant operating on a large scale explain to you how it was that even in a material sense we profited by this.

Ours was the only theatre in which the labour of rehearsals consumed not merely no less, but often more, creative effort than the performances themselves. I have dwelt on this point at length because in these labours new quests were carried out, the authors' profoundest thoughts revealed, the actors' individualities broadened, and the harmony of all stage parts established. In our eighteen-hour conversation our conviction of the tremendous importance of this reform remained unshaken. All the rules of life behind the scenes, the whole discipline, mutual relations, rights and responsibilities—everything contributed to forging the unity so essential to our endeavour. In this manner was formed the group of theatrical workers which eventually would be called the *collective*.

Once I happened to ask Yuzhin, when he began to manage the Small Theatre, how he could reconcile himself with the old methods of rehearsal, considering the fact that he had already had before his eyes the many years' trial of the Art Theatre? He answered thus: 'I am ready to give my *régisseur* as much time as he wants for a production, but he does not see in a play anything requiring more than three weeks, or a month!'

This was inaccurate. The *régisseur* may not see it, but the actors will. Who knows at what point will come jolts to their creativeness? It is necessary that the working atmosphere shall help them.

Ah, if only my dream were to come true, and that in all your theatres—of America, of Italy—such a system were not an exception, but the first rule of every theatre!

I have already mentioned that coryphaeus of our literature—Piotr Dmitrievitch Boborikin. With him, as with Chekhov, I used to converse a great deal concerning the new 'literary' theatre. Of an ardent temperament, possessed of immense erudition, he was capable within five minutes of outlining the most brilliant repertory of our promising theatre; he could recount how this matter progressed in all the capitals of Europe, where he felt himself at home, where he knew all the best actors, actresses, authors, critics; he wrote essays on the theatre, read lectures . . . I never succeeded, however, in drawing him into a detailed analysis of the 'kitchen' of the theatre. It bored him. He glowed over results, but did not possess the tenacity that produces results. Although he was above all a novelist, he devoted considerable time to the theatre, and was even an outstanding dramatist. But he was not 'a man of the theatre'. He loved the external showy aspect of the theatre, but skimmed over what might be called its 'craft'. It is this, precisely, that we men of the theatre love above everything in the world. This craft is a tenacious one, persistent and many-faceted, filling the stage, from the upper bars to the trapdoors; it is the craft of the actor at his rôle. And what does this mean? It means labour over oneself, over one's gifts, nerves, memory, and habits. . . . Kachalov once said that for the actor of the Art Theatre each new rôle is the birth of a new person . . . This labour is a tormenting, sacrificial one, often thankless to the point of despair; nevertheless, it is a labour from which the actor, once he has given himself to it, will never willingly tear himself away, and which he will never in this life exchange for a more tranquil occupation. If this feeling does not exist, it is better to avoid the theatre.

This indeed was at the very root of the coming together of Stanislavsky and myself. It is possible that the more business-like, seemingly tedious details crept into our conversation

[102]

the less we avoided them, and the more faith we had that our undertaking would prosper.

In what measure was Stanislavsky ambitious? More than once this question arose in my mind, when, behind the intonations of his deep, always warm, somewhat hoarse voice there sounded either satisfaction (what was it that pleased him?) or vexation (what was it that distressed him?) or apparent restraint (what emotion did he avoid revealing?). Many undertakings, with excellent prospects, I have seen dissipated before my eyes because of histrionic ambitions. Now, in our conversation there was a fragment of this ambition.

We were discussing the question of a repertory. Before opening the doors of a theatre, with an immediate programme of daily performances, it is necessary to have several productions ready. The American and French system of repeating the same play as long as it continues to attract the public was unknown to the Russian theatre; nor would it have found acceptance: it smacked too much of a trade. We went over the plays already given by Stanislavsky's Circle, and tried to evaluate them from the point of view of our future theatre. We paused to consider two of the most significant productions—'Othello' and 'Uriel Acosta'. I made no effort to conceal my doubts. Notwithstanding their worthiness, the question touched on the quality of the leading actor. The undertaking which we were entering upon was too serious an affair for us to begin with spurious compliments. Our conversation had reached a moment of psychological poignancy.

And Stanislavsky did not utter a single word in his own defence. He humbly left it to me to decide whether or not he was fitted to play these tragic rôles. And we actually excluded 'Othello' and 'Uriel Acosta' from our repertory. I may boldly say that no other major actor would have been capable of such a self-sacrificing gesture.

Was it possible for me to draw any other conclusion from this single episode than that this mighty creator of dramatic productions would be capable of submitting to the same discipline that he was creating for others? The sacrifices he was prepared to exact from others he was ready to make himself.

It goes without saying, I was not so naïve as to consider such a major theatrical personage wholly lacking in ambition. But as with every passion, the force of ambition can be destructive as well as creative. Under its urging, the artist can create the best of which he is capable, yet every one knows the evil behaviour to which this passion may lead. It depends a great deal, too, on certain qualities of character . . .

Finally, from a whole series of separate petty cues I gathered the impression that whatever ambition Stanislavsky had—whether as an actor to become a Lensky (who from youth had attracted him) or a Rossi or a Possart (European tragedians, meetings with whom he loved to tell about and who apparently had imposed upon him their Germanic monumentality), or as a *régisseur* to create out of himself a Russian Kronek (the *régisseur* of the celebrated Meiningen company—Stanislavsky had in fact cited examples of the elegant productions upon which Kronek exercised his monarchical authority)—he had excellent taste and sound judgment; I was growing confident that the vision of the undertaking as a whole would swallow up what had been the source of that vision.

And suddenly something wholly unexpected occurred: We were already near the end of our conversation when one morning, during coffee, I said: 'There's another thing which we must establish—we must each tell the other the whole truth to his face!' After everything that we had discussed I expected a brief answer such as 'It goes without saying', or 'We've already made a good start in this direction.' Consider, then, my astonishment when Constantin Sergeievitch, throwing himself against the back of the chair and fixing me with a glance, said: 'I can't do that.'

At first I failed to comprehend his meaning, and I made haste to say: 'Ah, no! I give you this right in all our mutual relations.'

'You don't understand. *I* can't stand hearing the whole truth to my face.'

The frankness of this admission was as remarkable as its contradiction of everything that had preceded it. I tried to soften the condition: 'It's always possible to find a means for speaking the truth without provoking the *amour propre* . . .'

Often afterwards, in the course of decades of collaboration, the memory of this acknowledgment returned to me. Sometimes it seemed prophetic. Yet it was not strictly accurate: often it was possible to say to Constantin Sergeievitch's face the most painful truth, and to see him accept it simply and with courage. At other times he was deeply perturbed and wounded; still more often he was driven to exasperation by a truth relatively trivial.

For a long time his ardent, devoted admirers referred to him as 'the big infant', but this had no final bearing on the matter; it lacked definiteness and had no serious meaning. Stanislavsky's nature was, indeed, a passionate and a com-

[105]

plex one. It unfolded itself before us through the years. For a long time it was impossible to grasp much of what was going on within him, thanks to the contradictions which perpetually astonished us. Stencilled definitions of a single colour were never applicable in any characterization of him.

And our first meeting was too full of an ardent desire to gain the affection of the other, and to give it; there was little room for calm analysis. He also must have made surmises concerning my character. He even went so far as to acknowledge that for over a year and a half he had been 'walking in circles' round me with the thought of meeting me to discuss the undertaking. . . .

Two bears won't get along together in one den!

Eyeing each other with a trusting smile we boldly, without any pharisaism, brought up this question: how were we to divide our rights and responsibilities? As far as the administrative side was concerned it was possible to fix some sort of boundary. To Stanislavsky's lot was to fall a great deal of actor's work; hence, though there were powers and duties connected with it which involved his looking into all administrative matters, the larger share of the administrative burden fell upon me. We decided that I should be what is known in the juridical 'Society' as the director-manager.

To begin with, we were both of us in our groups absolute *régisseurs* and pedagogues. Both of us were accustomed to impose our sole will; more than that, we accustomed our pupils to submit to it. Furthermore, we were convinced that it could not be otherwise. And if in the matter of production Stanislavsky had had more experience than I—he had already revealed new methods in *mise en scène*, in characterization, in human-crowd effects, and I could not but acknowledge

[106]

his decided pre-eminence over me—it followed that in the carrying out of the inner, histrionic direction of the production we could not avoid finding ourselves in the position of the two bears in a single den.

Constantin Sergeievitch, however, had already prepared a solution of this difficult problem. This is what he proposed:

The entire artistic realm was to be divided into two parts —the literary and the productional. Both of us were to take possession of a whole production, helping each other and criticizing each other. How this would work out technically was left for later discussion. In any event, in the artistic region we would have equal rights. But should there be a difference of opinion and a decision had to be made, he would have the right to veto what he thought objectionable in the productional part, and I have the same right in the literary part.

It came to this: he had the last word in the region of *form*, and I in the region of *content*.

The solution was by no means a wise one, and it is scarcely possible that we were not aware that same morning of the impracticability of such a plan. The practice itself would soon show, and show at every step, that form could not be torn from content; that I, insisting on some sort of psychological detail or literary image, ran the danger of running foul of their productional expression, i.e. of the form; while, on the other hand, he, affirming his discovered favourite form, might find himself in conflict with my literary treatment.

It is precisely this point that was to become the most explosive in our future mutual relations . . .

[107]

MY LIFE IN THE RUSSIAN THEATRE

None the less, on that remarkable morning we snatched at this artificial device, so intensely did we desire to banish all hindrances, so endlessly attractive, so tremendous and precious seemed that visionary edifice which we had adorned inwardly and outwardly, infecting each other from two o'clock of the previous day with our temperaments, beautiful dreams, and closeness to realization. Both of us honestly and without calculation was ready to take upon his own shoulders the sacrificial burden of making the concession, if only to keep the divine conflagration in us from being forthwith extinguished.

Sometimes such trifles are recalled, such seemingly insignificant trifles!

For the whole of life there has remained in my memory the silence before the dawn in the farmhouse, upon my return from Moscow. Days on the noisy railway; a detour, and the immediate silence of the Ekaterinoslav steppes, the train running so slowly that it seemed possible to jump off, pick some flowers, and overtake the train; then the journey of fifty 'good' versts [1] with horses, through the warm Southern night, amid clouds of dust, rising in the darkness and attacking the nostrils; on either side, the whole way, the crisp sound of unharvested barley—the right-hand horse is trampling upon it in the road—and then, at last, the village and the farmhouse, plunged in sleep.

My wife and I are walking before the terrace of the house —from the wing occupied by the servants, where is also the stable, we walk as far as the park. I have already recounted to her my meeting with Alekseiev, and am continuing to recall details. Separate features, observations, are interrupted

[1] A verst is about two-thirds of a mile.

by businesslike reflections, and are thus bound up with the visions, as though merged in them. Neither in the farmhouse nor in the steppe is the slightest sound audible. Now and then the snort of a horse is heard—the horses are in the open, close to the stable, by the cart containing oats; it is stifling in the stable; on the river, there is the sudden cry of a duck startled by the diving of a fish. One of the big yarddogs approaches us, licks our hands. The dogs somehow appear to be acutely conscious of the pre-dawn silence, and seem, as it were, apprehensive of violating its final hour. There, behind the garden, strips of light have already made their appearance. We approach the well, make a detour of the puddles round its new framework, lower the pail for fresh water.

Dreams and plans . . . plans.

In what consists the remarkable power of the theatre? Why does it draw the girl from the remote provinces, as Nina Zaretchnaya in 'The Sea Gull', and the *gymnasium* student, and the merchant's son, and the princely offspring, as for example Prince Sumbatov, and the famous doctor, who abandons his immense practice, and General Stakhovitch, friend of Grand Dukes on terms of 'thou', who takes off his uniform to become an actor, and the young count who leaves his parents' house, and the most gifted writers before whom all doors are flung open, all preferring to give their best emotions to the theatre and the actors? Within ten years the Art Theatre would become a big share-holding corporation, and consider who the shareholders would be: a citizen of the city of Odessa, a remarkable actor; a marvellous actress, a peasant of the Saratov province, Butova; a teacher of calligraphy, the enchanting Artem; 'Riurikovitchi' [1], Count Orlov-Davidov, Prince Dolgoruky; Her Excellency Jerusolemskaya—this was our *grande dame* Rayevskaya; an esteemed merchant, still another merchant, the Countess Panina, Prince Volkonsky, the doctor, Anton Chekhov . . .

The music of life; the spirit of easy, free intercourse; the uninterrupted nearness to the glow of lights, to eloquent speech—all that is best in me comes to life; the ideal reflection of all human relations—of family, of friendship, of love, of still more love, of love without end, of politics, of heroism, of pathos, of laughter. And the behind-the-scenes existence of actors is always tremulous, always tense, and everything comes together—the joy, and the tears, and the exasperation.

The kingdom of dreams. The power over the crowd.

Across my entire life, as also across the entire life of Alekseiev, like a commanding broad river running across the steppe, there flows by this theatrical existence, this theatrical atmosphere, tense and restless, with power of attraction and repulsion, and always holding you in thrall to its enchantments.

The nine-year-old lad holds his daily performances in the pasteboard theatre on the window-sill: he himself is the actor and the programme-maker, he is also the musician and the orchestra conductor swinging the baton; his favourite occupation is rummaging among the rubbish of a summer theatre in process of construction; his favourite odours are the smells of printer's ink on the play-bills and of the gas behind the scenes; he makes friends with the box-office keeper. At thirteen years of age he is a dramatist, the author of a five-act melodrama, 'Jacque Noel Rambert', of

[1] Descended from Rurik, ancestor of Russian Nobles.

[110]

a four-act comedy with couplets, and of a vaudeville sketch with songs, 'The Bridal Coiffure'—all three of them written in a single summer! His first diversion is a horsewoman of the circus, the first woman he falls in love with at sixteen is an actress. Then he is an amateur, with the best connections —behind the scenes; and so it goes.

Whence all this? By what theory of heredity? My father was a provincial military man, a landowner in the Chernigov province, not at any time having any acquaintance with the theatre. My mother came from some quite remote corner in the Caucasus; she married at fourteen, knew nothing of the theatre, was a mother at fifteen, but simultaneously with the nursing of her babe she played with dolls. It is true, father subscribed to periodicals and possessed a fairly good library. But he did not anticipate, of course, that she would poison his first-born; while in the military cadet corps brother Vassily was given a sound birching for a whole series of poems against the authorities; afterwards, in face of the strongest opposition on father's part, he abandoned the corps and ran away to St. Petersburg where, in stormy loneliness, he developed into a brilliant writer, making known to the whole world the humble name of the lieutenant-colonel.

Let us say that this was due to the library—to Pushkin, Lermontov, Marlinsky, the *Sovremennik* (*The Contemporary*) —but whence the passion for the theatre? The second son, Ivan, an Adonis, also abandoned the cadet school and became an actor. Poor fellow, he fell a victim to tuberculosis just as he was on the threshold of brilliant successes. My only sister, one of the most fascinating women of the theatre, became a famous actress.

And now—the fourth.

[111]

Whence such a flow to literature, to the theatre, to music? Where is its source?

Did it come only because my mother up to her sixteenth year had played with dolls? . . .

Neither Chekhov's name nor his writing image was near us, near Alekseiev and me, in that conversation. It goes without saying that I mentioned him, but my remark brought forth not the slightest response. In repertory Constantin Sergeievitch revealed very good taste and an obvious inclination to the classics. And he was indifferent to contemporary authors—they did not enter at all into his theatrical calculations. Naturally, he was familiar with Chekhov's tales, but as a dramatist Chekhov made an impression on him no greater than the other authors with whose names he was familiar: Shpazhinsky, Sumbatov, Nevezhin, Gneditch. At best, he regarded his plays with the same perplexity with which the theatrical public regarded them.

Apart from this, we discussed *our* theatre, Stanislavsky's theatre and mine, in an egoistic, even deeply egoistic, mood. It was to become the theatre of Chekhov only later, and wholly unexpectedly for us.

As for Anton Pavlovitch (Chekhov), he was at this time, in the summer of 1897, in hiding from the theatre, and doing it with all the resolution he possessed; he imagined that from the theatre and its friends he was now safe for ever. He went on writing, practising medicine in his own village, Melekhovo, and rarely gave heed to his barely healed wounds: 'Never will I write these plays or try to produce them, not if I live to be seven hundred years old!'

That very spring, during lunch with Suvorin, he had suddenly begun to spit blood. He was taken to the clinic, where he was kept for a month and a half, and where even his own sister was not allowed to see him for a long time.

'How could I have been so stupid as to overlook this—and I a doctor!' he repeated several times.

The whole of that winter, 1897–1898, he spent in Nice.

CHAPTER SEVEN

Stanislavsky and I decided to spend a year in preparation. To an American manager or an Italian *direttore* this would have sounded preposterous; an entire year to be spent in preparing for the opening! But even this was scarcely sufficient for us.

The difficulties which gave us the greatest concern may be divided into four sections: (1) the unification of the two groups, his and mine, by means of a survey of the performances, his and mine; this was the main artistic function; (2) the technical preparation, i.e. the finding of a suitable theatrical structure, the arranging of contracts, the creation of all required supply and administrative departments; (3) the preparation of the so-called 'community spirit'; and (4)—oh, what a nightmare!—the most necessary thing of all: money, money, and money!

This, surely, is comprehensible to every one; it comes before everything. There still sounds in my ears the pure Moscow intonation, with frank sympathy and a suppressed smile: 'Yes, my good gentlemen, and where do you propose to find this money?'

Now, as I write these lines, the question of means in the Soviet Union has taken quite a secondary place. The slightest artistic undertaking, however modest, whether a theatrical group working honestly and sincerely, or one engaged in a wholly fantastic experiment having no connection whatsoever with art, all this promptly receives support from the Government itself: in one fashion or another everything is done to make it possible for you to establish yourself at the start.

At that time, Alekseiev and I felt ourselves in the situation of those regarded with suspicion by servants: 'Have these gentlemen some design on the silver, or a hat belonging to some one else?' I recall how one day we shared the same feeling as we left the magnificent entrance of the house of Varvara Alekseievna Morozova. She was a very generous, philanthropic woman, a remarkable character in her way. She was handsome, and she owned a factory, but she conducted herself modestly and did not flaunt her money. Closely associated with a professor, who was the chief editor of the most popular newspaper in Russia, it is even possible that she was building up her life according to the taste of the noble restrained tone of this journal. As a patroness of higher education for women, of student bodies, of libraries, one invariably saw the name of Varvara Alekseievna Morozova. And it seemed natural for us to ask who would respond to our theatrical dreams if not she? As it happened, both Alekseiev and I had had a previous acquaintance with her; I was certain that she thought well of us both.

But a theatre! Moreover, a theatre composed of amateurs and pupils!

When we timidly, as though suffering embarrassment for our ideas, reported our plans to her, there came into her eyes such a look of frozen intentness that all our fervour promptly departed and our best thoughts remained unspoken. We felt that the more vigorously we tried to convince her, the less she was inclined to believe us; we were increasingly

[115]

conscious of appearing in her eyes as men who had come to persuade a rich woman to invest her money in a worthless undertaking. With a cold smile she refused us. As a matter of fact, we had not come to ask for some preposterous sum like a hundred thousand; we merely proposed that she should become a stockholder in our theatre, to the extent, say, of 5,000 rubles, the equivalent of £500 in English money.

Private theatrical undertakings seem to have become the thing at this time in cultured Moscow. There were opera seasons supported by the wealthy mercantile class. There was the theatre of the suddenly enriched actress Abramova; in this theatre Chekhov's 'The Wood Demon' was performed. In the building which now harbours the Art Theatre there was supported for a whole season the theatre of another actress, Goreva, whom chance had made wealthy. Here perished more than 250,000 rubles of some feminine admirer of this very beautiful but cold actress. Her theatre began in a very elegant fashion. She had the auditorium remade, invited the best provincial actors at handsome salaries, and appointed my Boborikin as art director. The latter announced a brilliant repertory, but he remained in his position twenty-three days in all. At a rehearsal he quarrelled with an actress, who, in some sort of classical play, refused to utter the words: 'I fell into a sweat.' She maintained that it was a coarse, improper expression. Boborikin, who was easily inflamed—his whole bald head usually reddened when he was in a rage—retorted: 'It's for me to say what's coarse and what's not, and certainly the famous dramatist understood this better than you!' The actress held to her own opinion, and the directress Goreva took her side. Boborikin

MARYA LILINA, HIS WIFE

STANISLAVSKY

*At the time of the founding of the
Moscow Art Theatre*

resigned. The undertaking ultimately proved to be the most wanton folly.

But all these ventures burst like bubbles; and there developed the conviction that rarely does the expression, 'the all-consuming Moloch', apply so fittingly as to a theatrical undertaking. Wealthy, solid folk knew this very well, and avoided all theatrical visionaries. Alekseiev and I were conscious of this, and it caused us embarrassment. The quest for money required not only the possession of excellent ideas and confidence in them, but also some other quality, which, it was evident, both he and I wholly lacked.

Alekseiev himself was a man of means, but not at all wealthy. His capital was in his 'business'. He received a dividend and a salary as director. This enabled him to live well, but did not allow him to indulge much in 'whims'. He also had a private fund, but this he had put aside for his children, and he did not dare touch it. He had told me all this quite frankly during our first meeting. To the present undertaking he was ready to contribute a sum of approximately 10,000 rubles. Quite apart from this, his wife, Marya Petrovna Lilina, who was later to prove an excellent actress, promised her services for an indefinite period, without compensation.

On the other hand, our visit to Varvara Alekseievna Morozova threw us into consternation. When she refused, what was to be expected of other responsible persons? Then we tried something else: I composed a report to the City Council, petitioning it to assist us with a subsidy. We wanted our theatre to be generally accessible, we wanted the main part of our audience to consist of the intelligentsia in moderate circumstances, and of the student bodies. Moreover, we had no intention of following the customary rule, that of providing poor places for little money. No, we wanted to provide cheap places in the neighbourhood of the most expensive ones. Thus, for example, the first four rows were to be for very well-to-do people at four rubles a seat. This was more expensive than in other theatres; but immediately behind them there were to be seats for a ruble and a half and even for less, while the front rows of the first balcony, usually the best places in all theatres, were scheduled at a ruble a seat; as for the boxes of the first balcony, we would not charge for them the usual price of ten or twelve rubles, but only six.

Again, we planned to dedicate our morning holiday performances to the Society of National Diversions: it was to be the same repertory, and the actors were also to be the same. The workers, for whom these performances were to be given, would be asked to pay quite low prices. Such a theatre, it seemed to us, should be very much in the spirit of the city government, which we called upon to give some consideration to the population. That is why during its first year our theatre bore the rather awkward title of the 'Art-Accessible Theatre'.

Alas! My report was placed on the board of the Council for discussion only after the Art Theatre had existed a full year and more! It had simply remained waiting its turn in a completely stationary state for eighteen months or so.

In this fashion did the cardinal question of our undertaking—the question of money—remain hanging in the air. Month after month had passed by speedily. The snow had already thawed out, the droshkys had replaced the sleighs;

the intoxication of the season, 'the smoke and the fumes' [1] of first nights, balls, opulent evening parties—all these were already left behind; the visits to the Yar and the Stryelna [2] had become, as always before the end of the season, more suffocating, more inebriated; the militant students' concerts were by now a thing of the past; there was already talk about the coming spring exhibition of the *Peredvizhniki*,[3] soon 'the rooks will be here'.

And what then? Shall we have our theatre or not? Shall we find the necessary money? And how shall we find it when, strictly speaking, we are not even looking for it? Abashed, we avoided this question, as if we actually feared to ask it, one of the other, and face it fairly and squarely.

But the happy solution came from an altogether un-expected quarter.

During all this time we continued the process of acquaint-ance: I with his Circle, Stanislavsky with my pupils. We did not reveal our plan to the young people, but murder will out. I remember how Moskvin, who had left the provinces for Korsh's theatre in Moscow to play in vaudeville, quietly said to me: 'I dream of your theatre almost every night.' The perturbing news soon penetrated both groups. A sort of rivalry arose. During that winter Stanislavsky presented his best production, Hauptmann's 'The Sunken Bell', while my pupils accomplished the impossible: they prepared for final performance no less than six productions! Stanislavsky scented in Hauptmann a writer who was

[1] From a comedy by Griboyedov.
[2] Very popular restaurants on the outskirts of Moscow.
[3] A society of painters.

[119]

'our own'. I may add that Chekhov intensely admired Hauptmann, and at the same time had no liking at all for Ibsen.

The dress rehearsal of 'The Sunken Bell' immediately revealed all the high qualities of the Circle as well as its basic shortcomings. The *mise en scène* astonished one by its wealth of fantasy, novelty, and resourcefulness. Every inch of the tiny club scene was utilized with extraordinary skill; instead of the customary small, level stage square there were mountains, crags, and abysses; there were effects of light as well as of sound; the pauses, in particular, created a whole bacchanalia of new stage achievements. The sounds of the choruses, the inhuman outcries and voices, the whistling of nocturnal birds, the mysterious shadows and spots, the wood demon, the elves—all these filled the stage with a very diverting fancifulness. I remember well how Fedotova said to me: 'I'm afraid Kostya [1] will go out of his mind.'

This was the most impressive thing in the performance. Moreover, the tints and designs in the decorations, costumes, and stage properties were created by distinguished artists. Finally, the figures of the artists were original, spirited, and free from stereotyped quality.

In this fashion the pictorial side of 'The Sunken Bell' was singularly strong, while the first two acts could not have been bettered. As the performance continued, however, there was also revealed its basic shortcoming: the instability of the inner lines, the obscurity and even weakness of the psychological motivation, and because of this an essential faultiness in its dramatic base. This performance served to strengthen the view I had of Constantin Sergeievitch at this

[1] Short for Constantin (Stanislavsky).

period; his managerial palette possessed an immense supply of external tints, but he made no use of them according to the demands of inner necessity; he responded only to the whims of temperament and chance outbursts of fancy. This continued for a sufficient number of years; sometimes it seemed as if, to the point of eccentricity, he attached little importance to the spoken word and to psychology.

I recall that even in the fifth or sixth year of the Art Theatre, in a heated discussion—in one of those, as it were disquieting and nervous, but extraordinarily useful discussions, which customarily took place at the end of rehearsals, when all had departed, the stage was being prepared for the evening, the theatre attendants were going back and forth putting the auditorium in order, and we moved from one unoccupied corner to another—I formulated for him the following criticism:

'You are an exceptional *régisseur*, but so far only for melodrama or for farce, for productions full of dazzling stage effects, but which bind you neither to psychological nor to verbal demands. You trample upon every creative production. Sometimes you have the good fortune to fuse with it; in such an instance the result is excellent, but more often after the first two acts the author, if he happens to be a great poet or a great playwright, begins to call you to account for your inattention to his play's deepest and most significant inner movements. And that is why with the third act your performances begin their downward turn.'

Stanislavsky himself, in his book, *My Life in Art*, speaks more than once about this, without sparing himself; and it becomes comprehensible why he took the trouble to anticipate me by yielding the content to me, and taking charge of the form himself. But it is easier to impress the public pictorially, so that in one sense Alekseiev was right. In any event, the production had a great success, and the public at the dress rehearsal was very kindly disposed: I left at half-past one in the morning, and there were two long acts yet to be played. Yet another peculiarity stamped the man: he had tremendous perseverance—it was perhaps the most dominant trait of his character—and this perseverance, which was now a manifestation of a powerful will, and now of an obstinate artistic capriciousness, was responsible for a complete absence of the sense of time and space in his mental make-up. On the stage he was definitely conscious of every inch, but in life he frankly acknowledged that he could not imagine what one hundred yards represented, or what five hundred. Nor could he say what a quarter of an hour was, or a half. There was, for example, a rehearsal of 'The Merchant of Venice', which I persuaded him to stop in the early hours of the morning before the third act was begun. It was all because during the intermission Constantin Sergeievitch had given instructions to an actor how to wield a sword, or how to make a bow.

Thus it was in Alekseiev's Circle, but in my courses there was also a keen sense of rivalry. This happened because in the final course there were several particularly gifted pupils, and also because among them was Meyerhold.

This young man, who was later to become a celebrated *régisseur*, had been promptly accepted at the Philharmonic in the second course and displayed considerable activity in the school labours, especially in the direction of co-operative labour. It was an unheard-of fact in the schools: after five prepared and acted performances my pupils asked for permission to prepare my play 'The Last Will' almost independently. As I now recall, I turned over the whole production to the nine classes, and in the course of a month the big play was put on as the Commencement performance, which, among other things, gave a great opportunity to Olga Knipper to come forward. The 'leader' of the whole undertaking was Meyerhold. I recall yet another performance—that of the French comedy, '*Le Monde où l'on s'ennuie*', by Pailleron. Meyerhold, with a comrade, adorned the tiny school stage with excellent directing quality and not a little technical skill.

As an actor, Meyerhold gave no indication of being a pupil. He showed a measure of experience and mastered his rôles with unusual quickness. Moreover, he managed a remarkable variety of rôles—from the tragic part of Ivan the Terrible to one in a vaudeville act with singing. He played them all equally well and with accuracy. It was not given him to create any sort of specifically brilliant part. He was really very intelligent. Chekhov said of him (in Hauptmann's 'Lonely Lives'): 'It is very pleasant to listen to him, because one can believe that he understands all he says.' And is this not rare when an actor plays the rôle of a shrewd or cultured person? Meyerhold was conscious of Chekhov-the-poet more than others.

It was least of all to be expected that material welfare would come to us from this tiny school stage; actually, such was the case.

The Philharmonic Society and school were under the patronage of the Grand Duchess Elizabeth Feodorovna. In the cultural life of Moscow private initiative always tried to

find support in some sort of patronage. Elizabeth Feodorovna loved the theatre, attaching herself to my school performances, and in an abashed sort of way even tried to be
present in the ordinary classes. She usually maintained a
modest, almost timid, demeanour. The attitude towards her
in Moscow society was very friendly, not at all like its
attitude toward her husband, the Grand Duke Sergey Alexandrovitch, then the Governor-General of Moscow.

The Moscow Governor-General had always played an
important rôle in the life of Russia. St. Petersburg was considered the brain of Russia, Moscow its heart. Peripherally,
Moscow was nearer to the provinces, nearer to Russia's
depth, the land's womb. Aside from military and administrative nuclei, two important strata were concentrated here
—the nobility and the mercantile class. The nobility was
gradually becoming poorer, while the mercantile class, ever
more deeply and boldly, spread its tentacles to embrace the
whole of national life. These two classes regarded each other
with external amiability and concealed hatred: on the side
of the first was illustrious birth, on the side of the second,
capital. Each with skilled diplomacy tried to flaunt its
superior virtues before the other.

Moscow has been necessary to St. Petersburg in all the
most important stages of history. Before the war the Tsar
inevitably came to Moscow, as though to make a bow to the
mercantile class, and, following an imposing conference, the
representatives of this class made subscriptions to the war
fund. They did this very solemnly: the manufacturer
walked up to the list, made the sign of the Cross, and wrote
his name and the amount of his contribution, approximately
3,000,000 rubles. As he inscribed these facts, he knew only

too well that if his contracts during the war netted him only 100 per cent. he would be doing badly.

The merchants had bonds with the Grand Dukes; I well remember how the prominent merchant Khludov lent the Grand Duke Nikolai Nikolaievitch the elder several hundred thousand rubles, without, of course, expecting to be paid back. For what particular undertakings he needed the protection of the Grand Duke I do not know. As the Khludovs were the most considerable representatives of the textile trade, such connections were absolutely essential. I remember Khludov's own account of how he had received permission to make the Empress Marya Feodorovna [1] a gift, a magnificent young Danish hound (the Empress was inordinately fond of dogs), and of how, when she went out to a reception, surrounded by a host of small dogs, the big dog made a dash for them; Khludov, who was possessed of great strength and had once before our eyes downed a tame tiger, restrained the dog, but not before it had succeeded in tearing a splendid heavy, silken cord; the tiny dogs, to save themselves from the fierce animal, ran to cover under the Empress's skirts; the dog went after them, and Khludov went down on all fours in order to seize the disobedient beast. . . .

The nobility envied the merchants; the latter flaunted their aspiration to civilization and culture, their wives received their dress finery from Paris, spent their winters in the French Riviera, and, at the same time, for some secret psychological reason, tried to curry favour with the higher nobility. The richer a human being becomes, the more opulent his ambition grows. This circumstance sometimes found expression in strange forms. I remember a merchant,

[1] Wife of Alexander III.

a very elegant fellow of about forty years old; he would not buy his clothes elsewhere than in London, where he had his regular tailor. . . . He spoke thus concerning a certain aristocrat:

'Why, he's by far too proud. Of course, he'll ask me to a ball in his house, or to a rout—but what's that? No, you let *me* invite you, let *me* show you the sort of party I can give. But what's he—with his visiting-card!'

The Governor-General was under the obligation of maintaining excellent relations with one and the other. This was sometimes agonizing for the refined aristocratic taste. One of the Governor-Generals, Prince Vladimir Dolgoruky, bore with great fortitude the necessity of frequent contact with elements not belonging to the nobility. This was the tale told about him:

For the *rapprochement* between opposing camps, he had no less than twenty persons to dinner each day, and in connection with this affair he had a special adjutant, whose duty it was to attend to the selection of prospective guests and to appoint the time for their invitation.

'Whom have you on to-morrow's list?' the Prince asked.

The adjutant showed him the list. At one of the names the Prince frowned. 'Can't we manage without him?'

'Impossible, Your Excellency. He's not been asked in a long time, and he's rather important.'

'I know that, but he drinks red wine with fish, and he cuts asparagus with a knife!'

In order to give the position of Governor-General of Moscow greater prestige, Alexander III appointed the Grand Duke Sergey Alexandrovitch to the position. It was the first instance of the kind. The nobility was much gratified with the appointment; it felt that the Grand Duke would show it preference over the mercantile class. The latter was more cool towards him; when they spoke of him they let no chance go by to hint about his inclinations toward his young adjutants.

Twice a year the Governor-General was under obligation to give a big reception to Moscow society. That particular winter the Grand Duchess conceived the idea of giving a theatrical performance in her house in place of the customary party, and amateurs among higher society were to participate in it. She had been especially pleased with Alekseiev's production of 'The Sunken Bell'; she had scarcely seen it more than twice. She must have, by some chance, heard of the growing intimacy between Alekseiev and me, and she asked us both to assist her in staging the performance. She entrusted Colonel Aleksey Stakhovitch, adjutant to the Grand Duke, with the task of making arrangements with us.

The family of the Stakhovitches were large landowners; they were the neighbours and friends of Count Leo Tolstoy. One of them—Mikhail—was a member of the National Duma, a minister in the Provisional Government; he was the most gifted member of the family. Our Stakhovitch was captivated by Constantin Sergeievitch; he called him an eagle; afterwards, when our theatre was already enjoying success, he wholeheartedly joined us; he resigned his position as general and became one of the largest stockholders of the Art Theatre; later he became one of its directors, and finally an actor. He was a typical courtier, handsome, one of the most elegant of men, educated almost to excess, but a slave of his education and his aristocracy. He gave himself up to

[127]

the theatre; nevertheless, he held his noble birth and his connection with the upper social caste higher than the theatre. He was to have a tragic end: he did not accept the revolution and, having lost all his substance, felt himself solitary even among us, and—hanged himself.

It goes without saying that neither of us had the least desire to occupy himself with an amateur performance in high society, but to refuse was impossible. With our customary scrupulousness we tackled the undertaking. Constantin Sergeievitch, however, after the first effective conferences, was forced to desist, as his home was invaded by scarlet fever. I was left alone to carry on. The Grand Duchess herself did no acting in the play, but contented herself with the pleasure she received from busying herself with the arrangements for the performance.

Americans say: 'It is difficult to say when and where anything begins and when and where any end will come.' The performance was a complete success, and proved to be the first dawn of our future theatre.

There were further happenings:

The more deeply and agonizingly the doubt gnawed at me of any likelihood of obtaining money for our theatre, the more powerfully the thought matured that a school without a theatre is a thoroughly futile phenomenon and a waste of time, that pupils should develop in a theatre, that only there can they receive the first stage experience in a crowd, in making exits and entrances, playing minor rôles; hence, if I did not succeed in creating a theatre that very year, I decided to abandon my school and place a tombstone on this activity.

I candidly told the directors of the Philharmonic of my intention. They valued me, but their attitude toward my announcement was one of indifference; they showed the same indifference in a general way toward the school. For them the Philharmonic Society was valuable for its concerts, at which they occupied seats in the front rows and could flaunt before all Moscow their patronage. Thus it looked as if my connection with them would come to an end. But it turned out differently. As it happened, during a visit of the Grand Duchess to the school one of the directors quite casually remarked that everything was going very well, except for one petty unpleasantness—Nemirovitch was abandoning the school. To this the Grand Duchess is said to have replied: 'Why, I can't imagine our school without Nemirovitch!'

This was sufficient to cause a sudden and sharp reconsideration of the whole question. Among the directors was the rich merchant Ushkov. In his study he had an authentic Rembrandt; the floor of his reception-room was encrusted with mother-of-pearl. There was a custom among the merchant class generously to reward the poor at the funeral of a wealthy merchant, in order that they might pray for the salvation of the dead magnate's soul. When in Ushkov's house the former occupant died, the gathering of beggars was so great that many of them were crushed to death.

Ushkov himself manifested in his person a splendid combination of artlessness, guile, and vanity. Shortly before this I had had an amusing experience with him. I had not been using the ordinary decorations on my tiny school stage, but had substituted a kind of cloth. This cloth gradually grew more and more tattered, whereupon I applied several times to the school administration, always to be refused on the ground of lack of means. One day, however, I seized

[129]

the opportune moment and said to Ushkov: 'Well, don't you think it would be a good idea to contribute five hundred rubles or so? Here the Grand Duchess comes in to see us, and what must she think when she sees the stage all in rags!'

'Very well,' said Ushkov. 'Five hundred, thou sayest?' (In a cheerful mood he frequently changed over from the formal 'you' to the more intimate 'thou'.) 'I'll give thee the five hundred thou askest, but remember: tell the Grand Duchess without fail that I contributed it. Dost thou agree?'

'I agree.'

'All right, then. But don't forget to mention it to her that Constantin Ushkov contributed five hundred rubles!'

And now, as the first stockholder, he subscribed to the extent of 4,000 rubles. Subsequently, he more than once asked that the fact that he was the first stockholder be emphasized; I complied with pleasure. He easily inveigled the remaining directors of the Philharmonic into subscribing, only small sums, to be sure—some 2,000 rubles, others 1,000. Stimulated by this success, Alekseiev and I then took another step, the most significant step of all for the future of our theatre: together we went to see the most prominent of all Moscow manufacturers—Savva Timofeievitch Morozov.

Boborikin called the important Moscow merchant families 'dynasties'; among these the dynasty of the Morozovs was the outstanding one. Savva Timofeievitch was its chief representative. His energy and will were tremendous; he by no means exaggerated when he said of himself: 'If any one should stand in my way, I would ride right over him without blinking.'

His footfalls were moderate and inaudible, as though he

wore no heels. And his mercurial eyes quickly tried to seize your thought and size up the situation. But he made no haste to make answers. His rule was: 'He who can wait will win out.' His voice was brusque, he laughed easily; he had the habit of interrupting his own speech with the question, 'Isn't that so?' Thus: 'I enter the vestibule of the theatre . . . isn't that so? . . . An inspector comes to meet us . . . isn't that so? . . .' His mind was always preoccupied with some sort of mathematical and psychological calculation. The expression 'a merchant's shrewdness' fitted him admirably.

On the spot where originally stood the house of the celebrated Russian Slavophiles, the Aksakovs, he built himself a magnificent palace. The actor Sadovsky, whom I have already mentioned, and who enjoyed a reputation for epigrams, composed the following verse:

> This castle wafts a host of thoughts,
> I muse upon the past, reluctantly and sadly:
> Here, where aforetime the Russian mind reigned,
> Now reigns the manufacturer's wit.

The epigram pleased the nobility, which strongly envied the 'dynasty' of the Morozovs its cool 3,000,000 annual income.

Morozov conducted himself with extraordinary independence. This was told of him:

Rumours of his *palazzo*, decorated in the best of taste, reached the Grand Duke, and one day an adjutant appeared before Morozov with the request that Sergey Alexandrovitch be permitted to see the house. Morozov very amiably answered: 'With pleasure. Whenever it's convenient for him.' He added: 'He'd like to see my house?'

'Yes.'

'To-morrow at two, then.'

On the following day the Grand Duke and his adjutant arrived, but they were met by the majordomo; the master himself was away. This was a very subtle snub, which was equivalent to saying: 'You have a desire to see my house, but you're not coming to see me. The house is at your service, then. Have a look round. But don't imagine that I'll be here to meet you with genuflections.'

He knew the good taste and value of that simplicity which is more costly than luxury. He understood the power of capitalism when applied on a broad national scale, and he worked with energy, often disappearing for weeks to spend the time at his factory, which maintained 30,000 employees. He knew the secret ways of St. Petersburg governmental departments. He once told with a smile how necessary it had been for him to carry out a certain undertaking. For a long time everything went wrong, but one day it was whispered in his ear: 'Go to such and such an address. A handsome woman will come out to see you. Don't be astonished, and do exactly as she tells you.'

He went to the address given. And, actually, a handsome woman came out to see him.

'You've come to see me about my remarkable cow?' she asked cheerfully.

'Yes, yes,' he replied, understanding nothing.

'You've been warned, of course, that it's the only one in existence—highly bred, from Kholmogorsk? I can't let you have it for less than 5,000 rubles!'

Without demanding any explanation, Morozov gave her 5,000 rubles. To be sure, he did not receive any kind of cow in return, but everything that had to be done was done the following morning at the department concerned.

But the human race cannot endure two equally strong but contrary passions. The merchant should not allow himself to be captivated by any other interest; he must be faithful to his element—the element of survival and reckoning. A betrayal will inevitably lead to a tragic conflict. And Savva Morozov was capable of becoming captivated by a passion— to the point of intense love.

No, not with a woman. This did not play any considerable rôle in his life. But with a personality, with an idea, with some social aspiration. He enthusiastically played the part of the leading representative of the Moscow merchants' class, endowing this rôle with a broad social significance. for two years he was captivated with me, then with Stanislavsky. While the enchantment lasted he completely yielded his powerful will into the hands of the enchanter. When he spoke, his quick eyes seemed to seek approbation; they gleamed with ruthlessness, with the consciousness of capitalistic might, and with the devoted desire to please the object of his enchantment.

How often had the two of us met in a private room in a restaurant, for hours discussing not only matters concerning the theatre, but also literature,—even Ibsen! Who could have believed that Savva Morozov, with perturbation, entered the revolutionary atmosphere of Rosmersholm, taking no notice of the speeding hours? He did this to the tune of two glasses of tea, a portion of ham, and a bottle of Johannisberger—and this only in order to maintain the ethics of the restaurant.

But his most tremendous, all-consuming attraction was Maxim Gorky, and later the revolutionary movement . . .

At the beginning my acquaintance with Savva Timofeie-

[133]

vitch was very superficial. We used to meet at evening parties, at picture exhibitions, or at *premières*; on one of these occasions we were introduced. Once there was announced a big charitable performance, in which my pupils played parts. Meeting Savva Timofeievitch somewhere, I suggested to him that he buy a couple of tickets from me. He willingly complied, but with a laugh said that he had no money with him. I replied: 'You can owe it to me. All the same, it gives me a peculiar satisfaction—me, a cultured proletarian—to have the millionaire Morozov as my debtor!' We were both of us gratified with the jest. Two months passed by, we again met somewhere, when he said: 'I owe you ten rubles, and again I have no money.' I responded: 'Please, please, don't let that worry you! Let this state of affairs continue longer.' Thus, on meeting each other several times in the course of two years, we kept up the jest. Once I even said to him: 'Never mind. One day I'll look in on you and collect the money!'

And, actually, when with Alekseiev I called on him, I said: 'Well, Savva Timofeievitch, I've come to collect the debt. I've come for the ten rubles!'

Morozov agreed to take shares in our company—promptly, without making inquiries. He made a single condition: that our company should have no higher patronage of any sort over it. He subscribed 10,000 rubles. Subsequently he took all the material responsibilities of the theatre upon himself. He erected the building, and assisted the Union of Actors in getting on its feet. In the history of the Art Theatre his name occupies an outstanding place.

He contributed considerable sums, I think, to the revolutionary movement. When in 1905 the first revolution broke out and reaction followed, something happened to his mind, and he shot himself. This happened at Nice. His widow brought for burial in Moscow his sealed metal coffin. Moscow scandalmongers spread the rumour that the coffin did not contain the body of Savva Morozov. Persons avid for mystery kept up the legend in Moscow for many, many years that Morozov was alive and was hiding somewhere in the depths of Russia.

During this period the journalists brought into fashion the following mode of discourse: 'A little philosophy.' Or on another occasion: 'Yet a little more philosophy.' Thus, on this occasion, I too, turning away briefly from my narrative, must interject 'A little philosophy!'

Who among you, I ask, does not know of the full-chested, joyous sigh of relief when money, the absence of which had at one time so oppressed you, was at last found?! Ah-h . . . ! Or, Oh! Ah-h . . . what a burden is off one's shoulders! Oh, what happiness! . . .

The permanent frown has disappeared from the face. In its place there is a clear, tranquil smile. The veins and muscles are filled with confidence, with firmness. Worried thoughts, of which there were so many, have melted away like tiny clouds before the summer sun. There is faith not only in one's undertaking and its success, but in oneself, which grows with each hour. With each boldly uttered phrase, one seems to onself to be extraordinarily endowed with talent. One feels that success and happiness have already once and for all settled somewhere beside one.

So then, from the philosophic point of view: really, is this sort of happiness so necessary in the existence of a human being? In order successfully to develop one's life problem, is it really necessary to pay for it with a whole series of depressing doubts, of experiences humiliating to one's pride, fits of dejection, moments of deep pessimism? According to Schopenhauer, happiness is negative; it is merely an escape from unhappiness. And there we were in this position—we breathed with joyous relief, because we had escaped from depressing obstacles, from barriers, ravines, all manner of hindrances which life had put in our way in the course of the year and a half, from the eighteen-hour conversation to the opening of the theatre. Was it really so necessary for us to have gone through all the sufferings from the beginning? Why should it be necessary? That we might the more value the successes in life? That is to say, in order to create out of a Chekhov play a high achievement in art, we had not only to carry out a creative labour of many years over ourselves, over our natural, born gifts—because 'even spiritual fruit is not born without agonies'—but also to suffer humiliation in Varvara Alekseievna's reception-room, to seek out and genuflect to the 4,000 rubles of Ushkov, to the 2,000 of Vostryakov, to the 1,000 of Firgang—human beings, whom, canididly speaking, with a hand on our hearts, we did not respect—neither them nor their capital.

As if our social life could not be arranged differently!

CHAPTER EIGHT

A nd so, the means have been found. We shall have our
theatre!

The most magnificent, perhaps the only, fervour in life
seized upon all our future actors—that which Tolstoy called
'the banked-up fires of life'.

It is true that there was at our disposal all in all only
28,000 rubles! But then our budget was not very large.
There was a distinguishing peculiarity about this. The
salaries to the members of our company were designated not
according to rôles, but according to the personal factor; not
according to the wage supposed to be paid an actor playing
such or such a rôle, but according to the wage that such or
such of my pupils or such or such of the amateurs from
Alekseiev's Circle might at this time expect to receive in the
best theatre. Moskvin, for example, was receiving at this
time at Korsh's theatre the sum of 100 rubles a month for six
months in the year; during the summer he could expect to
earn an additional 300 rubles. We, on the other hand, agreed
to pay him 100 rubles per month the year round, but he
would be playing leading rôles. The performer in these rôles
in the ordinary theatre was usually paid 500 rubles a month.
But Korsh had not as yet sufficient faith in Moskvin and did
not entrust him with leading rôles; moreover, without Stanislavsky's assistance and mine, he would not as yet have been
able to achieve his best in the playing of these parts. When

gradually, from year to year, he would have sufficiently developed his skill to require less and less of our creative assistance, and less and less of our effort at rehearsals, his salary would steadily increase in ratio to his improvement. And that is exactly what happened. Within several years he attained to an income which was beyond the capacity of any other theatre to provide. This, of course, occurred simultaneously with the growth of the Art Theatre itself and with the corresponding growth of its budget.

Under the same rule, for example, Olga Knipper received during the first year only 900 rubles, i.e. 75 rubles a month, playing leading rôles.

There were so many difficulties to overcome, so many negotiations to carry through, that I cannot now remember the details, and even generalities have vanished from memory. I recall how we examined available theatrical buildings and paused at a smallish, not particularly attractive structure in the neighbourhood of the Summer Garden. . . . I recall the difficulties we encountered in making the censorship release for production Alexey Tolstoy's tragedy, 'Tsar Fyodor Iohannovitch.' Luckily, Suvorin was at the same time trying to obtain the play's release for his own theatre in St. Petersburg. Success was wholly due to his influence. . . . I also recall how at this very time a competitor suddenly, as it were from the ground, or like a jack-in-the-box, bobbed up his head—indeed a child of our own not quite yet born. And what a competitor! In the Imperial Theatres! That meant that he would be financially quite independent. This is how it happened:

A new director was appointed for the Imperial Theatres. He arrived in Moscow, where he stumbled upon the ques-

A. G. LENSKY

IVAN MOSKVIN

Two talented actors of the Moscow Art Theatre

tion of 'the overproduction of acting forces'. Some one thought it necessary to taunt him: 'Here you are sitting, considering things. You are wondering what to do with your young actors. Yet at this very moment two sufficiently well-known personages in Moscow are organizing a young company and opening up a theatre!'

These words acted as a spur. In the course of the next twenty-four hours the new director sent a telegram to a minister of the Imperial Court, leased the best theatre in Moscow, on which I also had my eyes, and offered it to Lensky—with whom you are more or less familiar—for the purpose of showing his students' dramatic performances there.

Lensky was of very much the same mind as I. He nurtured the same hopes of the theatrical youth and of the renewal of the dramatic theatre. I therefore experienced a dual feeling: on the one hand, I should have rejoiced because of Lensky's new position; on the other, I had reason to fear a powerful rival.

In all modesty, however, I must say that precisely from the point of view of artistic competition I had no apprehensions. In the first place Lensky, himself an artist, was bound to be very much of a prisoner in the old Russian theatre; in the second place I knew very well the nature of the directorate of State theatres, and I might have foretold that Lensky would have an impossibly hard task in organizing the new undertaking, so alien in spirit to the old institutions.

But after all, what's the odds? The Roman adage says: 'To live means to fight.' We felt very bold! And very courageously, even cheerfully, we gathered and discussed our plans.

[139]

Somehow, many years afterwards, Stanislavsky, when he was inspiring the actors at a rehearsal by saying that it was possible to find splendid stimulation in a modest setting, that for dazzling feelings it was not necessary to have all this dazzling theatrical tinsel, recalled the cold beet soup and the young roast chickens he had for dinner in my small, modest garden:

'Instead of reception-rooms and salons we passed through a tiny yard, instead of armchairs there were benches, instead of palms in tubs there were living bushes of lilac; on the other hand, in all my life I have scarcely eaten such a tasty dinner—such a tasty and friendly one . . . everything depends on one's mood. . . .'

Across these buoyant activities, however, there blew a brief but malignant whirlwind, so brief that I scarce remember it. I was reminded of it by the latest Soviet edition of Chekhov's works. There, in the supplement, are some fragments of my letters to Anton Pavlovitch, found in the Chekhov Museum.

To my request for permission to produce 'The Sea Gull' Chekhov answered with a categorical refusal. I had completely forgotten about this. And now, in order to recall the circumstances of the episode, I have taken copies of my letters from the museum. Chekhov not only preserved all the letters to him, but he numbered them and filed them alphabetically. Here is my first letter concerning 'The Sea Gull':

DEAR ANTON PAVLOVITCH!

You know by now that I have drifted into a theatrical undertaking. For the time being, in our first year we (Alekseiev and I) are creating a theatre exclusively devoted to art. For this

purpose we have leased the 'Hermitage'. We have in view
for production 'Tsar Fyodor Iohannovitch', 'The Merchant of
Venice', 'Julius Caesar', 'Hannele', several plays of Ostrovsky and
the better part of the repertory of the Society of the Fine Arts
and Literature (Circle of Alekseiev). From among contemporary Russian authors I have decided to cultivate *only* the most
gifted, those as yet insufficiently understood. For Shpazhinksy
and Nevezhin we can do nothing. Nemirovitch and Sumbatov
are sufficiently well understood. But of you the Russian theatrical public is quite ignorant. You must be shown in such a way
as is only possible to a *littérateur* with taste, capable of understanding the beauty of your productions, who is at the same time a
skilful *régisseur*. I consider myself to be such a person. I have
made it my goal to show the marvellous pictures of life in the
works 'Ivanov' and 'The Sea Gull'. The latter especially inspires
my enthusiasm, and I am ready to defend the statement that
the latent drama and tragedy in *each* figure of the plays will also
inspire the enthusiasm of the theatrical public, provided they are
shown in a skilful, unhackneyed, conscientious production. Perhaps the play will not provoke storms of applause, but that
a genuine production with *spontaneous* qualities, *liberated from
routine*, will prove a triumph of art—this I can guarantee. It only
awaits your authorization. I ought to tell you that I already
wanted to produce 'The Sea Gull' as a Commencement performance at the school. All the more was I attracted to the idea
because the best of my pupils were in love with the play. I was
only stopped because Sumbatov and Lensky spoke of arranging
a production of the play at the Small Theatre. The conversation
took place in the presence of Goltzev. I expressed myself to the
effect that the big actors of the Small Theatre, having already
formed their mould, were incapable of appearing before the
public in a wholly new aspect, of creating that atmosphere, that
aroma and mood, which envelop the characters of your play.
But they insisted on my not putting on 'The Sea Gull'. All the
same, 'The Sea Gull' has not been put on at the Small Theatre.
And thank God for that—I say this with all the whole-hearted

[141]

admiration I have for your genius. So let me have the play. I assure you, you will not find a *régisseur* or a member of any company who holds you in greater admiration.

I am too poor to pay you adequately. But believe me, I will do everything to satisfy you even in this respect. Our theatre is beginning to awaken the strong . . . indignation of the Imperial Theatre. They fail to understand that we are out to challenge the routine, the mould, the acknowledged geniuses, etc. . . . And they scent the fact that here all forces are being employed for the creation of an *art* theatre. This is why I should feel sad if I could not find support in you.

A quick reply is essential: just a simple little note that you are authorizing *me* to produce 'The Sea Gull' where I find it convenient to do so.

As I now recall, Chekhov rejected my proposal because of his confessed sensitiveness and self-consciousness: he wrote that he had no desire and had not sufficient strength to experience again the theatrical perturbations which had in the past caused him so much pain; and he repeated, not for the first time, that he was no playwright, that there was something in life better than writing plays, and so forth. I then wrote him another letter, in the course of which I said:

If you refuse me your play, you will wound me, as I consider 'The Sea Gull' the only contemporary play that possesses me as a *régisseur*, and you as the only contemporary writer that can have any great interest for a theatre with an exemplary repertory.

If you like, I'll come to you before the rehearsals take place, to have a talk with you about 'The Sea Gull' and my plan of production.

We are to have 20 'mornings' for the young people, with a conference before the play. During these mornings we shall present 'Antigone', 'The Merchant of Venice', Beaumarchais, Ostrovsky,

Goldoni, 'Uriel Acosta', etc. Certain professors will read brief lectures before the performances. I want to devote one of these mornings to you, though I have not yet decided who is to talk about you—Goltzev or some one else.

Please reply at once.

A greeting to your house from my wife and myself.

On Saturday I leave Moscow—or Sunday at the latest.

And finally:

DEAR ANTON PAVLOVITCH!

I received your letter here, in the steppe. It means, I will produce 'The Sea Gull'!! Because I shall make the journey to see you without fail.[1] I was planning to go to Moscow on July 15 (the rehearsals of the other plays will begin without me), but in view of your charming request I will see you before that date. Thus, you may expect me between the 1st and 10th of July. I will write you more precisely later. I am not afraid of *tarataikas*,[2] so don't take the trouble to send any horses to the station.

I am poring over 'The Sea Gull' and I am constantly seeking those tiny bridges across which a *régisseur* should lead his public, making a detour away from its favoured routine. The public is not yet capable and perhaps never will be capable of yielding to the mood of the play; it is necessary that it should have a strong vehicle for conveying it. We will do our best!

Good-bye.

A greeting to you all from my wife and me.

I made the journey to see him in Melekhovo. Notwithstanding his illness I found him, as always, in a mood for a smile, for a jest. Recently an infant had been born to his brother. It was brought to be shown to my wife.

---

[1] It is quite evident that in return for authorization I had to pay him with a journey to his farm in Melekhovo.

[2] A two-wheeled cart.

'What do you say to buying it, say for two and a half rubles?'

It is remarkable that a human being with such a fund of cheerfulness and humour could have written 'Ward Number Six' and permeated his short stories and plays with such infinite sadness!

On the jubilee of the twenty-fifth year of the Art Theatre (the 27th of October, according to the New Style: the 14th according to the Old, then prevailing), Stanislavsky in his speech, dwelling on our close twenty-five-year alliance, several times referred to me as his 'wife'; he added that he was leaving with the company for America, but that his 'wife' would remain at home to look after the household; hence, the rôle of the wife was not so apparent as that of her husband. In responding to this in my speech, to the laughter of our jubilee audience, I protested. I said that he was the wife and I the husband, and that this was very easy to prove. The day of October 14 (27), I said, was the day of the first performance, the day of the christening, so to speak, of the Art Theatre, and not of its birth. The birth had taken place several months before in the village of Pushkino, not far from Alekseiev's farm, Liubimovka, in a specially fitted-up isolated house with a stage. It was there that the whole company first gathered; it was there that the first introductory word was uttered; it was there, at the first rehearsals, that our babe gave vent to its first cry. Therefore the place of the theatre's birth must be considered Pushkino, and the date of birth June 14 (27). These rehearsals had been arranged by him, Constantin Sergeievitch, who also directed all the first meetings of our general company; at this time I was not even in the neighbourhood; indeed, I was on my own farm. As every one knew, it was possible for a birth to take place in the absence of the father, but in no case in the absence of the mother. It quite evidently followed that the mother of the Art Theatre, and consequently my wife, was none other than he, Stanislavsky. That the infant might resemble the mother more than the father was quite another question.

We made this arrangement: for a month and a half he would be with Sanin in Pushkino, while I would conclude my literary duties. Afterwards I would arrive to take charge of the rehearsals where they had been left off, while Constantin Sergeievitch would go somewhere for a rest preliminary to the most difficult winter in his life.

The main thing: before my return they were to prepare as many scenes as possible of 'Tsar Fyodor'. We did not even discuss 'The Sea Gull'.

I have always considered the month of August the best time of the year in Moscow and its environs. It is very difficult to convey this 'perception of August'; there is in it something lighthearted and softly joyous. Perhaps it is the caressing sun, perhaps the clear bright air. Perhaps it is because the summer mood of rest has not yet wholly vanished, and the winter anxieties have not yet quite arrived; or because the hopes stored up during the summer unconcern are full of fresh courage. The weather at this time is magnificent. And it seems as though the deepest lyricism which has possessed the poets in Russian nature glowed brighter during August.

Pushkino is five versts from Liubimovka. At my disposal at the house of the Alekseievs was a balcony, overlooking the garden above the running stream called the Klyazma. A complete silence always reigned in the house and all around it, so that when in the early hours I sat alone I could listen to the same tiny bird, of whose name I was ignorant, which at precisely the same time always invited some one with its very modest call in two tiny notes. I experienced a real wealth of fulfilled reveries. In Pushkino, where it became necessary to pass the larger part of the day, everything was filled with excitement, the very best, to be sure, that was in the souls of our young people. The company lived communally; they themselves had to clear the stage and the auditorium, prepare their samovars, and take turns at housekeeping. Nothing lowered their high spirits. Even marriages were soon arranged—something like a dozen within the first half year. The actor Darsky, a provincial tragedian, who had forsaken his career as a star and come to us, took advantage one day of the absence of Stanislavsky and began to shout at me, taking me to task for not using my position as director to forbid Stanislavsky from repeating twenty times the rehearsal of bowing to the ground, which to his mind was making mock of an actor.

It was all so earnest, so comic and so fiery—everything was imbued with youth, spirit and faith. This atmosphere did not suffer even when suddenly there was a threat of a catastrophe: we were preparing the production of 'Tsar Fyodor', but discovered there was no actor for the rôle of Fyodor himself!

Moskvin, who was later to shine in this rôle, of whom they were yet to write in Vienna, 'Forget all the names of actors famous to you, but keep in mind the name of Moskvin' (with what surprises does the theatrical art furnish us!), this same Moskvin at the first rehearsals, before my own

THE HOUSE AT PUSHKINO WHERE THE MOSCOW ART THEATRE
REHEARSED THE FIRST SUMMER

p. 146]

appearance at them, had left Stanislavsky so dissatisfied that
he promptly took the rôle from Moskvin and gave it to
another, then to a third. He wrote me in the village in terms
of despair. Then still another letter came: Hurrah! Fyodor
has been found!

And—oh, horror!—this lucky fellow did not at all meet
with my approval. I can recall how after the rehearsal Constantin Sergeievitch and I travelled late at night in the train,
how he did not even attempt to argue with me or to defend
the impossible Fyodor, but only kept repeating: 'Well, what
are we to do now? What are we to do?'

Then I took hold of my favourite, Moskvin. Evidently
in ignorance of his personality, Stanislavsky had approached
him in the wrong way. The rehearsals in the tiny theatre did
not cease; while I, for lack of space, occupied myself with
Moskvin in the yard porter's hut, while the porter himself
sat on a small bench just outside the open window and
listened to us, understanding nothing, but smiling.

We opened the theatre with 'Tsar Fyodor'. As the card
experts say, 'When you have the queen of trumps, begin
with the ace of trumps.' There was something sure about it.
There was, to start with, a great interest in a tragedy which
for thirty years had been forbidden by the censorship; there
was also the devotion of the public to national, historical
plays ; and it was easier, as Stanislavsky loved to express it, to
épater les bourgeois, i.e. to stupefy the public with almost
museum pieces in the matter of costume, with remarkable
embroideries, made under the direction of Alekseiev's wife
(the actress Lilina), with a bright-coloured throng and audacious mises en scène. In a word, in every respect it was running little risk, with the greatest chances of success, to begin

with this play. And as we had excellent performers selected for the main rôles, there was all the more reason for 'Tsar Fyodor' to occupy a respected place in our repertory.

The announcement of our repertory was very effective. It included the following names: Sophocles ('Antigone'); Shakespeare ('The Merchant of Venice'); Alexey Tolstoy ('Tsar Fyodor Iohannovitch'); Ibsen ('Hedda Gabler'); Pisemsky ('They Who Take the Law Into Their Own Hands'); Hauptmann ('The Sunken Bell' and 'Hannele'); and Chekhov ('The Sea Gull'). Considering the historical reputation of each play, the list was a very imposing one, forming a whole fleet of cruisers and dreadnoughts, with heavy artillery—howitzers and mortars. Among them Chekhov with his 'The Sea Gull' seemed no more than a 5,000-ton vessel with some sort of 40-inch weapons.

Among the Moscow theatrical critics I had the best relations with Nikolai Efros. He was yet to occupy perhaps the first place among theatrical journalists. He possessed two excellent qualities for a critic: great perception with regard to the inwardness of a performance, its lyricism; and the knowledge of how to praise—he was capable of enthusiasm, which is more difficult than criticism. When I published the first announcement of the repertory I asked Efros: 'And what do you think is the most valuable thing here?' Without the least hesitation he replied: ' "The Sea Gull", of course!' So I was not alone! I was happy to feel that I was not alone. But I had yet to inspire Stanislavsky with this faith.

According to our agreement, the power to veto the staging of a play rested with him. It was for him to prepare the *mise en scène* of 'The Sea Gull'. On the other hand, having read the play, he did not understand at all in what way it could interest any one: the people in it seemed to him to be only half human, the passions ineffective, the words perhaps too simple, the images failing to give the actors any good material.

Before me was a *régisseur* who, out of decorations, cos- tumes, all manners of properties and human beings, was capable of creating bright, enchanting stage effects. He had excellent taste in the matter of choosing colours, a taste culti- vated in museums and from association with artists. But he directed the full force of his gift only toward creating something which should astonish with its novelty and originality, something—it goes without saying—which was above all unusual. And my problem was to awaken his interest in the depths of things, in the lyric qualities of the workaday world. It was necessary to divert his thought from fantasy or history (an inexhaustible source of effective themes), and to plunge him into the most ordinary everyday realities, filled with our most ordinary everyday emotions.

When we had calmed down on the subject of 'Fyodor'— for Moskvin, who had been rehearsed in the yard porter's hut, created such a furore in the part as to move every one to tears—we arranged to leave further rehearsals in charge of Stanislavsky's right-hand man, the *régisseur* Sanin, well known to all for his labours on the American and European stages; Stanislavsky himself was to depart for a rest and the preparation of a *régisseur's* copy of 'The Sea Gull', while I was to begin my work with the actors.

In approaching a new production, Stanislavsky sooner or later would say to me: 'Now fill me up with what you think I ought to have especially in mind in making up my *régis-*

[149]

seur's copy.' It fell out that there was one such happy day: neither he nor I had any rehearsal on our hands, nothing external diverted us, and from morning till late at night we talked about Chekhov. To be accurate, I spoke, while he listened and made notes. I paced up and down, then seated myself, then paced again; I sought the most convincing words. When I saw by the tensity of his expression that my words were gliding past his attention, I reinforced them with gestures, intonations, repetitions, while he listened with an open mind, trustful.

Alekseiev had always lived in Moscow. As a Moscow manufacturer, he possessed an immense fund of impressions of the life of the mercantile class. Later he began to associate with the artistic world, again that of Moscow. He knew the classical repertory, was acquainted with the best actors, Continental as well as Russian. When he journeyed abroad he studied the theatrical art there, visited the museums, and in the rôle of *régisseur* tried to pillage anything that appealed to him for his theatrical projects. Of the immense mass, however, of the Russian provincial intelligentsia and semi-intelligentsia, of all that many-millioned stratum of Russian life which served as material for Chekhov's productions, he knew nothing. Equally alien to him were their perturbations, their tears, envies, grudges, quarrels, all that which makes up life in the provinces. And of the meaning of need, of earning one's livelihood, he was also ignorant. And the main thing: he did not perceive the tremendous witchery of the author's lyricism which enveloped these Chekhovian workaday realities.

There, somewhere, within the broadest circles of the intelligentsia, amidst human beings dreaming of a better life,

[150]

amidst those whom this drab existence has sucked in, those who live in inertia, yet cannot reconcile themselves with the coarseness of life and suffer from oppressive injustice in the most comfortable and purest corners of their souls—there Chekhov was beloved, there he was considered their own, incredibly close to them. And he was close to them not as an abstract poet, but as one of ourselves who walked among us, as if he were not one little inch higher than we—and he loved what we loved, he smiled with us and laughed; he was not always deeper than we, but he was far more sharp-sighted, and possessed the magnificent gift of being able to reveal to us our sins and our dreams.

CHAPTER NINE

I must confess that this part of my book has cost me a great deal of time. How often have I been on the point of refusing to go on with it! But suppose my reader—some sort of vexed playgoer, or still better an actor—should suddenly ask me: 'In what lies the real essence of your method ? Of your art? Now you have come to the rehearsals of "The Sea Gull"; apparently you will work on it not at all as in the theatre in which this play had failed. Well, in what lies the difference? In the preceding chapters you have examined the difference in organization: in the old theatre they immediately enter upon the stage and immediately start rehearsing the entire play, while you at the beginning sit for a long time at a table discussing it, and when at last you begin rehearsals you do it by fragments. It is evident that it is not this alone that matters. It is evident that there is also something in the very essence of your directorial work with the actor. What is it, precisely?'

The answer to this question is a very complex one. A single chapter is not sufficient; a whole book would be necessary. It will have to be given here in a very compact form, as a brief synopsis of the art of the *régisseur*. Is it possible to do so?

Quite apart from this, in the thirty and more years our methods have been subjected to changes and modifications; it would be so easy to ascribe present traits to the past. If it were only possible to show photographically what we did then and compare it with our present methods, the difference would be immense.

Finally, I shall be impelled to speak of myself, and that is always awkward. . . .

Really, this is a difficult matter.

Simultaneously with the rehearsals of 'The Sea Gull' the atmosphere in our theatrical 'shed' underwent an abrupt change. Up to now, every day from morning till night all our strength was concentrated on furnishing a reflection of Russia of the sixteenth century ('Tsar Fyodor'); of land-owners' estates of the eighteenth century ('They Who Take the Law Into Their Own Hands'); of Venice hundreds of years ago ('The Merchant of Venice'); finally, of Greece two thousand years ago ('Antigone'). We had to show varied costumes, a bright colourful existence, pictures and feelings, all quite remote from us and having little in common with our own time. Stanislavsky with his collaborating *régisseurs* quickened the interest in his brilliant and astonishing *mises en scène*, in his discovery of movements, costumes and proper-ties, by no means always historically accurate, and little re-sembling the effects to which the playgoer was accustomed. If the original hats were high, he must make them exces-sively high; if the sleeves were long, he must make them so long as to necessitate their being continually tucked in; if the door in the manor was small, he had to reproduce a door so small as to force the actors to bend low in order to pass through. He had read somewhere that the boyars, in appear-ing before the Tsar, bowed thrice to the ground. Well, in our rehearsals the boyars got down on their knees, touched the floor with their foreheads, rose and went down again—

[153]

not less than twenty times!—for which, if you will remember, the actor Darsky once called me to account in a loud voice. In a word, everything must be, as Alekseiev was inclined to say, 'curious'.

And from this bright piling up of colours, images, outcries, we had to turn about-face to the sad everyday realities of Chekhov. Nothing extravagant in the costumes; no violent make-up; a complete absence of crowd scenes; no cascade of external tints—in a word, nothing with which the actor might protect himself against revealing his individuality to the point of nakedness. As for the rest: silence, concentration, a relatively uninhabited world.

Before anything else I had to consider the motley composition of the performers. Of the personages in 'The Sea Gull' (ten in all), four were my pupils, three were amateurs from Alekseiev's Circle, and three were actors outside our groups. Constantin Sergeievitch's wife, the actress Lilina, fitted marvellously to the tone of Chekhov's play. Another important member of the Circle, Luzhsky, full-heartedly and trustfully followed me and quickly was master of his rôle. My main props were my pupils, Knipper, Roxanova, and Meyerhold. Among them, at the beginning a kind of white raven, appeared the American favourite, Vishnevsky. He was a provincial actor with all the earmarks of the old theatre. But he so passionately fought to get into our theatre, so blindly believed in Stanislavsky and me, that he refused a good contract and worked obediently and with zeal, which any other old-school actor would have been scarcely capable of doing. And, as you will observe further, he believed in Chekhov before any one else. The rehearsals were hindered by the absence of Stanislavsky, and he was to play the rôle of

ALEXANDER VISHNEVSKY

VASSILY KACHALOV

Two leading Russian actors

the writer. We were forced to hold the first ten, and again another ten, rehearsals without him.

You must know that a *régisseur* is a triple-faced creature:

(1) the *régisseur*-interpreter; he instructs *how* to play; so that it is possible to call him the *régisseur*-actor or the *régisseur*-pedagogue;

(2) the *régisseur*-mirror, reflecting the individual qualities of the actor;

(3) the *régisseur*-organizer of the entire production.

The public knows only the third, because he alone is visible, in everything: in the *mises en scène*, in the design of the director, in the sounds, in the lighting, in the harmony of the crowd scenes. The *régisseur*-interpreter and the *régisseur*-mirror, however, are invisible. They have sunk themselves in the actor. One of my favourite conceptions, which I have often repeated, is the necessity of the *death* of the *régisseur* in the actor's creativeness. However much and richly the *régisseur* instructs the actor, it too often happens that the former plays the whole rôle to the last detail; it only remains for the actor to imitate and to transmute the whole in himself. In a word, no matter how deep and rich in content the *régisseur's* rôle may be in the shaping of the actor's creativeness, it is absolutely essential that not a trace of it be visible. The greatest reward that such a *régisseur* can have comes when even the actor himself forgets about what he has received from the *régisseur*, to such a degree that he enters into the life of all the instructions received from him.

'Except a corn of wheat fall into the ground and die, it abideth alone; but if it die, it bringeth forth much fruit.' This Biblical expression, in the deepest sense, applies to the joint creativeness of the *régisseur* and the actor.

[155]

Is it necessary to say that for this the *régisseur* should possess the potentiality of an actor? Essentially, it should be said, he ought to be in a profound sense an actor of diverse parts. And if the better *régisseurs* before us—Yablochkin, Agramov —like me did not remain actors, it is evident that we were hindered by the limitation of our external expressiveness and our tremendous demands upon ourselves.

The *régisseur*-mirror's most significant ability is to perceive the individuality of the actor; to follow it uninterruptedly in the process of work; to observe how the intentions of the author and the *régisseur* are reflected in him, what he does well and what he does badly, the direction in which his imagination leads him, his desires, and to what limits it is possible to insist upon one or another solution. Simultaneously it is necessary to watch the actor's will and to direct it, without his being conscious of it; to be able without inflicting humiliation but with love and friendliness to mimic: 'This is how you are doing it; is that what you intended?' so that the actor may see himself face to face, as in a mirror.

The *régisseur*-organizer brings within his horizon all the elements of the production, giving first place to the creativeness of the actors, and merges them with the whole setting into one harmonious whole. In this organizing work he is all-powerful. The servant of the actor where it is necessary to submit to his individuality, adapting himself also to the individual qualities of the artist-decorator, constantly taking into account the demands of the direction, he appears in the final reckoning the real dominator of the production.

In this, then, lies the first and most significant difference between the new and the old theatre: a single will reigns in our theatre. The production is permeated with a single spirit, whereas in the old theatre, even to this day, there reigns the fullest divergence of directing forces. Say, the *régisseur* has sensed the true inwardness of the theatrical essence of all the elements of the performance, say he has fused the author with the actor—hence success. Again, he has not sensed this essence, he has entangled himself in it, he has broken it up into divergent elements; there may be excellent fragments in it, but in a general way it is at odds with itself, a failure.

As I recall my activities with pupils and actors thirty years ago, I find that the essence of my method was then what it is now. To be sure, I have become immeasurably more experienced, my methods have become more deliberate, more shrewd; a certain 'craft' has developed; but the basis remains the same: it is *intuition* and the *infection* of the actor by it. What is this? How is it to be explained in brief?

Once a short but remarkable dialogue passed between me and Leonid Andreiev. When I worked over his plays, he, with unconcealed sincerity, was delighted because I had succeeded in revealing his most sensitive intentions to the actors. 'Amazingly accurate. I couldn't have done better myself!' he exclaimed. And one day he kept his eyes fixed on me for a long time; then suddenly, with great earnestness, he asked: 'How could you have stopped writing plays yourself, when you are in the possession of such a gift, of being able to sense a human being and of analysing his behaviour?'

I answered something like this:

'It is possible that this gift of intuition does not go beyond literature in me, and does not extend to life as it is. It is possible that I—forgive the high-sounding words—penetratingly see *your* attitude to the world, your observation of life, as I also see those of Chekhov, Dostoievsky, and Tol-stoy. It is you, the author, who from behind the lines of your play whisper to me your knowledge of life, while I, with merely a kind of sixth sense, perceive where it is the truth and where falsehood. It is even possible that I shall enter into a dispute with you and even prove myself to be in the right. But without your prompting as the author, it is very unlikely that I should have paused before these living appearances, which I now so excellently analyse. But in order to create plays oneself, it is necessary oneself to grasp at life.'

When, some years afterward, we worked over Dostoiev-sky and we invited several scholars from the Psychological Society to the rehearsals, they invariably said that we had nothing to learn from them, but that they had much to learn from us.

Forgive me, reader, for bragging, but in questions of theatrical art this comprehension has such a tremendous significance: true intuition! Without it, all is falsehood, all is a mutilation of the author's intention and style. But as it lends itself only with difficulty to analysis, as 'images' prompted by intuition do not allow licence and demand a rigid control in the selection of theatrical resources, so to this day the lords of theatrical undertakings are afraid of it and avoid it; often they simply drive it from the theatre as though it were the plague. Without it matters are simpler, especially for *régisseurs* with 'ingenious ideas', which is the term applied by Heine to all sorts of rubbish that finds its way into men's heads.

This conception—of accurate intuition—has to this day found no scientific formulation in the theatrical art. For this reason there remains but the single alternative for rehearsals: to *infect* the actor with the intentions, images, the subtlest nuances, now by means of interpretation, now by the simple method of *showing* the actor how to execute a rôle.

There is but a single foundation, which very much later I formulated thus: *The law of inner justification.* But this is far too complex to be discussed in the present chapter.

Later, after Stanislavsky had transferred his *régisseur's* attention from the outer to the inner, he occupied himself, together with his assistant, *régisseur* Sulerdzhitsky, with a precise definition of the elements of the creativeness of the actor. The so-called 'system' of Stanislavsky found its approximation at this time. There appeared his now popular expression, 'transparent action'. It answers the question I have earlier put: where should the actor's temperament be directed? The deepest essence of a play or rôle was defined in the word 'seed', more particularly the seed of the scenes, the seed of a fragment.

A rôle was composed during the rehearsal out of a multitude of conversations of a semi-dilettantish character. At present, during the labours with my actors, I use precise definitions: 'atmosphere', in which this or another scene takes place: the 'physical self-consciousness' of a given character—gay, sad, ill, somnolent, indolent, cold, hot, etc.; 'characterization'—an official, an actress, a society woman, a female telegraphist, a musician, etc.; the 'style' of the entire setting—heroic, Homeric, epochal, comical, farcical, lyrical, etc.

But the most important domain of the rehearsing labours was something which, as it happened, Chekhov was the first to hit upon. Do you remember what I said about the rehearsals in St. Petersburg? It was during these that Chekhov said: 'They act too much. It would be better if they acted a little more as in life.' In this is contained the most profound difference between the actor of our theatre and the actor of the old theatre. The actor of the old theatre acts either *emotion*: love, jealousy, hatred, joy, etc.; or *words*, underlining them, stressing each significant one; or a *situation*, laughable or dramatic; or a *mood*, or *physical self-consciousness*. In a word, inevitably during every instant of his presence on the stage he is *acting* something, representing something. Our demands on the actor are that he should not act anything; decidedly not a *thing*; neither feelings, nor moods, nor situations, nor words, nor styles, nor images. All this should come of itself from the individuality of the actor, individuality liberated from stereotyped forms, prompted by his entire 'nervous organization'—that which our Professor Speransky but lately defined by the word 'trophica'. For us the individuality of the actor is the immense region of his imagination, his heredity, all that might manifest itself beyond his consciousness in a moment of aberration. To awaken the features of individuality, such is the problem during rehearsal. There is yet another very important requirement: in such a degree to read and incarnate oneself into a rôle that the words of the author become for the actor his own words; i.e., if I may repeat what I said about the *régisseur*, the author must also be lost in the individuality of the actor.

For in the end, when you watch a performance you must forget not only the *régisseur*, you must forget even the author; you must yield wholly to the actor. He can gratify you, or distress you. The actor speaks, and not the author, and not the *régisseur*. Both one and the other have died in him, even as have died and become resurrected the innumerable observations and impressions experienced by him in the course of his whole life, from childhood to this very evening. All this, as though long since passed away, is resurrected under the pressure of that force which is embodied in a theatrical performance.

In our rehearsals there was still another force, an immense, unifying force: enthusiasm; devotion to the whole undertaking, to the work itself, without petty vanity, with tremendous faith. One of the actors, by the way, refused to yield to the common enthusiasm, though in his own fashion he was suited to the given rôle. He did not even try to conceal his ironic attitude to the new methods of Chekhov the dramatist. Without much hesitation I gave his rôle to some one else. Among my letters, which I found in the Chekhov museum, I discovered the following:

DEAR ANTON PAVLOVITCH!

To-day there were two readings of 'The Sea Gull'. If only, invisibly, you could have been present. Then, you know what? You would have promptly begun writing a new play!

You would have been a witness of such a growing, absorbing interest, such a profound meditativeness, such interpretations and such an intentness, that for this one day at least you would have succumbed to self-admiration.

To-day we've admired you beyond measure for your genius, for the sensitive perceptions of your soul.

We are in the process of polishing. We are testing the tones, or more accurately the semitones, in which 'The Sea Gull' should be played. We are discussing the ways and means of staging your play, so that it shall possess the public as it has possessed us. . . .

Speaking seriously, if our theatre ever gets on its feet, then you

[161]

who have made a gift to us of 'The Sea Gull', 'Uncle Vanya', and 'Ivanov', must write for us yet another play.

Never have I admired your genius more than to-day, when it has become necessary to penetrate into the innermost depths of your play.

Two or three weeks went by before Alekseiev began to send us from the village the *mise en scène*, according to the acts. This *mise en scène* was very audacious, different from the kind to which the public was accustomed, and it was very much alive. Basically, Stanislavsky did not feel the real Chekhovian lyricism; nevertheless his scenic imagination prompted him to devise the most fitting fragments from real life. Excellently he caught the mood of *ennui* of the day at the farmhouse, the half-hysterical irritation between the characters, the pictures of departure, arrival, the autumnal evening, and skilfully filled out the course of the act with appropriate objects and characteristic minutiae for the persons of the play.

One of the considerable elements in the scenic novelty of the *régisseur* Stanislavsky lay precisely in this utilization of objects; they not only occupied the attention of the spectator, assisting in endowing the scene with a mood of reality, but in still greater measure they were useful to the actor, whose greatest misfortune, perhaps, in the old theatre was the fact that his whole being found itself, as it were, outside time and space. This *régisseur's* trait of Alekseiev was an elementary response to Chekhov's requests; there was not yet in this anything of the aroma of the author's charm. Such things still manifested a naturalism of the first water, Zolaism, even the spirit of the theatre of Antoine in Paris, or of Reinhardt in Berlin, which were already infected with naturalism. But in Russia this took place on the stage for the first time: the match and the lighted cigarette in the darkness, the powder in Arkadina's pocket, Sorin's plaid, a comb, studs, the washing of hands, the drinking of water in gulps, and so forth, *ad infinitum*. The actor's attention should be trained to make a note of these things, and this should have the effect of making his speech simpler. Later, within perhaps not more than seven or eight years, there would come a reaction, a conflict precisely with these things. At this time, however, Stanislavsky proposed to utilize them in large measure; he was even lavish in the use of everyday colours. Like every innovator he fell into extremes, but as every detail went through my direction I was in a position to cast aside anything that seemed superfluous or questionable.

Within a year, in 'Uncle Vanya', he would cover up the head against mosquitoes, would stress the chirp of the cricket behind the stove; for these effects theatrical criticism would go to great lengths to abuse the Art Theatre. Even Chekhov, half jesting, half in earnest, would say: 'In my next play I'll make the stipulation: "The action takes place in a land which has neither mosquitoes nor crickets nor any other insects which hinder conversation between human beings." ' For the time being, however, these things did me a great service in my capacity as a *régisseur*. Another important stage innovation consisted in the pauses. In this, too, there was an elementary closeness to Chekhov, who on every page of his plays had two or three pauses.

In the art of the Art Theatre these pauses would have an important place: the nearer to life, the farther from the gliding, uninterrupted 'literary' flow so characteristic of the old theatre. In the *mise en scène* of 'The Sea Gull' we were to

[163]

grope our way to the most profound pauses which belong to life itself; they were to manifest the completion of an immediately experienced perturbation, to prepare the outburst of an approaching emotion, or to imply a silence charged with tensity.

A pause is not something that is dead, but is an active intensification of experience, sometimes marked by sounds stressing the mood: the whistle of a factory or steamer siren, the warbling of a bird, the melancholy hoot of an owl, the passage of a carriage, the sound of music coming from a distance. With the years the pauses entered to such an extent into the art of the Art Theatre as to become a characteristic feature, often fatiguing and even irritating. At that time, however, they were alluringly new. They were attained with difficulty, and only through persistent and involved research, not merely external but also psychological; the quest was for harmony between the experiences of the characters of a play and the entire setting.

I have more than once stressed the fact that Chekhov saw his personages as inseparable from nature, from the weather, from the external world.

Finally, the third element of the *régisseur's* novelty was the artist, not merely a decorator, but the authentic artist. In that scenic 'wonder', which was yet to come to pass, the important rôle was played by Simov. He was of the flesh and blood of the realistic school in Russian painting, the so-called school of the 'Peredvizhniki'—Repin, Levitan, Vasnetsov, Surikov, Polenov, etc. Alive, ardent, always smiling, he rejected the word 'impossible'; everything was possible in the opinion of this splendid 'Russian', who intensely felt both historical 'Muscovy' and Russian nature.

[164]

During one of the performances of 'The Sea Gull' the following incident took place. In the audience sat a mother with a five-year-old child. The youngster insisted on making loud observations, and though he bothered people he proved so diverting that he was forgiven. As he surveyed the garden on the stage, he turned to his mother and said: 'Mother! Let's go into the garden there for a walk!'

And what was still more important, we established a new lighting system for the stage, something different from the monotonous lighting employed in the government theatres, but more nearly conforming to the time and having some relation to reality. In this respect, at the beginning we went to extremes. There were times, indeed, when the stage was so dark as to render invisible not only the actors' faces, but even their figures. . . .

CHAPTER TEN

The autumn came; the cottage at Pushkino was cold to live in; the shed which we used for rehearsals was not heated. We transferred the rehearsals to the Hunting Club in Moscow, where some years before Alekseiev's Circle had played. At this time the stage rehearsals of 'Tsar Fyodor' had already begun; they were conducted by Sanin under the most difficult circumstances. The auditorium was being re-painted, the footlights were being rebuilt and the chairs removed; but at least there was some cleanliness and order behind the scenes.

Chekhov arrived in Moscow during this September period. He was tranquil, self-contained; he evidently was in that mood of smiling equilibrium when a human being knows that he is liked by some, loved by others, and even idolized by a third group.

I showed him fragments from 'The Sea Gull', without decorations, without costumes, at a simple rehearsal. I do not remember how the actors met him, but here is how Olga Knipper recalls it:

To this day I remember everything to the slightest detail, and it is difficult to tell about the intense perturbation which seized me and the other actors of the new theatre at the meeting with the beloved writer, whose name we—brought up as we were by Vladimir Ivanovitch Nemirovitch-Dantchenko—had become accustomed to pronounce with veneration.

I shall never forget the tremulous excitement which possessed me on that eve when I first read the note of Vladimir Ivanovitch announcing that on the morrow, September the 9th, A. P. Chekhov would be present at the rehearsal of 'The Sea Gull'. . . .

. . . We were all taken with the singularly sensitive charm of his personality, his simplicity, his inability 'to teach', 'to show'. We did not know how and of what to speak. . . . While he looked at us, now smiling, then suddenly with an unusual seriousness, with a kind of embarrassment, he pinched at his beard and took off his pince-nez. . . . He seemed perplexed as to how to answer certain questions. . . .

During the same days I took him to a rehearsal of 'Tsar Fyodor', in the regular theatre, in full dress, and with complete stage settings. He sat in the so-called director's box, attired in a light overcoat. The rehearsal took place in a cold theatre without electric lighting. We used candles and candle-ends, and kerosene lamps, which appeared from I knew not where. During the summer the theatre had been used for comic opera, which, I must add, was largely supported by the buffet run in connection with it. The room in which my study was situated was permeated with the odour of wine, and there was nothing we could do to eliminate it. None the less, the rehearsal produced an excellent impression. Chekhov at once appraised the high culture of the performance; but he was especially enthusiastic—so far as it was possible for him to express himself with fervour—about Olga Knipper.

Under what 'auspices'—the popular way of expressing it in those days—did our theatre have its opening? What attitude did the public manifest toward it?

One human being is a wolf to another.

[167]

Rumours concerning our theatre had, of course, long since penetrated into society, but the newspapers either maintained a silence or published short notes, one of which ended thus: 'Is it not true, that all this is a whim of grown-up but naïve human beings, the wealthy merchant-amateur Alekseiev and the delirious *littérateur* Vladimir Nemiro-vitch?' For the most part the newspapers were silent. It is necessary to state that Russian newspapers in their theatrical departments never had any resemblance to the French news-papers, in the sense that 'publicity' could be bought. And I immediately established toward the newspaper critics an attitude which I deemed the correct one. I made no attempt to curry favour. I did not even follow the example of private theatres in reserving permanent seats for the critics; I sent to the editors but a single ticket for the first perform-ance. In a word, no support could be expected from this quarter, and in the sanctums of the editorial offices the attitude was either frankly hostile or definitely mocking. I do not, as a general rule, nurse my wrongs, and even now I cannot recall the pamphlet about which Stanislavsky speaks in his book and which I met with in *The History of the Art Theatre*. The pamphlet, I seem to remember, was aimed chiefly at Alekseiev:

> The laws of art are to me nothing,
> I've devised my own to take their place,
> Tradition's tireless foe am I,
> The actors' scourge, the stage's ruin—
> I have no curbs, nothing to restrain me,
> I am in the fullest sense a 'gentleman'.

At that time a play by Sumbatov, called 'The Gentleman', which had for its leading character a stupid merchant, was very much in the fashion. Do you think that such sentiments were expressed by a personal enemy? By no means. The author was an important critic, who was a collaborator in one of our best newspapers. And this mocking attitude was evidently quite strong, because as *The History of the Art Theatre* informs us the pamphlet was printed in a large edition and enjoyed a wide circulation.

There were other theatrical critics whose attitude could be thus defined: 'Well, well! We shall see. If you conquer, we shall be very pleased. If not, get out of your hole the best you can!'

There were friends of the old theatre who had been previously irritated by the mere thought that here a new theatre was about to open which would compete with the famous Small Theatre. These and the others prophesied for us, of course, a brief career. 'You've said good-bye to your money,' they said to my directors of the Philharmonic, who were stockholders. The majority of them hypocritically replied: 'Well, I haven't been caught with much. I gave a mere two thousand, and that only out of respect.' We could count on friends only among the young.

Even the admirers of our previous activities, while ready to support us, were on their guard.

October 14 (Old Style) was definitely settled as our opening day. This date was due to a gypsy woman. I never indulged in superstition, nor in 'predestination from on high', yet nowhere did superstition rule with such power as in the theatre. And the circumstances and the whole activity of the theatre are so constituted as to cause human beings to yield to it; it would be beyond me to make a count of all the numerous instances that came within my experience. There

[169]

was, for example, the composer Blaramberg. He was a very honest, very charming man, who counted even Maxim Gorky among his friends. He composed the opera 'Marya Burgundskaya' ('Mary of Burgundy'), which ran exactly three times at the Big Theatre and was then removed because during every performance some misfortune occurred. Once the curtain collapsed, then the prompter died, the third time something else happened.

Gneditch, whom I have already mentioned, once wrote a one-act play called 'Foul Weather', which was not at all bad. Just as it was about to be put on in St. Petersburg, before the raising of the curtain, Svobodin, the actor who was to play the chief rôle, died behind the wings; so the play was abandoned. Later I wanted to present it at one of my school performances, but during a rehearsal the brother of the leading actress met with a tragic death. Many years went by. Somehow I happened to ask our actress Muratova, who was engaged in the school of the Art Theatre, 'What do you intend to put on next?' She replied: 'I've just distributed among my pupils their parts for Gneditch's "Foul Weather". Do you know, it's a very good play.' Involuntarily, I cried out; though right after that I laughed. And, of course, I made no explanation for my outcry. But this time, again, the play did not go on, because, as it happened, Muratova herself died.

When we produced Maeterlinck's 'The Intruder' things went wrong from the start, and the play had no success. During every performance something happened: either the curtain refused to close, or the iron curtain collapsed, or the understudy of the leading lady fell dangerously ill. The actors began to implore us to take the play off.

[170]

I conceived the idea of producing 'Faust', having Stanislavsky in mind for the rôle of Mephistopheles. Stanislavsky smiled, shrugged his shoulders, and said: 'But I must tell you, I've wanted to play Mephistopheles quite a number of times, but each time I tried it some kind of misfortune took place in my family.'

One prominent actress won such renown for *porte malheur* that they began to avoid her in all the theatres.

Particularly susceptible in this respect among our actors was Vishnevsky. When the news arrived of the death of our splendid actress Savitskaya I heard him cry in the corridor: 'Well, there! What did I tell you? Vladimir Ivanovitch had driven into the yard of her house in a carriage harnessed to a *white* horse. I told you what would happen!'

The landlord of our theatre, Stchukin, a simple merchant, who would not even destroy rats for fear of vengeance, brought a gypsy woman to me in order that she might foretell on what day the theatre should be opened. In response to my jesting tone he touched my shoulder and said: 'Believe me, there'll be "*antoniasm*"—instead of "enthusiasm".' The gypsy gave me a list, as she expressed it, of 'decisive' days, which meant dangerous or risky days. And she said: 'When you begin a big business, remember this: take a day that's of "no particular account" '; by which she meant that it mustn't be a Saturday, a Sunday, a Monday; 'take a kind of middle figure', i.e. not a five, or a ten, or a fifteen. So Stchukin and I chose for the opening day a Wednesday, the 14th of October; and, oddly enough, it was revealed years afterwards, the famous Small Theatre of Moscow had had its opening 74 years before also on Wednesday, October 14.

Thus, on October 14 (27) the Art-Accessible Theatre was opened. 'Tsar Fyodor' had a great success. It was something of an event; after all, the Russian tragedy, forbidden for thirty years by the censorship, was new to the playgoing public! The play caught on; Moskvin, of whom but yesterday every one was ignorant, awoke the following day to fame. Our admirers triumphed; those who had been hostile and had sneered were silenced. To be sure, in various corners they still raised their voices: 'Well, what do you think of the decorations of the garden? They are right along the footlights, and they shut off the view! Isn't that enough to destroy the actor? Why, we scarcely see the people on the stage!' And some one else: 'What a darkness! . . . And what hats on the bodyguard! . . . And what sleeves on the boyars! . . . Doesn't it all hide the actor's creativeness?'— 'An imitation of the Meiningen players, and nothing more!' —'Archaeological details. What a rummaging in the museums!'

On the other hand, side by side with these grumblers were those who were enthusiastic precisely over the 'art' of the costumes, and the *mise en scène*; and many over the archaeological details. The main thing was that the play was exciting, while in the last act it was profoundly touching.

Success was also achieved in the Press. Yet the critics were restrained; it was as if they said: 'Let's wait and see what will happen next!'

The Art-Accessible Theatre was open, but the Art Theatre was not yet born! Throughout the city reports were broadcast concerning the new word, but the new word had not yet been said. There were small groups which desired it so intensely that they considered it as already said: it was indeed a case of the wish being father to the thought. The truth is, the performance lived only in the present, the excitement ended with the evening; it had pleased the eyes, but this pleasure glided by very much as the pleasure of a glimpsed landscape glides by. It had been a success, the play had been given before a full house, but the feeling that a new theatre had been born was lacking. It was to come to birth later, without pomp, in a far more modest setting.

And soon enough the dark days came. We had scarcely managed even to enjoy our success to the full. Apart from 'Tsar Fyodor', not a single performance attracted the crowds. I had enough to do to look after my responsibilities as a director and steward; our administration was a small one, consisting altogether of three or four persons. It was necessary to exercise rigid economy, and there was much to do in the way of official representation, arrangement of personal interviews, and business matters within the theatre. Stanislavsky with his assistants struggled on the stage, and I seem to remember that temporarily he even ceased visiting his factory. Upon his shoulders was the burden of a new production of 'The Merchant of Venice', and the revival of some plays of his Circle, as well as his participation in them as an actor. . . . Of the sum contributed by the stockholders —28,000 rubles—soon not a trace remained. It was possible to exist only through the sale of tickets at the box-office and through contracting new debts. For a long time I had to deny myself the joys of creative labour, the joys of that spiritual world 'into which no thief can penetrate, and which no moth can corrupt'.

'The Merchant of Venice' met with complete failure. The production contained some remarkably beautiful fragments, which justified our boldness in naming our theatre the 'Art Theatre'. There was much that was beautiful and original in it. If the production had been made in an amateur circle for the benefit of a limited number of artistically sensitive people, the interest in it would have been far greater. But as Leo Tolstoy has somewhere said: 'In art, subtlety and the power of influence are diametrically opposed.'

Stanislavsky, in this case, made a very startling experiment in naturalism: Shylock spoke with a Jewish accent. The playgoing public refused to accept this. What, a tragic rôle from Shakespeare—and an accent! Lovers of the rare appreciated it, but to the vast majority it seemed a desecration of the deep conception of the tragedy. We, of course, tried to console ourselves with the thought that 'the public understands nothing'!

Do you know, nowhere in the world does the relation between art and the public bear so 'ideal' [1] a character as in Russia. With Americans, for example, the matter is quite simple. Success—that is everything. 'You, Mr. So-and-So, have had your *chance*! You haven't made good use of it. Your train's gone. Good-bye! Good luck!' But what sort of *intentions* you have had and why they have not been fully realized—well, no one is interested in that. Good-bye!

Among us, however, it is very easy to meet the poet, the artist, the writer, the playwright who, lacking success, far from lamenting the circumstance, is even often proud of it. And this is not because he holds himself in such high regard —and his family also—but because the subtlest appreciators of art say at every step: 'The public understands nothing!'—

[1] The word 'ideal' is used here in the sense of embodying idea, and not in the more customary interpretation of perfection.—*Translator.*

'Do they know how to appreciate genius?'—'It has had no success because it is new and original, and the public loves only the commonplace!'—'The public has not yet been educated up to it!' Then, too, there were such popular aphorisms as 'What's fate? Nothing but an empty sound!'

Yes, the public bites at its favourite banalities, as the fish at the worm; yes, the public is susceptible to many effects, the use of which is forbidden by the artistic conscience of the exacting artist; yes, many remarkable things have for a long time remained unacknowledged; yet, for all that, I have never forgotten the phrase of the critic Flerov-Vassilyev, whom I have already mentioned: 'The public is never to blame.' Yes, the public again and again fails to appreciate the value of some pearls; it fails to be enthusiastic because it has been cooled off by an awkward ending, unsuccessful half-minutes, a shocking-sounding morality; yet you must seek those guilty of failure in other places: in the actor, in the author, in the *régisseur*; some one among them, when he created a part, was not conscious of any resonance, was not aware of the mood of the public in the auditorium. I have always thought that to blame failure on the fact that the public has failed to understand is to deceive oneself. During my own career, to express myself bluntly, I have more than once fallen down as an author and as a *régisseur*, but for all my condescension toward myself I must say that I do not recall a single instance in which I had the right to put the blame of my failure on the public.

Whether it happened in this way or that, the fact remains that we lost one of the high trumps of our repertory. We then began to count on that enchanting play by Hauptmann,

'Hannele', with its half-realistic, half-fantastic mood; Stanis-lavsky's Circle had already played it several years before; now it was revived in a wholly new setting. At this time there occurred one of the most painful incidents in the history of the Art Theatre. It is worth while to go into detail.

In its first translation, 'Hannele' was forbidden for production on the stage. Two censorships existed side by side: one for printed works, the other for the theatre. The play was permitted to be printed, but not played. The chief cause of the ban was that the village teacher appeared to poor Hannele in her dreams in the form of Christ. Later another translation was made, more suitable for the Russian stage; the censorship sanctioned its production. It was this translation that we used. In a word, in the matter of censorship we had not the least concern. Then, suddenly, on the eve of the final general rehearsal I received an order from the Chief of Police, Trepov, to remove the play from our repertory. What was the matter? I learned that the play was forbidden in response to a protest from the Metropolitan of Moscow, Vladimir. Without making head or tail of the business, we managed to procure an appointment with the Metropolitan and made haste to visit him at his home. The floor and the walls were immaculately clean; out of the windows I glimpsed little paths, and monkish figures passing along them; and, again, there was the aroma of incense and cypress; upon everything was the stamp of severe simplicity. Presently there came out to see us a tall, dry, ascetic-looking individual, inspiring respect; in his hands there was a small book—'Hannele' in its *first* translation. We immediately grasped the cause of the difficulty. Softly yet sternly he spoke of the impossibility of allowing Christ to appear on the stage, of allowing such phrases to be uttered—he quoted from the volume he held in his hand. Several times we tried to interrupt him, to point out to him—however awkward it was for us—the source of his misunderstanding in the present instance, i.e. that we were not producing our play from this particular translation—which, as I learned later, had been deliberately put into his hands by an informer who worked on a newspaper. We wanted to impress upon him the fact that we were using another copy, permitted by the theatrical censor, that we had it right here in our hands. But the Metropolitan would allow of no interruption, and even began to show anger. Finally, we had an opportunity to explain the misunderstanding to him. To our great mortification, he not only failed to grasp our meaning, but became increasingly angry.

'How can you say that the play in this edition is forbidden when it says right here that it is permitted by the censorship?'

I replied: 'Your High Grace, there are two separate censorships—one for books, the other for the theatre; this edition is permitted to be published in book form, another is permitted for production on the stage.'

He interrupted me: 'What do you mean by saying that when it states here plainly: "Permitted"? How then can it be permitted if . . .' And once more he began to repeat his earlier accusations against 'Hannele'.

The more trouble we took to explain to him his very simple misunderstanding, the angrier he became. It was becoming clear that he took us for speculators, human beings from a vicious *milieu*. He rose to his feet, giving us to understand that the audience was over.

[177]

Stanislavsky and I left the Metropolitan's presence very much shaken, not so much with our failure as with the thought: what an abyss existed between the theatre—which was a civil institution—and the highest representative of religion! It was an abyss so deep as to be beyond understanding. With all the caution we had exercised in expressing ourselves, now that we were alone but one word—'stupidity'—went on repeating itself on our lips.

Well, what were we to do?

Stakhovitch arranged for us an interview with the Grand Duke. The latter listened to us and promptly understood everything. Nevertheless, far from encouraging us, he nervously went on rubbing his hands, as though he were trying hard to keep down a surfeit of seething unhappy feelings. 'I'll try, but I warn you: it'll be hard.'

We were amazed: 'Why should it be hard, Your Highness? All that is necessary is to explain to the Metropolitan the cause of the misunderstanding.'

'I'll try,' the Grand Duke replied briefly and lapsed into enigmatic silence. He could do nothing. Either that, or he did not wish to irritate the Metropolitan. The matter ended there. 'Hannele' was removed from our repertory because of this slight misunderstanding, and all the labour we had put into it was lost.

I imagine that I shall not find a better place for relating another outstanding incident. This happened much later. Quite apart from the censorships then existing for printing and stage production, there was also the Church censorship. The Art Theatre conceived the idea of producing Oscar Wilde's 'Salome' and Byron's 'Cain'. The general censorship and even the theatrical censorship granted the necessary

[178]

permission, but they warned us that in these particular instances it was absolutely necessary to obtain the permit of the Church censorship. The matter reached the highest religious department, the Most Holy Synod. There the production of both plays was forbidden. I employed all means at my command; by this time we had achieved a great success, and we had some valuable connections in St. Petersburg. Our efforts finally obtained for me an audience with the chief personage who protested against the proposed production —the Exarch of Georgia. He, even as the Metropolitan Vladimir, assumed an angry tone:

'What's this you're proposing to do? Bring on the stage a sacrifice? And to whom this sacrifice? To God? And whom do you propose bringing on the stage for this purpose? Adam! Adam, who is accounted among the holy! And Abel! Don't you know that Abel is counted as two degrees higher than Adam in the hierarchy of the saints?'

Thus, we were not allowed to produce either 'Cain' or 'Salome'.

There was still another episode in the spirit of the episode of the Metropolitan Vladimir.

We gave a production of 'Anathema' by Leonid Andreiev. The chief acting characters in the play were the old Jew Leizer, a man of ideal goodness, enacted by Vishnevsky ; and Satan, in the guise of the unknown who mocked the goodness of Leizer, a rôle played by Kachalov. The play had an enormous success. We suffered no qualms on the score of possible censorship. One day I received a telegram dealing with matters of publication from St. Petersburg from the chief of the Head Department, Bellgard, requesting that a seat be reserved for him at the next performance of 'Ana-

[179]

thema'. Bellgard had been always favourably inclined toward us, in so far as a censor could be favourably inclined.

He arrived. He watched the stage. It was the thirtieth-odd performance. During the intermission he sat in my study and with suspicious caution asked questions.

'Tell me . . . Has Vishnevsky changed his make-up?'

I did not understand the question.

'I mean, did he have a different make-up in the earlier performances?'

I shrugged. Where did he get the idea?

In any case, upon my desk lay a pile of photographs of the performance—of the *mise en scène* and of the actors.

There! The photographs had been taken during the general rehearsal and since then no change had been made.

'It's strange!' said Bellgard, examining the photographs. 'I'll tell you what the trouble is. Some days ago Pobiedonostzev demanded my presence and strongly reprimanded me: "What's this that's going on at Moscow? Shirinsky-Shakhmatov has arrived from Moscow, all stirred up. He says that the Art Theatre is showing Christ on the stage." Vishnevsky in "Anathema". That's what brought me to Moscow to find out for myself.'

Shirinsky-Shakhmatov was an important figure among the nobility, intimate with court circles.

There was nothing left for me to do but laugh gaily at the ways of gossip-mongers who do not take the trouble to confirm rumours they have heard. Bellgard sat through the entire performance, and walked behind stage to interview Vishnevsky and Kachalov; he expressed himself as fully satisfied. And he left Moscow with the gratifying feeling, not without spite, that he would expose Shirinsky-Shakhmatov and avenge the undeserved reprimand he had received from Pobiedonostzev.

Nevertheless, within three days we received the order to remove 'Anathema' from our repertory.

All my efforts and my journey to St. Petersburg were of no avail. Thus it was that we no longer played 'Anathema'.

At this time our idea for making our theatre generally accessible miscarried. I have already related how we had come to terms with the Society of National Recreation and promised to present morning performances for the working-men. I knew that there was a fourth censorship—for people's performances! But I thought that with the assistance of the Educational Department our performances would encounter no opposition. Yet, lo! one day I was asked to appear before the Chief of Police, Trepov. It was the same Trepov who was to make a brilliant career and win renown by his expression, 'Don't spare the bullets!' when on the 9th (22nd) of January the factory workmen of St. Petersburg marched to the palace with a petition to the Tsar (Nicholas II), in consequence of which there occurred the disgraceful slaughter now celebrated in history.

'Surely you know that for people's performances there's a special censorship?' Trepov asked me. 'But,' I protested, 'this is not a people's performance in the official sense, as it takes place neither in a factory nor in the village, but in the very heart of the city.' 'Nevertheless,' he replied, 'it's a fact that the Society of National Recreation takes half the theatre for one factory and the other half for another factory. That simply means that there is a change of locality, but the principle remains the same. You understand, of course, I can commit you for trial in the courts. But I'll be lenient, if you stop the performances.'

Some one has made the excellent comparison: 'Popular enlightenment holds the same relation to the Tsarist régime as the sun to the snow: when its rays are weak, the snow gleams with the light of diamonds and rubies; but when they are strong, the snow melts.'

Thus, holding my indignation in check, on returning home and falling into a fit of coughing which almost choked me, I realized how powerless we were to struggle with the arbiters of our destiny. And we did not know, nor did I know, what manner of brake would arrest the downward flight of our chariot. The box-office takings went on diminishing; how I managed to borrow money I do not know.

Such was the situation on the eve of the first performance of 'The Sea Gull', a comedy in four acts by Anton Chekhov. The fact is, our theatre was on the verge of complete collapse.

CHAPTER ELEVEN

The atmosphere was charged with excitement and perturbation, not only among those participating in 'The
Sea Gull', but in the entire theatre. There was the sense of
an impending storm. The whole existence of the young
theatre depended on this performance. There was nothing
in the rehearsals to give confidence in success; singularly
lacking were those encouraging incidents when actors sitting
within the darkness of the auditorium, actors having no rôles
in the play, and others friendly to the theatre, suddenly,
after some particular scene or act, rise from their seats and
walk over to the *régisseur's* table to express their enthusiasm.
Such incidents usually cheer the *régisseur* and the actors; the
atmosphere grows stimulating. This time there was nothing
of the sort—those in the darkened auditorium listened in
silence, and departed in silence. There was, however, an
extraordinary tension, and no one seemed to be able to make
up his mind to offer any prognostication. Moreover, the
general nervousness was intensified by the presence of Chekhov's sister, Marya Pavlovna. Anton Pavlovitch lived at
this time in Yalta, and she knew the nervous mood in which
he awaited this performance; she went on saying that her
brother would curse himself for yielding to me. She was
greatly perturbed herself, and infected every one in the
theatre with her nervousness. She was acquainted with the
actors and tried to find encouragement in them, but received

[183]

no consolation. Again and again she came to implore me not to proceed further, reminding me of my promise not to allow a performance of 'The Sea Gull' to take place unless there was some definite assurance that the play would prove a success.

The day before the performance, notwithstanding the fact that the dress rehearsal had been satisfactory, Stanislavsky turned to me with an almost official demand concerning the necessity of postponing the performance and of carrying on further rehearsals. I replied that in my opinion the play was fully ready, that I saw no purpose in postponing it, and that if it should for all that prove a failure there was nothing now that could materially alter the fact.

'Then remove my name from the bills!' he said. (On the bills, in the rôle of *régisseur*, were both our names.) I do not remember whether I convinced him or simply refused to listen to him, but I did not remove his name. And on the eve of the *première*, during the performance of a play whose name I do not remember, as I was passing behind the wings, there twice approached me the pacing Vishnevsky, who was about to go on. In a stage-whisper he said to me: 'To-morrow there will be a great success!'

And for the second time, flourishing his fists before his chest, he said: 'Vladimir Ivanovitch, believe me, to-morrow there will be a tremendous success! Yes, a tremendous success!'

It was the only voice of encouragement. This brief episode has remained among the unforgettable things in my mind.

And now it was the 17th (30th) of December. The theatre was by no means full; the *première* of Chekhov's play did not fill the house.

At the very start the *mise en scène* of the first act was a bold one. According to the author, there should be a straight path, intersected by an estrade with a curtain: this is the stage upon which Treplev's play would be given. When the curtain goes up, instead of decorations only the lake and the moon would be visible. Of course, in every theatre, for the characters watching the play within the play, a bench would have been erected on the side to the right or to the left; while we had a long bench stretching the length of the footlights, quite near the prompter's box; to the left of this bench was a stump, on which Masha was to sit. Besides this, there was a bench to the left. And upon the long bench, their backs to the public, sat the stage audience. As the moon was behind the curtain, the stage was still in darkness.

Now, the darkness and the disposition of the benches were sufficient to put our enemies in the proper frame of mind for their little jokes. On the other hand, those who were in a mood to see the performance simply, without any precon-ceptions, saw before them the simplicity of life itself. Later the moon would illumine all. What decorations there were filled the stage with the living mood of a summer evening; the figures moved slowly, without the slightest artifice, the least affectation; simply and slowly, because the whole life which passed by on the stage was simple and ductile; the intonations were simple, the pauses by no means empty but charged, as it were, with the breath of this life and of this evening; they were pauses in which were expressed un-spoken feelings, insinuations as to character, the semitones. The atmosphere gradually deepened, gathered itself into one harmonious whole, became, as it were, the music of life. Various particulars, to which the playgoer's ear was unaccustomed, as when Masha smells the snuff, goes about in black ('This is in mourning for my life'), the *leit-motif* of each figure, speech in all its simplicity, clear and beautiful— all this gradually attracted the attention of the auditor, forced him to listen, and, unperceived by himself, wholly to yield himself to the spectacle before him. The public lost all sense of the theatre; it was as if this simplicity, this powerful, all-compelling mood of the evening and of semitones had cast a spell upon it, and the notes of secret affliction which had broken through in the actors' voices had bewitched it. There was on the stage that of which *littérateurs* who loved the theatre had long dreamed: the life they now beheld in these simple human contacts on the stage was 'real', not theatrical.

Chekhov sympathized with the Symbolists, and Treplev was without doubt under the influence of this literary current, then fairly popular.

The most hazardous thing in the play was Nina's monologue. She sat there, on the stone, an afflicted figure. How would those words sound from the stage?

Men, lions, eagles and partridges, horned deer, geese, swans, silent fish inhabiting the waters, starfish and others which it is impossible to see with the eye; in a word, all lives, all lives, which, having achieved the melancholy circle, have become extinguished. Already a thousand ages have passed since the earth has ceased to bear upon it a single living creature, and this pale moon in vain lights its lantern. In the meadow, no longer do the cranes awaken with their outcries; nor are the cockchafers heard among the groves of lindens. It is cold, cold, cold. Empty, empty, empty. Awful, awful, awful . . . I am alone. Once in a hundred years I open my lips, to speak, and in this emptiness my voice sounds mournful, and no one hears me: and you, poor flames, do not hear me . . .

This monologue, which in the first performance at St. Petersburg had awakened laughter, which to such a degree is permeated with the lyrical mood of a real poet that in our production there could not have been the least doubt of its rightness and beauty, now resounded in the deep, tense silence and held attention. And there was not the shadow of a smile, not the least hint of anything untoward. Then ensued the bitter outburst between mother and son; then, as scene followed scene, the more intimate these people became to the spectator, the more perturbing became their fits of anger, half-phrases, silences, the more powerful there rose from the depth of the spectator's soul the perceptions of his own unhappiness and anguish. And when at the end of the act Masha, restraining her tears, said to Dorn: 'Please help me, or I'll commit some stupidity, I'll laugh at my own life,' and then flung herself on the ground near the bench, weeping, a repressed, tremulous wave swept through the audience.

The curtain was drawn, and something occurred which can occur in a theatre only once in a decade: the curtain closed, and there was silence, a complete silence both in the theatre and on the stage; it was as though all held their breath, as though no one quite understood: had it been a vision? a dream? a sad song from some familiar melody? Whence had it come? From what memory of every one there? This mood lasted quite a long time, so long indeed that those on the stage decided that the first act had failed, failed so completely that not a single friend in the audience dared applaud. A nervous chill seized the actors, close to hysteria.

Then, suddenly, in the auditorium, something happened.

[187]

It was as if a dam had burst, or a bomb had exploded—all at once there was a deafening crash of applause from all: from friends and from enemies.

I have always forbidden the opening or the closing of the curtain to be done quickly and frequently, as is done in the *cafés chantant*—in order that later it might be said that there were many curtain calls. For this reason our curtain did not open quickly, and a long time was allowed to elapse before it was drawn again, so that if this was done two or three times it was an indication of a very great success. On this occasion the curtain was drawn no less than six times; then suddenly the applause ceased, as if the spectators were in fear of dissipating the magnificence of what they had just experienced.

The entire play maintained this mood. Life unfolded in such frank simplicity that the auditors seemed almost embarrassed to be present; it was as if they eavesdropped behind a door or peeped through a window. As you know, there is no heroism of any kind in the play, no stormy theatrical experiences, no lurid spots to invoke sympathy, such spots as usually serve the actor to display his talents. Here was nothing but shattered illusions, and tender feelings crushed by contact with rude reality.

There was the tremendous success of the third act and the triumph in the end, after the concluding scene between Nina and Treplev, and the magnificent finale.

Even immediately after the first act the actors in the audience, and friends of the theatre, rushed upon the stage. They were all excited to such a degree that they could scarcely wait for the end to celebrate the triumph. But after the third act there was undoubtedly a state of emotion on the stage which was like that prevailing on Easter Day: the actors embraced, wept, and could find no words for the expression of their tremendous joy. At the end of the performance the triumph was so definitely acclaimed that there could no longer be any doubt of it, and when I went on the stage and suggested to the public that a telegram be sent to the author the ovation continued for an incredibly long time. It was remarkable that even the indifferent execution of certain rôles did nothing to hinder our triumph.

The New Theatre was born.

The following telegram was despatched that same night:

To Anton Pavlovitch Chekhov, Yalta:
We have just finished performance of Sea Gull. A colossal success. From the first act the play so possessed every one that there followed a series of triumphs. Endless curtain calls. My announcement after third act that the author was not in the theatre called forth demand from audience that a telegram be sent you. We are mad with happiness. We all affectionately embrace you. Will write in detail.
Nemirovitch-Dantchenko, Alekseiev, Meyerhold, Vishnevsky, Luzhsky, Artem, Tikhomirov, Fessing, Knipper, Roxanova, Alekseieva, Rayevskaya, Nikolaieva and Ekaterina Nemirovitch-Dantchenko.

Another telegram followed the next day:

All the newspapers with astonishing accord call the success of Sea Gull brilliant, uproarious, tremendous. Criticisms all enthusiastic. Success of Sea Gull far exceeds success of Fyodor in our theatre. I am happier than ever I was at productions of my own plays.
Nemirovitch-Dantchenko.

[189]

Anton Pavlovitch at this time either had already bought or was on the verge of buying a plot of land for the erection of a house, and was working out a plan for its construction with some young architect. He had no particular affection for the Crimea, but knew that it was essential for him to live in the South; the preceding winter at Nice had left him dissatisfied.

The first telegram about the success of his play stunned him. He did not believe it, and thought that it was merely a show of friendship, which exaggerated the truth. On the same day, however, he was showered with congratulatory telegrams in such numbers, and expressed in such strong terms, that his doubts quickly scattered.

A letter from the Chekhov Museum:

DEAR ANTON PAVLOVITCH!

From my telegrams you already know of the general success of 'The Sea Gull'. In order to paint for you a picture of the first performance, I must tell you that after the third act there reigned behind the wings a kind of drunken atmosphere. As some one has aptly said, it was just as on Easter Day. They all kissed one another, flung themselves on one another's neck; all were excited with the mood of the supreme triumph of truth and honest labour. Just consider the reasons for such joy: the actors are in love with the play, with every rehearsal they discovered in it more and more new pearls of art. At the same time they trembled because the public was so unliterary, so poorly developed, spoiled by cheap stage effects, and unready for a higher artistic simplicity, and would therefore be unable to appreciate the beauty of 'The Sea Gull'. We gave up our whole soul to the play, and we risked everything on this one card. We régisseurs, i.e. Alekseiev and I, bent all our efforts and capabilities so that the astonishing moods of the play might be intensified. We had three dress rehearsals, we examined every corner of the stage,

[190]

we tested every electric-light bulb. For two weeks I lived in the theatre with the decorations, the properties; I made trips to the antique shops, seeking out objects which would give the necessary touches of colour. But why dwell on this? I am speaking of a theatre in which not a single nail has been overlooked. . . .

At the first performance, I, as at a jury trial, 'challenged' the jury, so that the public should consist of persons capable of valuing the beauty of truth on the stage. But I, true to myself, did not do a thing to prepare a spurious success.

From the first dress rehearsal there prevailed a spirit in the company that promised success. Nevertheless, my dreams *never* went that far. In any event, I anticipated that at best the success would be one of serious attention. Then suddenly—I cannot convey to you the whole sum of my impressions—not a single word, not a single sound escaped me. Not only the general mood reached the public, not only the *legend*, which in this play it was so hard to stress with a red line, but each separate thought, everything indeed that makes you what you are, both as an artist and as a thinker, everything, everything—well, in a word, every psychological movement—everything reached the public and possessed it. And all my fears that only a few would understand the play vanished. There could not have been more than a dozen persons who failed to grasp something in it. Then I thought that the general success would express itself merely in a few friendly curtain calls after the third act. Actually, what happened was this: after the first act the audience demanded no less than six curtain calls (we do not respond promptly to such demands). The auditorium was enthralled and excited; while after the third act not a single auditor left the theatre, but remained standing, and the calls became an endless uproarious ovation. There were calls for the author, and I informed the audience that you were not present. Then came voices: 'Send him a telegram!' . . .

You can see how busy I've been. I began this letter on Friday morning, and until Monday I couldn't snatch a single hour to finish it! And you tell me: 'Come to Yalta.' On the 23rd I'll

[191]

make my escape to Chernigovskaya, just in order to get a good sleep!

But to continue. . . . So I asked the public: 'You authorize me to send a telegram?' At this there was loud applause and cries of 'Yes!' 'Yes!'

After the fourth act the ovation was renewed. You have probably seen the papers. Thus far, the most favourable reaction to the play has appeared in the *Moskauer Deutsche Zeitung*, which I will send you to-day together with a fairly intelligent article in the *Courier*—'The Diary of a Nervous Man.' The *Russkiye Viedomosti* has, of course, been rather in a fix. Poor Ignatov— he's always at a loss when a play happens to be even a trifle above the ordinary.

We played . . . in this order: Knipper is an astonishing, an ideal Arkadina. To such a degree has she merged with the rôle that you cannot tear away from her either her elegance as an actress, or her bewitching triviality, *stinginess*, jealousy, etc. Both scenes in the third act—with Treplev and Trigorin, the first in particular—had a tremendous success. And the departure which concluded the act was an unusual piece of staging, without superfluous people. After Knipper comes Alekseieva—Masha. A marvellous image! Very characteristic and remarkably touching. She was a great success. Then Luzhsky—Sorin. He played like a major artist. Then Meyerhold. He was tender, touching and definitely a decadent. Then Alekseiev. He used a successfully mild, will-less tone. He spoke the monologues of the second act excellently, marvellously. He was a bit sugary in the third act. Roxanova was not so good; Alekseiev disconcerted her, forcing her to play the rôle of a little fool. I was angry and demanded a return to the previous lyrical tone. The poor woman got all mixed up. Vishnevsky has not yet quite merged with his rôle of the tender-hearted, shrewd, observing and all-experiencing Dorn, who was however very well made up in the style of Alexey Tolstoy and superbly ended the play. The remainder of the cast maintained a harmonious ensemble. The general tone was restrained and highly literary.

The public listened to the play with such absorbed attention as I have rarely witnessed. Moscow is in an uproar over it. In the Small Theatre they are ready to tear us to pieces.

The play is sure of a run. You'd have enjoyed the first act— and, in my opinion, the fourth, in particular.

I am infinitely happy.

I embrace you.

     Yours,
      VLADIMIR NEMIROVITCH-DANTCHENKO.

What about letting us have 'Uncle Vanya'?

CHAPTER TWELVE

This chapter might be called 'Chekhov's Treachery', or 'How Chekhov Betrayed Us'.

The rehabilitation of 'The Sea Gull' was so astounding that the question naturally arises: which was greater in the triumph, the creation of the Art Theatre or simply the success of the playwright Chekhov?

Writers do not usually express well their feelings of satisfaction in the matter of some professional triumph. The greater and the more undoubted the success, the more modest is any manifestation on the author's part. He leaves the more fervent expressions to those who indulge in them. This is neither embarrassment nor modesty, but something quite different. Chekhov, generally, was not a man of many words, and he quite locked in within himself any definite feeling of satisfaction which he must have experienced when people praised his works, and in particular those which, in his opinion, deserved praise. I often saw him at moments when friends piled thick their praise of his work; I did it myself. I said to him—how well I remember the conversation!—that he did not quite grasp not only the artistic but also the general social significance of his stories and plays. He listened the whole while in silence, not letting a single word slip from his lips. I often even thought that actually he did not understand, but only pretended that my words were for him no new thing. That is why I can imagine his great

happiness in Yalta, almost in solitude, amidst a few acquaint-
ances, amongst whom he was most fond of conversing with
the owner of a book-shop on the quay.

After this a correspondence developed, full of the most
tender feelings, 'tender feelings, like unto flowers'. The intimacy between the theatre and Anton Pavlovitch bore itself
along, as in two confluent streams. The financial side apparently did not interest him in the least. It is remarkable. Chekhov often said: 'Write plays, write vaudeville sketches;
they bring in a good income'; or 'One should write plays,
because the Society of Playwrights can in its own fashion
serve as a pension.' Actually, he thought only of vaudeville
sketches in this light. Towards serious plays, however, his
attitude was one of scrupulous, jealous artistry: even when
opportunities arose of receiving more and more honorar-
iums, he sharply refused if it involved possible failure. Following our production of 'The Sea Gull', the actress Yavorskaya asked for permission to produce the play in her theatre
in St. Petersburg. Chekhov replied that the play belonged
to the Art Theatre, and while this did not sound like a
definite refusal—for actually we had exclusive rights only
for Moscow—he immediately wrote me, for heaven's sake
not to allow Yavorskaya to produce 'The Sea Gull'. The
Alexandrinsky Theatre, after our own production of 'Uncle
Vanya', asked to be allowed to produce the play. And again
came a letter from Yalta, which implored us not under any
circumstances to grant rights of production, etc. . . . In any
event, all this happened later; but immediately after our
success with 'The Sea Gull' it was different. . . .

Anton Pavlovitch's feeling for the Art Theatre grew
steadily. I remember the dates when there were letters from

[195]

him containing such expressions: 'I am ready to be a door-keeper in your theatre'; or 'I envy the rat which lives under the walls of your theatre'; or, in answer to a perturbed letter of mine (this was already in the second year), 'A trembling note is audible in your words. Oh, don't give up! The Art Theatre is the best page of that book which will one day be written about the contemporary Russian theatre. This theatre is your pride; it is the only theatre that I love, though I haven't been in it even once.'

In the spring he arrived in Moscow, when the theatre was already closed. At this time those devoted to Chekhov were developing contacts with the actors who participated in 'The Sea Gull'.

While Anton Pavlovitch was in this manner swimming in his success, we were faced with the stern question of further existence. The season had ended with a loss; what were we to do now? Again there began for us a period of worry, and this in spite of such big successes as 'Tsar Fyodor' and 'The Sea Gull'. We had produced, besides, Ibsen's 'Hedda Gabler'; this was not an event, yet nor was it an ordinary, insignificant production. Around us there arose a din, and how full of import! From mouth to mouth there passed a word new to the stage—'atmosphere'. As you will remember, it had already flashed in my letter to Chekhov. It was evident that it had attained its purpose. The artistic idea which this word made an effort to reveal had reached the public in its complete sense. Even more than this, there flew from mouth to mouth such expressions as 'new forms', 'the theatre of new forms'. But this already belongs to the fame of Stanislavsky.

In editors' offices, in various artistic circles, in reception-rooms, where people love to talk of artistic and musical events, they were beginning to use such words as 'naturalism' and 'realism'.

Simultaneously with all this, the question of the significance of the *régisseur* in the theatre reached its full seriousness. Before us his rôle had been a very modest one, more administrative than anything else. Three or four *régisseurs* of great consequence might be counted, and no more. With the appearance of the Art Theatre the rôle of the *régisseur* became a primary one. There began endless discussions about the rights of the actor, the author and the *régisseur*. . . .

Through all this din, buzzing like a mosquito about the ear, there circulated the phrase, 'It's the vogue!' Our whole success was explained as simply a modish diversion: 'Just wait a little and see. It will all pass off like a bad headache! It's the vogue!'

And again we were without money. Nor was it all a matter of money. It was not sufficient to gain a victory; it was also necessary to reinforce it. If we were unable to pronounce the letter 'b' it had been all to no purpose to utter 'a'.

It was necessary to intensify, to stabilize, to render more precise all that our art manifested. It was necessary to strengthen our success, put ourselves in a position to stand on our own feet. We already had in view for our second season another tragedy by Alexey Tolstoy, 'The Death of Ivan the Terrible'; another play by Chekhov, 'Uncle Vanya'; still another beautiful play by Hauptmann, 'Lonely Lives'; then Ibsen's 'An Enemy of the People', and other marvellous things besides, which hitherto had suffered neglect.

[197]

It was necessary to give an opportunity to the gifted persons among our youth to perfect themselves.

On the other hand, our shareholders behaved ambiguously. Upon meeting them every one of them made compliments, but their actions resembled glidings across a polished floor: you scarcely mentioned, even remotely 'But, old chap, how are we to continue to exist?'—and—well, he was no longer there—simply vanished! And once more, as a year ago at Varvara Alekseievna Morozova's, our words congealed on our lips. As if this were not enough, rumours began to reach me of how one of our shareholders, with aggressive loudness, was abusing our theatre: 'There's really nothing interesting in it. Nothing but eccentricities. A bagful of tricks, I call it! In short, they're trying to keep up the vogue. And, of course, they can't expect any money for such stunts!'

But 'the little old woman told us our fortune', is an old saying that consoled us.

At this time Savva Timofeievitch Morozov was already strongly attracted to the theatre. I shall make no secret of it; I took advantage of this and tried to direct his powerful will where it should go. There was a meeting of shareholders, at which we reported: (1) The artistic results of our productions; (2) plans for the future; (3) the sad figures—debts to the extent of 45,000 rubles. Morozov proposed to the shareholders that they approve the report, liquidate the debt, and double their shareholdings. And as Morozov was the biggest manufacturer among them, they were afraid of displaying their miserliness before him.

Incidentally, there was the extraordinarily characteristic mercantile trait—well, what was, in Morozov's eyes, the mere

3,000 rubles of Ossipov or even the 10,000 or 15,000 rubles of the remaining shareholders? No: it was necessary that the business should be organized into a company. Let each take at least another thousand rubles' worth of stock, while he—well, he'd take 200,000 worth. This was in order that some sense of unity might exist. In this fashion, the matter ended in a victory for us.

Then suddenly the news: Chekhov says that he cannot let us have 'Uncle Vanya', as he has already promised the play to Lensky and Yuzhin for the Small Theatre; that it would be very awkward for him to take it away, and that he does not care to quarrel with them.

What! Despite the success of 'The Sea Gull' at our theatre! Despite the fact that until we achieved our success the Small Theatre could not decide to produce even a single one of his plays! To sacrifice to personal relations his own *amour propre* and all of us—to Lensky, above all men, who once thought that Chekhov had no business writing for the stage!!

The news so stunned me that I did not even protest to Chekhov, and I did not send him any of these exclamations. I knew whence the wind came. Yuzhin, as you know, was my first, my only friend, while Lensky was also close to me; nevertheless the pair held the Small Theatre above friendship: '*magis amicitiae veritas*' ('Truth is higher than friendship'). Quite apart from this, they were jealous of Stanislavsky and me, and together with the *régisseur* Kondratyev wanted to prove that the enormous artistic forces of the Small Theatre were capable of giving Chekhov a success not less great than we had had with our 'Sea Gull'.

What was to be done? For the time being we would continue without 'Uncle Vanya', all the more—as the truth forces me to admit—as Chekhov quite definitely promised to write a new play for us.

And again 'the little old woman told us our fortune'. In order that the play might be produced at the Imperial Small Theatre it was necessary for it to receive the approval of the so-called 'Theatro-Literary Committee'. And suddenly this committee approved 'Uncle Vanya' but on condition that Chekhov be requested to rewrite the third act! This was an outrageous demand. It goes without saying that Chekhov, making no response to it, gave 'Uncle Vanya' to us.

And the production of this play once and for all consolidated the foundations of the Chekhov theatre.

Posterity need not delve too deep into these things in our life, the life of men who have done a little in their time; posterity alone ought to know what good the average man has done and to preserve what remains. And what has remained is something fragile, something not too deep. Surround this heritage with tales of the author's envy, vengefulness, conceit, duplicity, and everything of any value that has remained of him will lose itself as the light of a lantern in a sea fog. But when the heritage is considerable, it cannot be dishonoured by any number of tales of absurd or worthy censure. Neither from Pushkin, nor from Oscar Wilde, nor from Gogol, could anything be taken, no matter how many new historical anecdotes should appear concerning the dissoluteness of the gifted Pushkin, the unnatural passion of Oscar Wilde, or the demented religiosity of Gogol. On the contrary, in the imagination of posterity they will only appear the more human, the nearer to us. And this, too, is necessary. It is needful that men should remember that it is not the gods who model the pots; what is wanted is realistic optimism, and not idol-worship.

In all sincerity I can say that in Anton Pavlovitch I never noticed anything that might throw a shadow on his nobility, taste, love of truth. To be sure, here and there flashed unfair jests of professional jealousy, jests which might with greater fitness have been directed at a man of lesser calibre; but this was very rare. To me it seemed that quite the opposite was the case, that in actual life Anton Pavlovitch watched over himself with the same rigid captiousness that he did in his literary works. How superbly he once expressed himself when he said that a literary production should be gifted, wise, and noble; but with us, alas, it was either gifted and noble, but not wise; or wise and noble, but not gifted; or wise and gifted, but not noble!

And it was this also that he carried into life. But sometimes he appeared to wear the armour of indifference. He would say something like this:'Don't imagine that this pleases me to the point of forgetfulness'; or 'I value this greatly, but it does not effect any change in my soul.' It was as if he was afraid that he might be somehow deprived of his independence. 'Don't attribute to me feelings too great in connection with such a minor matter.' He was afraid of exaggeration.

In this fashion, for quite a long time, continued his relation to the Art Theatre. Yet this theatre had entered his life. With all its interests and projects, with all its peculiar *milieu*, it entered the very existence of the writer Chekhov, however his biographers may avoid this issue, however Anton Pavlovitch himself may have at times tried to minimize it.

The Art Theatre filled his life with joys such as otherwise would have been lacking, and which were profoundly necessary to him. From his youth he loved the theatre scarcely less than he loved literature, and he aspired to the theatrical *milieu* perhaps even more than the literary; but the theatres cooled his ardour. And here had come a theatre which provided him with the highest joys for his personality as author, a theatre dedicated to the highest aims and wholly free from insipidity. And his intimacy with this theatre and its actors expelled from Chekhov's workaday existence those tedious and unnecessary people who used to fill the emptiness of his days.

At the same time, behind the wings of the theatre, in its very *milieu*, more and more solidly and more and more definitely there came into being a region—if it is possible thus to express oneself—of the Chekhovian world-perception. Later, within five years, there would appear upon it, protuberant, as it were, in relief, the swelling vein of the Gorkian world-perception.

Most firmly of all, this Chekhovian world-perception seized upon the group which participated in his plays. The deepest force of spiritual communion on the stage united the group; the author had insinuated himself into the tiniest corners of the actors' psychology, and remained to reign there even after the actor was off the stage. The group was welded even more compactly, and its members infected one another with the Chekhovian sense of life: there were things over which one should laugh and there were things over which one should weep. And the actors sat on the little green divan, waiting for their turn to make their entrance . . . the plays of Chekhov are quiet, with but little froth to them, and upon the stage there are quiet semitones set to a guitar, while behind the wings there is such a silence that a rat may be seen to stroll by with concentrated intentness ... and the actors exchange impressions, plans, and continue to find themselves in the power of Chekhov. . . . From this group the infection spread into the corners.

This had a potent influence on the whole art of our theatre. At the beginning it was positive and deep; later there was a negative element in it, as always happens with an art when it begins to fence itself off from life and becomes arrested in motion. . . .

With his marriage to Olga Knipper, Chekhov's intimacy with the theatre became, of course, even closer. It was engendered, it seems to me, quite promptly, at the rehearsal of 'Tsar Fyodor' in the unheated theatre. The attraction was instantaneous, and as always restrained. When Chekhov first arrived in Moscow (this was in the spring of 1899), he merely looked at her, allowed himself to be idolized; there was more as time went on. Olga Knipper was a fine young actress, but it was clear that a transient affair with her would have been impossible: she was a girl from a so-called 'good family'; her mother, a former singer, was almost the best teacher of singing in Moscow; one of her brothers was an engineer, another was an advocate. In her house everything was simple, modest, not at all bourgeois, yet also free from the tiresomeness of pretentious bohemia. The meeting between Chekhov and Olga Knipper was followed by a growing intimacy between the actress and the sister of Anton Pavlovitch; afterwards they met somewhere in the Caucasus; then there was a journey to Yalta, and from Yalta to Bakhchisarai. Friendly relations developed between the actress

[203]

and the poet, relations which were marked by a restraint of feelings and beautiful simplicity.

I sit at home and think of you. Journeying past Bakhchisarai I thought of you and recalled our journey together. Charming, superb actress, remarkable woman, if you only knew how your letter overjoyed me. I bow low to you, low, so low that my forehead touches the bottom of my well, which has already been dug a full fifty feet. [Chekhov was at this time building his cottage.]

. . . There is such fine weather at Yalta—which is neither here nor there—in fact, these past two days there has been nothing but rain. It is filthy, and it is necessary to wear galoshes. The walls are so damp that scolopendrines are crawling all over them, while in the garden you see jumping frogs and young crocodiles. . . . Well, I press your hand and kiss it. Keep well, gay and happy. Work, dance, enjoy yourself, sing, and, if possible—don't forget this poor writer, your ardent admirer.

At this time rehearsals of 'Uncle Vanya' were proceeding in Moscow. The actress was corresponding with the author. He writes her:

Art, especially the stage, is a region in which it is impossible to walk without stumbling. There are before you yet a good many unsuccessful days and even whole unsuccessful seasons; there will be great doubts and immense disenchantments; but you must be prepared for all that, you must expect it, and, without looking aside, must stubbornly go on, fanatically bending it all to your will.

Refined spiritual movements, inherent to intelligent people, should even in external matters be expressed in a refined way. Why, the vast majority of human beings are nervous sufferers, the minority experiences a sharp pain, but, where in the streets or in the houses will you find hysterical, jumping beings, clutching at their own throats? Sufferings must be expressed as they are expressed in life, i.e. not with the feet, not with the hands, but with a subtle glance; not by means of gesticulation, but by means of grace. You will say—the conditions of the stage? There are no conditions of any kind that permit falsehood.

After the first performance of 'Uncle Vanya' he writes:

The telegrams began to arrive on the evening of the 27th, when I was already in bed. They were delivered to me over the telephone. Each time I would awake and run to the telephone through the darkness, barefoot, chilled; afterwards I would fall asleep, only immediately to be awakened again by the bell. It was the first time that my own fame would not allow me to sleep. On the second day I took the precaution of placing near the bed both my dressing-gown and my slippers, but the telegrams no longer came. The telegrams were only about curtain-calls and the play's brilliant success, yet I felt in them something subtle, something very elusive, from which I concluded that the feelings of you all were not such as to assure me that everything was going exceptionally well.

There was the same experience with nearly all of Chekhov's plays: the prompt enormous success was achieved only in the rarest stratum of the public, among the particularly sensitive human beings who saw both farthest and deepest. Leonid Andreiev once wrote: 'I am not ashamed to acknowledge that I am in love with the present of this theatre, and even more with its future.' There was the advocate, Prince Urussov, a very considerable figure in the legal world, who saw 'The Sea Gull', if I remember aright, at least twelve times. Very many persons used to speak in this vein: 'Usually you leave a theatre to go to a restaurant, in order to sup, to listen to music, and to chatter. But after "Uncle Vanya" you have a desire to retire to a silent corner and

[205]

think and think, to the point of tears.' But neither 'Uncle Vanya' nor 'The Three Sisters' nor 'The Cherry Orchard' was accepted by the public promptly. Every one of these plays succeeded in winning a real triumph only from the second season, and only much later did any of them draw large houses. After 'Uncle Vanya', as always after a *première*, we drove to a restaurant to await the morning papers there, and actually we felt that everything was not going exceptionally well.

It is a very difficult ordeal for an artist, to experience undervaluation. Chekhov wrote:

No, actress, none of you, Art Actors, are satisfied with an ordinary, average success. What you want is noise, a discharge of guns, an explosion of dynamite. In a word, you are all spoiled, deafened by constant conversations about successes, about full and empty houses; you are poisoned with giddiness and in another two or three years you won't be good for anything else. So there!

Such relations between Chekhov and Olga Knipper continued until summer, and it was not till August of 1900 that he wrote:

'My darling Olga, my joy, I greet you. To-day I received a letter from you, the first since your departure. I read it and re-read it, then re-read once more. And here I am writing to you, my actress . . .'

The summer of 1900 proved a decisive one. In July the actress again visited the author's family, and when in the following month she left them she was his betrothed. Henceforth, his intimacy with our theatre grew increasingly close; our theatre infected him with the desire to write a new play. He planned it in a cheerful mood; he had in mind a very gay

OLGA KNIPPER, WIFE OF CHEKHOV

CHEKHOV AS A YOUNG MAN

p. 206]

comedy. In his letters to Olga Knipper he more and more often offered detailed observations on his labours.

Before he sat down to the actual writing of a play Chekhov spent a great deal of time preparing the material. He had before him a thickish notebook, in which he wrote down separate phrases caught in passing or read somewhere, characteristic of his personages. When there was accumulated a sufficient number of details, out of which, as it seemed to him, rôles might be constructed, and after he had found the proper mood for every act, only then would he begin to write the play according to the acts. The persons of the play were by now perfectly defined in his own mind, and, according to a letter of his, as the play proceeded they remained unchangeable. He did not believe in dragging things in, and this he scrupulously avoided. The events of the play crept along even as life itself during this epoch, in a tired sort of way, without any visible logic. Human beings acted under the influence of chance happenings; they did nothing to build their own lives. Here is the substance of his first act: a birthday party, the spring, gaiety, birds singing, bright sunshine. And of the second act: triviality gradually takes into its hands the power over sensitive, nobly inclined human beings. Of the third act: a conflagration in the neighbourhood, the entire street is aflame; the power of triviality grows intenser, human beings somehow flounder in their experiences. The fourth act: autumn, the collapse of all hopes, the triumph of triviality. Human beings are as chess pawns in the hands of invisible players. The absurd and the pathetic, the noble and the worthless, the intelligent and the stupid, are all interwoven and assume

[207]

a form of peculiar theatrical resonance, become a harmony of human voices and external sounds; somewhere there is a fiddle, somewhere a woman street-singer with a harp, elsewhere one hears the wind blowing down the chimney, elsewhere the fire alarms.

From letters:

When I am to come to Moscow is something I cannot say, because—can you imagine it?—I am writing a play—well, not exactly a play, but a kind of tangle: there are many characters in it; it is possible that I shall go astray and chuck it.

I am writing a play, but if it shall fail to please me, I will put it aside, hide it till next year or until such time as the desire comes to resume it. There is still no rain. A barn is now being built in the yard. . . . I love you.

By the way, 'Ivanov' alone of all my plays was put on by Korsh the moment I finished writing it. The other plays reposed a long time with me awaiting Vladimir Ivanovitch, and for this reason I had plenty of time to make all sorts of revisions.

As regards my play, I shall have it finished sooner or later— perhaps in September, even in October or even in November. But whether or not I decide to have it produced this season is unknown to me, my dear little woman.

Yalta is still without rains. The poor trees, especially those which are on the hills and on this side: not a single drop of rain have they received all summer, and they have turned yellow. Thus also it happens that in a lifetime human beings receive not a drop of happiness. It must be that that is how it should be.

He arrived in Moscow in the middle of October. He has remained very much in my memory during this visit. He was energetic, gay, grown younger. In a splendid mood, he sat down to make a clean copy of his new play. And do you

[208]

CHEKHOV MEETS A MOSCOW ART THEATRE GROUP

Chekhov in centre, with book

know, for a writer the best and perhaps the only pleasant part of his labours is when he writes his final copy, when the so-called 'throes of creation' are already behind him. Olga Knipper had already had a great success as an actress; very soon she would be known as one of the most interesting of women; which meant that the male *amour propre* of Chekhov had its gratification.

It was during this period that he made the final copy of 'The Three Sisters'. We in the theatre read the play in his presence. He fought with his own embarrassment and several times repeated: 'I've written a vaudeville piece!' Later he would say the same thing of 'The Cherry Orchard', that he had written a vaudeville piece. Really we could not understand why he called his play that, when on the title of the manuscript he called it a drama. On the other hand, within fifteen or twenty years irresponsible theatrical men would juggle with the phrase.

When the actors, who had listened to the reading of the play, asked him to explain, he answered, as was his habit, with phrases which explained little: 'Andrey appears in this scene in slippers,' or 'Here he simply whistles.' In this respect he was much more precise in his letters: 'Human beings who have long borne affliction in their hearts usually only whistle or lapse often into thought.' The rehearsals of 'The Three Sisters' began while he was still in Moscow. Above all, he insisted on the accuracy of everyday truth. For example: as certain artillerists appear in the play, it was necessary that there should be present at the rehearsals an acquaintance of his, a colonel in the artillery; he also insisted that the sounds of the conflagration off the stage should be extremely verisimilar; and so on.

[209]

In December he left for Nice. I met him there toward the end of the same month. As always, he concealed his nervousness. There I received from him some corrections in the text of the play, with which I returned to Moscow. At this time he wrote to his betrothed: 'I feel a rust in my soul. If the play should fail, I would go to Monte Carlo and play until I lost my last kopeck.'

But no matter how much he tried to hide behind a joke, he showed the true state of his feelings by leaving Nice a day or two before the first performance, without ostensible reason, and going to Algiers, then Italy, flitting rapidly from city to city—Pisa, Florence, Rome; in short, justifying the suspicion that he was running away from news of the results of the *première*. Or he would again put on his armour of indifference. After all, after 'The Sea Gull' this was his first new play, his return to the theatre. Not only a letter, but even a telegram failed to find him.

Towards the end of February he returned to Nice, where he first learned the details of 'The Three Sisters'.

This is what he wrote in a letter: 'It resembles a failure; well, it's all the same to me. . . . I am going to chuck the theatre and never again write for it. It is possible to write for the theatre in Germany, in Sweden, even in Spain, but not in Russia, where dramatic authors are not respected, are kicked with hooves, and their successes and failures not forgiven.'

'The Three Sisters' has remained the best production of the Art Theatre, not only because of the superb ensemble but also because of the fine *mise en scène* by Stanislavsky. It lacks the lyricism of 'The Sea Gull'; in 'The Three Sisters' the absence of spontaneity is compensated for by the wonderful craftsmanship. Quite apart from this, Chekhov did something in his play that is usually censured by the shrewdest dramatic critics: he had written a play for definitely designated actors. He, as a superb, if one may call him so, a dramatic, psychologist, excellently caught the artistic peculiarities of our young company and chose for this play, out of his literary baggage, such images as were closest to their artistic qualities. This also assisted the ensemble in no small measure.

When soon after this *première* our theatre paid a visit to St. Petersburg, Chekhov continued to maintain his casual jesting tone:

I've received an anonymous letter from Peter [1] that you've fallen in love with some one there up to your ears. Yes, and I myself have suspected it, you Jewess, you miser. You've evidently fallen out of love with me because I am not an economical person and asked you to ruin yourself by sending me one or two telegrams. Well, what's to be done? I still love you because of an old habit. . . . I've brought you some very good perfumes from abroad. You must come for them during Passion Week. You must make the journey without fail, my darling, my loved one. If you don't come, you'll hurt me deeply, you'll poison my existence. I have already begun to wait for you, I count the days and the hours. It's nothing that you've already fallen in love with some one else and have already betrayed me. Do you hear me, dog? Well, you must know that I love you. Write me. It is wretched without you. If you are ordered to attend rehearsals during Passion Week, then tell Nemirovitch that it's vile and swinish of him.

I have quoted from the letters to his widow, Mme Knipper-Chekhova, published in 1924, and I very strongly advise

[1] Short for St. Petersburg.

you to read the volume from which the quotations are taken. The widow decided to publish the entire intimate correspondence with Anton Pavlovitch, confirming indeed the opinion I have already expressed, that every trifle about a famous man is interesting, instructive, and can by no means deprive him of an iota of the tremendous heritage he has left to posterity. In truth, this book could scarcely avoid provoking much discussion. There cannot be the least doubt that had Chekhov known that his letters to his wife, even the most intimate of them, would be published, he would have avoided writing ninety per cent. of them, to say nothing of such intimacies as the names to which he treated her: 'my lovely little cachalot', 'exploitress of my soul'; but more often, 'my dog', 'infant', 'actressulya Knippusha', 'my booby', 'my joy', 'little cockroach', etc.[1]

Their marriage took place during the summer. It was altogether a private affair, of which we learned only on the following day, when they left on their honeymoon and sent us a telegram (I alone was in the secret). It was at this time that Morozov helped us to organize a company, consisting no longer of the directors of the Philharmonic, but of the actors themselves. Chekhov also became a shareholder, and grew even more intimate with the theatre.

I imagine that all this time was the happiest of his second youth. It was worse for him later: the more love the more sadness; they had to suffer separation; he was fettered to the South and was unhappier than before. To their common distress may be still added her tormented conscience. It was

[1] Nemirovitch offers other specimens of these absurd names, nearly all inventions absolutely untranslatable, if not quite meaningless.
—*Translator.*

as if she had been disloyal to her sacred duty: dare she take from him her nearness so dear to him, dare she leave him in his desperately unhappy loneliness for the sake of her stage career? Was this career worth these deprivations?

I can see her figure now as she was in winter behind the wings, before making her entrance. She sits at one side and avoids speaking with any one. Every instant she is on the verge of weeping. And in this so-called 'society' of all sorts there are gossips, enviers, female meddlers, and hysterical admirers of Chekhov's genius, to say nothing of the men who resemble these women, all of whom created an atmosphere full of reproach to Olga Knipper.

This from a letter from Chekhov:

You, my darling, continue writing me that your conscience is tormenting you because you are not with me in Yalta, but in Moscow. But what's to be done, my darling? Consider the matter sensibly: if you were with me in Yalta all winter your life would be quite spoiled for you, and then I should suffer the torments of conscience, which would be scarcely any better. After all, I knew I was marrying an actress, i.e. when I married you I was aware that you would be spending your winters in Moscow. Not an iota do I consider myself offended or neglected. On the contrary, everything seems to me to be going well, and as it should be; therefore, darling, do not make me feel badly about your pangs of conscience. In March we'll be together again, and we'll no longer feel the present loneliness. Calm yourself, my dear, and don't let anything distress you. Wait and hope. Hope, and nothing more.

Their happiness came in snatches: now she would go to Yalta for five days, now I had to replace her with some one else in the repertory in order that she might leave before the end of the season.

[213]

Such, it means, is my fate. I love you and shall continue to love you, even if you beat me with a stick. . . . There is nothing new except the snow and the frost. Everything is as it was. The rain is dripping from the roofs, there's the clamour of Spring, but when you look out of the window it is winter. Come to me in a dream, my darling.

He was writing scarcely any tales; in the course of two years he wrote two, I think. He was moralizing with a deep sincerity, yet with an astonishing artistic perception avoided the danger of falling into reasoning. In 'The Three Sisters' there is this remarkable, prophetic monologue:

The time has come, there is moving upon us all an immense mass, there is rising a mighty storm; it is very near, and before long it will sweep from our society its laziness, its indifference, its antipathy to work, its corrupt tedium. I shall work, but within twenty-five or thirty years every man shall work. Every man!

He was having a tremendous success at this time. This gave him a new charm; he was being read more and more, and as his readers became absorbed in him they fell in love with him. He might have refrained from writing another ten years, yet his fame would have grown. He was wholly occupied with the play. He had conceived it during the previous summer, while visiting Alekseiev in Liubimovka, in that same Liubimovka where Stanislavsky and I had had our first conversation. Chekhov was thinking of 'The Cherry Orchard'. Apart from that, he dedicated a good portion of his time to his favourite diversion—fishing.

Not a single play, not a single story, did he write so slowly as 'The Cherry Orchard'. The subject of this play actually seemed to him to be a vaudeville: 'I wanted to write a vaude-ville piece, but it was cold. It was so cold in the rooms that

I was forced to pace back and forth in order to keep warm.'
At first he saw the play not in four acts, but in three. At the
same time he did not think we had an actress for the leading
rôle.

If I write anything that resembles a play it will be a vaudeville
piece.

I manage to write four lines a day, and these with almost un-
endurable torments.

The weather is terrible, a roaring blizzard blows, the trees are
bending. I am fairly well. I am writing. Slowly perhaps, but
nevertheless writing.

I don't seem able to get warm. I tried writing in the bedroom,
but nothing has come of it: my back is hot from the stove, but
my chest and my arms are cold. In this exile I feel as though my
character has become spoiled, and all of me, for that matter.

Ah, my darling, I say it sincerely: what a pleasure it would
give me now if I could give up being a writer!

And he simply had to write, because we in Moscow insisted that at all costs we must have his play.

Yalta was a fine, enchanting little town. You could not
find such a gem either in the French or the Italian Riviera,
but it was remote from Moscow, remote from all those
persons who were close to his soul, remote from the metropolitan din and from the metropolitan interests, to which he
had become so used. Always cheerful, he did not feel himself
to be in his element here. He had never been a person of the
study. He always wanted to have people about him. Here,
with one or two possible exceptions, there lived perhaps
some nice enough persons, but he did not find them inter-

esting, and they came to him, as the saying goes, 'to let off steam'.

In one letter he wrote me: 'The tedium here is terrible. I somehow manage to forget myself by day in my work, but with evening despair comes. And when you are already playing the second act I am already in bed, and I rise while it is still dark. Imagine to yourself: it is dark, the wind howls and the rain beats against the window.'

Yes, imagine to yourself: during the hour when, in his imagination, Moscow is all ablaze with evening lights, when in his favourite theatre the second act is being played, perhaps even the second act of his 'The Three Sisters', at that point where the staid provincial Prozorov says: 'How pleasant it would be to sit at this moment in Testov's Tavern!' When the public, taking advantage of the simplest blessings of the metropolis, laments the lot of those forced to suffer in the sad, tedious backwoods, precisely then does the author who evoked these tears experience despair, as one undergoing imprisonment. And when all those whom the author speaks of have gone to sleep, he is already up; and here the wind howls, the rain beats against the window and it is still dark.

As it happens, I am writing this chapter at Yalta. I have just come from the house, which is now the Chekhov Museum. Thanks to the heroic efforts of Anton Pavlovitch's sister, the house has successfully survived the ravages of civil war. It is she, Marya Pavlovna herself, who maintains the Museum in model order. Hundreds of tourists from all the ends of the Union, young creators of a new life; daily fill it and with avid interest glance into every corner, at every portrait. The house is all white, with a white roof, it is a very good-looking house. During the thirty years following the death of the poet the garden has become astonishingly luxuriant; the trees which Chekhov himself planted have grown quite immense. His study has been left untouched. If it were not for the glass show-case on the mantel above the table, I could easily have imagined myself as speaking with Anton Pavlovitch there but a little while before. Even the calendar on his table, as it was on the last day, did not have the date torn from it. There was the familiar fireplace, upon whose stone was painted the landscape by his friend, the famous Levitan. Upon this fireplace there once used to lie the tiny paper funnels prepared each day for his spittle, which he used to throw into the flames. The immense window looked out on the garden, and from this window you glimpsed the distant sea. When Chekhov died, his sister planted a cypress before the window. Now it is tall, graceful, mighty; it is a handsome tree, and seems to guard the memory of the master, who once sat before the window and yearned.

Someone has said: 'That past is nearer to eternity. . . .'

Finally, on October 12: 'And so at last my patience and yours triumph. The play is finished, conclusively finished, and to-morrow evening, or at the latest on the morning of the 14th, it will be sent to you to Moscow. If any changes are necessary I cannot imagine them to be of any consequence. The worst thing about the play is that it was not written at a single sitting, but during a long, long period, so that it must give the feeling of being drawn out; well, we shall see.'

Afterwards he made a few changes in this swan-song, a song with the most delicate writing. The images of 'The

[217]

Cherry Orchard' are realistic, simple, and clear, and at the same time moulded in such a deep crystallized essence that they resemble symbols. And the entire play is so simple, so wholly real, but to such a point purified of everything superfluous and enveloped in such a lyrical quality, that it seems to me to be a symbolic poem.

After a hard struggle with his wife and the doctors, deceiving himself, imposing his own position as a doctor, Chekhov decided that it was perfectly allowable for him to come to Moscow in the winter, that for tuberculosis rain and snow were bad, and that the severe Moscow frosts did not matter. He wrote his wife:

My darling directress, sternest of wives. I promise to eat nothing but lentils; at the entrance of Nemirovitch and Vishnevsky I will rise in respect; only let me come. Really, it's revolting to live at Yalta, and I must run from the Yalta water and the magnificent Yalta air. It's about time you cultured people understood that in Yalta I always feel incomparably worse than in Moscow. If you only knew how sadly the rain beats upon the roof, and how strongly I desire to look upon my wife. And have I a wife? Where is she?

At the beginning of December (Old Style) he arrived in Moscow, during the very thick of rehearsals. He intensely desired to take a leading part in them, to be present at all their experiments, to see himself in the densest atmosphere of the theatre. He began by deriving great pleasure from this, but very soon, after four or five rehearsals, he saw that it was not so attractive for an author: at every step on the stage they irritated him, and he succeeded only in hindering the *régisseurs* and the actors. He stopped coming.

On the other hand, he felt very happy at home. His wife was near him, and the people who came were the sort he liked, the sort that brought something instead of taking from him. He was surrounded by them the whole time.

And again he was nervous over his play, and again he doubted its success. 'Buy my play for 3,000 rubles for all time,' he suggested to me, without jesting.

'I'll give you,' I replied, 'ten thousand for a single season, and that for the Art Theatre alone.' He rejected the proposal and, as always, merely shook his head.

'The Cherry Orchard' became the brightest, most expressive symbol of the Art Theatre.

The first performance took place on his name-day. This was quite accidental, without any divination or presentiment. Chekhov did not come to the theatre, but asked that any message be delivered to him over the telephone. But Moscow had the foreboding that this would be the last time in which it could see its beloved writer. They, in the city, knew that his malady of the lungs and intestines was becoming increasingly serious. All of literary and theatrical Moscow, as well as representatives of social institutions, were gathered in the theatre to do honour to the beloved writer. We telephoned to Chekhov asking him to come. At first he would not be persuaded, but when some of us went to his house and talked to him he was prevailed upon to change his mind. The tribute paid him was profoundly touching and profoundly sincere. I addressed him, speaking for the theatre:

'Our theatre is in such a degree indebted to your genius, your tender heart, your pure soul, that you can justly say: "This is my theatre, the theatre of Chekhov." '

[219]

In the middle of February he returned to his house in Yalta and from there, right through to the summer, his letters were no longer so tired as those of the preceding two winters; they were cheerful, gay, notwithstanding the fact that he was not quite satisfied with some of the actors in 'The Cherry Orchard'. It was as if a mountain had rolled from his shoulders, as if suddenly he felt he had a right to live, even as the simplest inhabitant—without any kind of literary or theatrical responsibilities. As a writer, it seems to me, he was afraid most of all of being tedious and repetitious. And now he was glad because neither the theatre nor any editor's office could violate his tranquillity.

In the spring war was declared with Japan. At this time we were playing 'The Cherry Orchard' in St. Petersburg. In that thin layer of the theatrical public which was most intimate with the actors in the midst of surrounding admirers, at the banquets dedicated to the theatre, as in all 'society' consisting of the *intelligentsia* and officials, severed from the popular undercurrents, there was scarcely a human being who doubted but that we would punish those impudent Japs as we might punish young puppies. The theatrical atmosphere in wartime is a bristling one. The theatres are always full. Consuming, poignant interests, the interests of war, commingling with theatrical emotions, still further prod human beings away from the roots of national life. One does not hear what is expressed in the mood of the soldiers going to war—'Somewhere to the world's end'— and in the murmurs of the peasants seeing them off. No one gave the least thought to the possibility of our losing the war. Only the more sensitive, looking into the near future, fore-

told that an end was approaching to this superficial unconcern, to the urban tinsel and the seeming peace and calm in
the village, the steppe and the factory. Only the sensitive
ear caught that which was already in the air: soon it would
all begin—here a Governor would be assassinated, there a
strike would take place; soon it would become impossible,
with such carefree unconcern, to go to one's place of useless
employment, to visit restaurants and evening parties, to take
journeys in dreamy calm to the farms and country estates.

'There is moving upon us an immense mass, there is rising
a mighty storm.'

How would Chekhov have borne all that we experienced
after his death? How would his lyrical gift have reacted to
the tremendous events after the year 1917?

On June 3 (16) he went abroad with his wife, and on July
3 I received a telegram from her from Badenweiler: 'Anton
died on the 2nd of July.' Subsequently she told me that he
had felt badly, and she called a doctor. Then: 'With as it
were, significant loudness, he said to the doctor in German:
"I am dying." Then he picked up the goblet, smiled his
wonderful smile and said: "It's long since I've tasted champagne." Calmly he drank it to the last drop, then turned
over on his left side, and soon was for ever silent.'

The town of Badenweiler erected a monument to Chekhov in one of its squares, but at the outbreak of war
between Russia and Germany in 1914 the German patriots
removed the statue.

Notwithstanding the dead of summer, the station platform in Moscow was full of holiday passengers gathered
from far and wide. When the train came in I, together with
the widow, who in full mourning stepped from the train to

[221]

meet me, walked in deep silence toward the goods wagon which contained the coffin. And ... surely, for the last time, from the other world, there flashed the humour of Chekhov: in that spot on the freight car where the contents are designated, there was written in large letters the single word: OYSTERS.

In Moscow we had had a common friend in the doctor N. N. Obolonsky. Quite recently his widow allowed me to see the hitherto unpublished jesting letter from Chekhov written from St. Petersburg:

'Your Excellency, my dear sir, Nikolai Nikolaievitch! I frequent the Miliutin Row [1] and eat oysters there. I positively have nothing to do, and I think of only what to eat and what to drink, and I regret that there is no such oyster as might eat me for my sins.'

[1] A restaurant.

PART III
MAXIM GORKY

CHAPTER THIRTEEN

After 'The Sea Gull' and 'Uncle Vanya' it became perfectly clear that of all authors Chekhov approached nearest to our theatrical dreams and that it was indispensable that he should write a new play. Chekhov, however, said that he would not write another play until he had seen the Art Theatre and seen with his own eyes just what it was in the art of this theatre that made the success of his plays. But the doctors refused to allow him to journey to Moscow; he was chained to the South. We therefore decided to travel to Yalta, taking the whole theatre with us, i.e. the entire company, with all the scenery, properties, costumes, stage-hands, and technicians. To reinforce our funds we planned several performances *en route* in Sebastopol. Only the wealthy company of the Duke of Meiningen permitted itself this unprecedented luxury—that of travelling with all its possessions. In Russia such a thing was not even thinkable. But we were, in the first place, audacious: it would have been difficult to stop us, since we saw before us a significant goal; in the second place, we were modest in our calculations: to pay the cost was something of an ideal with us.

The ardour of the young company was enormous. That joy of theatrical existence to which I dedicated the first chapters of this book, and which runs like a red thread through the life of an actor—oppressive, agonizing, yet unbrokenly joyous—gushed in a stream. The comradely com-

[225]

munion, the joint participation in personal and stage experiences, pride in success, a fervent faith in the future, a passionate and self-abnegating emulation of beloved leaders—
everything was ardent. Nothing was difficult, everything
surmountable. The hissing of the ever-increasing number of
foes merely serves to strengthen the fighting spirit of the
company. Even in cases of personal affront and mortification the tears which flow are so burning, so scalding, that
they quickly consume grief itself. And here, besides, was
spring, the gentle sun, the sea, the enchanting white towns
—Sebastopol and Yalta—the meeting with the writer towards whom the company cherished feelings of genuine
love. The whole journey was like a spring holiday. And the
time was coincident with Easter.

I left Moscow earlier than the rest, in order to inspect the
theatres. I wired Chekhov, telling him that I would leave
Sebastopol for Yalta by steamer and should arrive during
Passion Week, on Wednesday.

The steamer left Sebastopol at one o'clock in the afternoon. It was due in Yalta at six. But an unusually dense
fog arose. As we were approaching Yalta, the passengers on
deck could not see one another three paces away. The
steamer barely moved and for a long time could not dock.
The sirens wailed, the bells of the Yalta church dinned in-
cessantly, the steamer edged along the breakwater and found
it difficult to gain the entrance of the harbour. It was
already quite dark, about nine o'clock, when I reached the
hotel.

Chekhov had only lately erected his country house.
White, perching above the city, its ornamental front facing
seaward, it is the same house which so soon after the poet's

[226]

death was to become a place of pilgrimage for all tourists. At this time the town was but little acquainted with it. The cabby of the handsome native double-harnessed basket vehicle said that it was somewhere at the top, and we drove off to find it. The narrow, winding, sloping street of this eastern town was deserted. The fog was almost gone, but not a soul was visible. And there was no one to ask whether this was Chekhov's house, or that, or the one still farther on. I crept up against a fence, glanced into a lighted window, hoping to catch sight of the familiar figure. Just then, coming straight upon us down the ascending road, there appeared a human being. We waited for him to approach us. He eyed me very intently.

Above average height, lean but strongly built, with a markedly duck-like nose, and thick, reddish moustaches, he spoke in a very pleasant bass voice, with a light Volga-region accent on the 'o'; he was dressed in high top-boots and a sailor's cloak. No portrait of Gorky had yet appeared, and I was not acquainted with his appearance.

In a friendly manner, and with some precision, he explained where Chekhov's villa was to be found. As we continued our ascent, while he strode on his downward way, there lingered in my soul a remnant of his glance, which had so intently scrutinized me.

Chekhov himself opened the door, and his first words were: 'Gorky has only just left. He waited for you. He wanted to make your acquaintance.'

About Gorky there had already gathered rumours, of a tramp from the Volga with an enormous writing gift. This was my first meeting with the man who was to play such a tremendous rôle in the history of Russian culture, and this first meeting took place in the late evening, in the deserted lane of an eastern town, in the half-fog.

Do you remember the first appearance of Pugatchov in 'The Captain's Daughter' by Pushkin?

There was something overwhelming in the festal mood which had seized upon the whole company. Our faith that the future was ours had not infected merely the hardened followers of routine.

And now the actors were given a task: to inspire Gorky to write a play, to infect him with our dreams of a new theatre.

We brought with us to the Crimea four plays: 'The Sea Gull' and 'Uncle Vanya' by Chekhov, 'Lonely Lives' by Hauptmann and 'Hedda Gabler' by Ibsen. Hauptmann was very close to the soul of the most cultured Russian; little wonder Chekhov had such an affection for him. 'Lonely Lives' made a tremendous impression on Gorky. But 'Hedda Gabler' left the public cold, notwithstanding the fact that the rôle was excellently played by the beautiful Andreieva, while Stanislavsky gave an interesting interpretation of the genius, Lövborg. But it was the plays of Chekhov, of course, which were the centre of attraction and created the real new theatrical excitement.

The performances and the spirit of the young company enthralled Gorky.

We gave eight performances in Yalta and remained there ten days in all. The impressions and results were considerable. We performed in the evening, but the days were spent in walks, drives, and meetings with Chekhov and Gorky. The doors of Chekhov's house stood wide open all

MAXIM GORKY

this time. The entire company was asked to dine and to take tea there every day. If Gorky was absent from the table, it only meant that he was sitting somewhere on the balcony rails, surrounded by another group of our actors. Attired in his bright Russian shirt with leather belt, his thick rebellious hair prominent, he sat there intently listening, captivatingly smiling or narrating, deftly choosing picturesque, bold, characteristic expressions.

Here was a man of great gifts, such as makes an appearance once in several decades. Here was the brilliance of fireworks. From the very bosom of the nation he came, with a special destiny, clothed in legendary tales. In the direst poverty of childhood almost illiterate, then a youth in constant flight, later a tramp who had covered half of Russia on foot. Then suddenly his enticement by literature, his meeting with Korolenko, a writer of rare gifts. He achieved an immense success, and that immediately, by issuing simultaneously two or three works, in their way final and perfect, and then rested on his oars. To make up for this, during his whole life afterwards, to his sixty-fifth year, he preserved the charm of a clear, pure, serene man of the people. With the assistance of Korolenko, or rather on Korolenko's counsel, Gorky began to learn and to become a writer. Perhaps this was not so at all; but such was the rumour noised abroad.

At this time there had already been issued three volumes of his tales; *Malva*, *Chelkash*, and *Men With Pasts* had made their stir. Both their content and their form seized upon men's imaginations; a new galaxy from a little-known world, they seem to look out upon us from the sultry dusk of the steppe, or from the soot-steeped yards; their glance at strangers is restrainedly insolent, confident, as it were—intent upon to-morrow's foes to the death; figures mocking your respectability with contempt, flaunting the beauty of their muscular strength, and—what is more enviable—the free and bold solution of all your 'accursed problems'. Scarcely less infectious was the bright, life-loving radiance of these figures, the confident, challenging, courageous temperament of the author himself; to say nothing of his art: the hammered phrase, the glowing, picturesque language, the new, precise comparisons, the simplicity and lightness of poetical aspiration. A new romanticism. A new tocsin to the joys of life.

It was very interesting to observe the relations between Chekhov and Gorky. Two such different beings! The one —the sweet longing of the setting sun, the sighing reverie for freedom from this workaday world, the softness and tenderness of colours and lines; the other—he also strains at the dim 'to-day', but as with a war-cry, with taut muscles, with a bold, joyous faith in 'to-morrow', and not in 'perhaps two or three hundred years'. The affection our young actors felt for Chekhov had a chance to be put to the test; they were also strongly attracted to Gorky. The result of the experience was remarkable. Gorky proved to be as affectionate toward Chekhov as the rest of us. This feeling he cherished to the very end. We have now before us the whole life and activity of 'Maxim Gorky'. Replete as it is with revolts against 'lyricism', nevertheless we see him, throughout, unchanged toward Chekhov, the greatest of all Russian lyricists, whom he continued to cherish as in his youth in Yalta.

Often has this episode been told; it occurred in the Art Theatre, as it happens, in the winter following this Crimean journey. Gorky had received permission to visit Moscow, and came to our theatre to a performance of a Chekhov play. The public heard of it and was wild to see him. The interlude came. Gorky was in my study, while behind the door the entire corridor was packed with people. They so persistently demanded his appearance that he at last reluctantly yielded. What a disenchantment followed! Instead of the radiant face which the public was accustomed to meet in the hero of its ovation, it saw a face overclouded with anger. The ovation evaporated in confusion. The public grew quiet and he began to speak. He spoke simply, his head poised on one side, and he gesticulated with a single hand, using a persuasive tone:

'Well, why do you want to see me? I'm neither a drowned man nor a ballet girl, and when you consider what a remarkable play is being given, your idle curiosity is simply disgusting!'

In any case, Gorky detested this idle curiosity. I remember an incident. It happened at a railway station, I don't remember which. We were in the buffet, awaiting our train; we sat apart from the crowd. A company of merchants made merry around the table, and suddenly noticed Gorky. Their leader, a robust fellow, well-fed, tipsy, came toward him with a champagne bottle and glass in his hands, and rendered an effusive greeting, full of radiant welcome.

'Mister Gorky! Allow me to drink to your health! Allow me to offer a glass with our compliments! Gifted Mister Gorky!' Alexey Maximovitch motionlessly gazed at the man. Not a single muscle in his face moved. Then suddenly: 'If you could only see what a drunken mug you have!' he said simply and clearly.

The merchant was discomfited. 'As you like!'—And, his

[231]

face all red, he slunk away, muttering, 'When a man's as proud as all that, why, of course . . .'

The promise to write a play was given. We entered into a correspondence. Gorky always wrote on a large folio sheet, on the line, in an excellent even script, without a single blot; there was the legible signature: A. Peshkov. He was in banishment. He had the right to live only in Nizhni-Novgorod, while later his residence was limited to the district town of the same government—Arzamas. As he suffered continually from ailments of the chest, he was one summer allowed residence in the Crimea—under rigid surveillance, of course. And once he was given permission for a brief stay in Moscow.

I journeyed to see him in Nizhni-Novgorod, also in Arzamas. He was married. His wife, Ekaterina Pavlovna, was an engaging person. They had a six-year-old son, who was permitted anything he desired. For some particularly bad prank his father would punish him by placing him on top of a clothes closet.

'Anyhow, I'm taller than you now, Alexey!' the boy philosophized from above. He called his father 'Alexey'.

Many persons visited Gorky in Nizhni-Novgorod. One visitor impressed himself sharply on my memory. In appearance not unlike Sahtin in 'The Lower Depths', vigorous, picturesque; only yesterday a typical tramp, to-day a bit dressed up, with a distinguished, expressive face and handsome voice. After he left, Gorky said: 'Do you know, he'd make a fine actor!'

'What is he now?' I asked.

'He does anything that comes to hand. If he met you in

a lonely lane he'd demand a fifty-kopeck piece. "Hand it over," he'd say, "and be quick about it. Or I'll take more, if I have to take it myself!" . . .'

I recall this, because actually the man became a fine actor, one of the best in Russia to-day, and, moreover, he won for himself exceptional respect.

The impression Arzamas left on me was that of a typical little district town, scurvy, dusty, with unpaved streets, with rickety plank sidewalks. Beggars used to come to the open windows of Alexey Maximovitch's spacious room—beggars without end. Alexey Maximovitch gave to every one, gave with peculiar simplicity, without making much ado, neither in a spirit of pity nor of charity, but fulfilling—as it were— the simplest necessity, such as moving a chair, brushing the dust off, or closing the door flung open by the wind. There were so many of these beggars that they hindered conversation. The suspicion was born in my mind that they abused Gorky's kindness. Nevertheless, he did not allow one to pass by without giving him something. 'The devil, what a swarm of them comes here!' he would give loud vent to his feelings, even while distributing handfuls of petty coin. When he ran short of change or it was necessary to break a note, he used to look for his wife in one of the other rooms. Soon she ran short too; then he took what I had. All this was done quite simply, as one takes a match in order to smoke.

At twelve o'clock, midnight, to continue our unfinished conversation, we used to go to some dusty, deserted square, beyond which, from a dense, dark grove of trees, there gleamed the white crosses of a graveyard.

It was not until August, 1902, that Gorky finished the

[233]

play 'The Lower Depths of Life' (subsequently he abbreviated the title to 'The Lower Depths'). And it was during the former spring that I had visited him at Oleiz, a summer residence near Yalta, where he read to me the first two acts. I remember that when I arrived there I was obliged to wait for him. Ekaterina Pavlovna said that it was three days since he and Chaliapin, taking provision and wine with them, had directed their simple rowboat toward the open sea, and that they would not return to shore until that evening. There, in the immense water desert, they bathed, sunned themselves, ate, drank, slept and chatted. And, really, they returned with such a stock of oxygen, both physical and spiritual, so splendid in their mood of eagle-like freedom, so gay and inwardly plastic, so brotherly in their exchange of smiles—these two envoys from among the people, Chaliapin and Gorky—that to look at them was to believe in the most ardent romanticism.

There were years of external calm, of felicity, even of prosperity, while from the depths of the 160-million-peopled sea there were borne mighty, heaving waves, obscure and portentous. Here was St. Petersburg, the Court, the Royal Guard, the Grand Dukes, the high life, the demi-monde, the Maryinsky Theatre, the opera, the ballet, the parades, the balls, the *Novoye Vremya*, officialdom, Paris, London, the lustre of civilization; while from the invisible waves there came the odour of sweat, of smoke, and the harsh cold wind of ruthlessness. The edifice, the crown of which was St. Petersburg, appeared immovable, but the invisible waves were undermining it. Between the two worlds—one of them idle and indifferent, the other concealed, bearing tragedy—was a border zone. Every breath of this 160-

SCENE FROM GORKY'S PLAY 'THE LOWER DEPTHS'

p. 234]

million-peopled sea broadened and strengthened this zone.
It put forth new forces, new beliefs, a new courage. Millions
of sappers worked here, clearing the roads leading below, or
poisoning with doubts and weakening the will of the neighbours above.

Thus were Gorky and Chaliapin cast forth by a wave, in
order further to strengthen the faith in the creative forces of
the people! Through art!

Concerning Chaliapin, some one has said: When God
created him, He was in a particularly good mood, creating
him as a joy to all. Concerning Gorky we may say that
God, in creating him, must have been particularly vexed
with St. Petersburg.

As regards Gorky's relation to St. Petersburg there could
not have been two opinions. A sharp utterance of his lingers
in my memory. The cabinet minister Sipyagin had just been
assassinated. In Gorky's character there was known to be a
trait of deep compassion, so to speak—of easy response to
anything capable of rousing sympathy; it was not so rare to
see his eyes moist with pity. I cannot remember in what
form the news about Sipyagin came to him, but I remember
very clearly his answer and his gesture: 'Even with pleasure
I could poke a finger into this wound!'

At another time he spoke of the Constitution, then in
course of preparation, and of the conflict with it which
would ensue, and concluded: 'What we'll do will be to burn
at both ends!'—that is to say, at one end destroying those
against whom the Constitutionalists fought, while at the
other destroying the Constitutionalists themselves.

No one could possibly doubt that in relation to St. Petersburg Gorky was a determined, fierce class enemy; and no

one ever consoled himself with the hope that this enemy could relent. On the other hand, his admirers increased in numbers with every month, with every week. These included not only the youth, his natural partisans, but also, to speak precisely, members of the higher bourgeoisie, his most rabid foes. The residue of the bourgeoisie, the object of the revolution, were interested in Gorky, sought him out, and were enchanted with him.

We had a number of poor pupils in our theatre and wanted to help them. A benefit performance was out of the question; Gorky consented to read 'The Lower Depths' (he was a very good reader), but only on condition that the audience be limited. This reading was done at two o'clock in the afternoon, in the small foyer of the theatre, to one hundred 'invited guests', each of whom was charged 25 rubles for entrance! The price was absurd, but the result would have been the same if we had charged double that.

The insidiousness of art! The lofty production of art is always revolutionary, always destroys some kind of 'foundations'. The public, bedecked with gems, attired in furs and frock-coats, applauds the splendid spectacle; it is charmed by art and ignores the seed of revolution secreted in it. This was, with particular palpableness, felt in St. Petersburg at the performance of 'Smug Citizens', by Gorky.

What a curious political triangle on the ground of art: St. Petersburg, the Art Theatre, and Maxim Gorky! An elemental triangle!

CHAPTER FOURTEEN

Gorky's first play was 'Smug Citizens'. We all wished him to write a play from the life of the tramps—an existence at that time as yet untouched and of particular interest to us—but fear of the censorship made it necessary to begin with something more modest. Our Theatre did not find the opportunity to present 'Smug Citizens' in Moscow, for we were due each spring in St. Petersburg, where 'Smug Citizens' was scheduled for a *première*. During all this time —from our meeting with him at Yalta until the writing of 'Smug Citizens'—the fame of Gorky grew with such rapidity that he was elected an honorary member of the Academy. The president of the Academy was the Grand Duke Constantin Constantinovitch.[1] The higher administration brought pressure to bear upon him and he protested against the election of Gorky. This provoked heated discussions, and, as a counter-protest, Chekhov and Korolenko, themselves members of the Academy, sent in their resignations.

Demonstrations hostile to the Grand Duke were expected at the performances of 'Smug Citizens'. And, as usually happens in such instances, the solution was a very simple one: the play was forbidden.

[1] Poet, theatre-lover, himself an amateur. I have told elsewhere about his theatrical performances at court and his play, his translation of 'Hamlet', etc.

We began to make efforts. An audience was arranged for me with Prince Sviatopolk-Mirsky, Minister of the Interior, famed for his liberal projects. I succeeded in persuading him. The presentation of the play was permitted, conditionally (only for subscribers).

The Art Theatre enjoyed extraordinary popularity in St. Petersburg. It attracted all strata of the population to which the theatre was accessible. Members of the Tsar's Court, the higher circles, the entire immense intelligentsia, and the whole advanced youth patronized it. The last-named, in particular, considered the Art Theatre its own. During the first years we played in a private theatre adapted for performances of opera; its upper tiers contained many poor seats, from which it was possible to hear but not to see; these places were not put on sale; nevertheless they always filled up with an enormous number of 'hares' (the ticketless); there were as many as five hundred of these hares. We were aware of this, but we winked at it; after all, they were the student youth.

I often used to visit them up there and used to chat with them in the intermission. I remember that one of the performances of Ibsen's 'An Enemy of the People'—in which Stanislavsky played marvellously the leading rôle—coincided with the day in which a stormy, bloody manifestation took place at the Kazan Cathedral. It looked as though the demonstrating youth would have little thought for the theatre; there were so many wounded and maimed comrades being conveyed to hospitals or arrested; the general mood was satiated with politics. Nevertheless, the evening saw the upper tiers filled up, as always. The students came from physical skirmishes, frozen, wrought up, and hungry;

but to let the performance of the Art Theatre pass was not to be thought of. I remember one ardent, passionate girl, who said: 'This play, of course, in its political tendency, is not at all ours. It would seem that we ought to hiss it. But there is so much truth in it and Stanislavsky so warmly calls on every one to be true to himself, that for us this performance is a feast and is as much an "affair" to be attended as the manifestation at the Kazan Cathedral.'

Several evenings before the presentation of 'Smug Citizens', I ascended to the upper tiers to entreat the youth not to make any sort of demonstration. 'This performance is necessary to us, in order that Gorky may continue to write for the theatre,' I pleaded, 'but disorders would only call forth repressions, and we would lose such an author!'

The youth promised and kept their promise. Not until the final performance of 'Smug Citizens' did some one, in token of farewell, fail to resist his inclination; for his personal gratification, he gave a single shout, audible through the auditorium:

'Down with the Grand Duke!'

In such a manner the presentation of the play was made secure, as far as the youth was concerned. It was still necessary to guarantee its production against the assaults of higher officialdom, from the Ministry itself. This is where the elemental triangle begins.

We were helped by the St. Petersburg ladies, the wives of the ministers, and by one in particular who was more influential than the others, therefore also more ambitious—here ambition, and snobbism, and the vogue of the Art Theatre, and of Gorky, and the desire to show that she had great influence over her husband, all played their part.

[239]

Little wonder that men say that in the theatre and in creative literature it is the women who always achieve the success.

Before we could receive the final permit for public presentation, we were obliged to give a dress rehearsal for the officials. Here it was to be decided in what measure the play was dangerous. Then, with the rapidity so characteristic of worldly report, the news of this rehearsal spread like wildfire through the entire *beau monde*; we were overwhelmed with requests for boxes and front rows of stalls for the families of the higher officialdom and for the diplomatic corps; and the rehearsal collected such an elegant, fashionably attired, and politically influential audience as might be envied by any European gathering.

The mood of the audience was one of expectancy, but for the success of the occasion, wholly to our surprise, we were indebted neither to the play nor to the art of the Theatre, nor even to Gorky himself, as he was not in St. Petersburg, but to one of the performers—moreover, the most uncultured in our company and for the first time appearing in a responsible rôle.

That which in the course of another twenty years was to be called 'featuring', which was to become the basis of the actor's part in the cinema, upon which Reinhardt once constructed his spectacle (Artisten), the Art Theatre repeatedly tried. One of the chief characters in 'Smug Citizens' was a singer from a church choir, a bass. Among our beginners we found just the person we wanted, a big, robust, awkwardly set-up fellow, with a superb 'octave'. He was actually a singer, who found free time from his work to devote to the theatre. Gorky made an accurate picture of him in his Teterev. His name was Branov. Like all bass singers, he was capable of drinking a great deal and was often violent. Had he lived until the revolution he might have acted the rôle of Rasputin superbly.

It was he who created a genuine furore. It was precisely the women, precisely the women of St. Petersburg's highest social circles, who went into perfect ecstasies about him. From what? From a marvellous theatrical representation? From some sort of super-art? Or from the fact of life itself breaking into art and clashing with its naturalism? Of course, such was the case, but quite apart from that there was something else, because after the last curtain, behind the wings, these handsome, exquisite, perfumed women surrounded this bull and vied with each other in raptures over his 'presence'.

The play was granted a permit.

It was the elemental triangle.

A tragi-comedy.

Gorky took but little interest in the fate of 'Smug Citizens', for he was already at work on 'The Lower Depths' and was absorbed in it. The play immediately enraptured us; our theatre began to seethe with labour. The quest of a new 'tone' for the Gorkian dialogue passed by quickly. This quest of a special acting rhythm is a theme of great interest and importance in the theatre; I shall speak of it elsewhere.

During the whole time of the preparation of 'The Lower Depths' Gorky was among us, but here our rôles often changed: quite often he no longer dominated the theatre, but the theatre dominated him. I am not fond of busying myself with conjectures about another's psychology, but here it was quite clear that Gorky gave himself up to the success of his play, perhaps for the first time, body and soul. It was also necessary to meet a multitude of persons who genuinely desired to meet him, in a friendly way and with earnest questions. . . . I used to meet him at the Skirmunts; if my memory does not play me false, he lived with them. The Skirmunt-Blaramberg couple were among the best people I knew. Skirmunt was the editor of *Russkiye Viedomosti* (*The Russian Gazette*) and a composer, his wife was the artiste and singer, Blaramberg-Chernova. . . . These persons laboured a great deal for public enlightenment and were among Gorky's friends.[1]

Gorky was 'taken up', as the phrase goes. Most of all he frequented the Art Theatre, the composition of which was pretty variegated. Rehearsals, dinners, suppers, meetings, expressions of admiration, conversations, readings. . . . Always energetic, always superbly self-possessed, he used to eye his *vis-à-vis* intently, with the desire to understand him well, to give him immediate affection if he recognized him as one 'of his own kind'; in questions of what was good and what was bad he never wavered an instant; he was so unshakenly assured of himself. At the rehearsals he was simple, frank, trusting, but where necessary inoffensively

[1] I cannot resist a digression, in order to say a few words about this rare, noble couple, the mere memory of whom revives feelings of deep emotion. Their whole life and activity were permeated with probity, sincerity, intelligence, and unceasing labour. And their devotion to each other was fabulous. Paul Ivanovitch died abroad. Minna Carlovna returned to Russia, bringing the urn containing his ashes. She then decided to put her husband's productions in order, publish them, then follow him. She actually did this. She gave herself to the work for a year, fulfilled everything that was necessary; then departing to some remote place, quietly, without making much ado about it, she put an end to herself.

firm. He comes to my memory of this whole period—to be precise, this winter of 1902–1903—as energetic, pleased, as one at last rewarded for many years of hard life. During the *première* of 'The Lower Depths', which had as great a success as the Theatre has seen, he answered the calls for the author with the natural diffidence of one unaccustomed to appear in public, forming a contrast to the experienced actors; he was nevertheless much gratified.

'That's fine, the deuce take it!' he exclaimed, as he entered my study direct from the stage, after curtain calls, radiant, smiling, crushing in the ash-tray the cigarette with which he had appeared to bow to the public, or lighting a new one.

'There's history for you, and geography!' was an expression he loved to repeat.

There! The Theatre yields all its mastery, the maximum of its inspiration; the whole company is possessed with joy; yes—the whole company, both the best players, who play the leading rôles, and all those who appear in the throng of tramps, cut-throats and hooligans—they all find themselves in that highest state of tension, when a human being gaily and successfully fulfils the chief function of his life. The militant tone, the whiplashing words, the fierce revolutionary undercurrent, found a powerful, persuasive, theatrical incarnation; while the audience, which for the most part consisted of the author's most malignant class enemies, against whom the entire anger of the play was directed, responded with a unanimous, enthusiastic ovation.

The insidiousness of art.

The elemental triangle.

A quarter of a century would pass. In the same theatre, between the same walls, the same play would be played;

[243]

even the majority of the actors would be the same, only more polished. The rôle of Luka would be played by the same Moskvin; that of the Baron, by the same Kachalov; while the decorations and the *mise en scène* would also remain the same, untouched by a quarter of a century's evolution of theatrical art; in a word, the performance would not show the slightest change. Only the audience would change—unrecognizably. It would become wholly new; there would be women here with shawls around their heads and men in native shirts. Twenty-five years before, this audience had no entrance to this theatre, had scarcely even heard of it at their benches and machines. But now it has driven the previous hangers-on from the boxes and stalls and has itself taken possession of all the seats in the theatre, and with the gratifying feeling of mastery is there to listen to the same words, to watch the same passions, to go into the same raptures over the same art of the famed Art Theatre. With the same transports the auditors would greet the actors; they would offer the same ovation to the author. And when the author came forth, with grey-grown, somehow reddened, but still thick hair, and deeply furrowed face, it would become startlingly clear that the triangle had already lost its militant content. The arrows of the play would fly past the audience, in pursuit of the past. There would remain only the great art, but the political combustibility would be wholly gone.

CHAPTER FIFTEEN

'The Lower Depths' achieved universal success; for the art of the Art Theatre, this play, after Chekhov, became one of the most desirable in its repertory. The season of 1902–1903 might be called 'Under the Sign of Gorky', as out of the four plays presented, two belonged to him, while the other two—'The Power of Darkness' by Tolstoy and 'The Pillars of Society' by Ibsen—did not eclipse his success. Immediately thereafter, however, Gorky's creative association with the Art Theatre practically ended. Only one more play of his—'The Children of the Sun'—was presented; it proved to be short-lived. This was not until 1905.

During this time our Theatre had some significant experiences, and in the midst of them the presence of Gorky played no small rôle.

When you recall these three years, when the imagination pictures those performances, there comes back to you the sight of that auditorium, permeated with high art, with an atmosphere of artistic harmony, with joy, brought to the public by 'Julius Caesar' and 'Lonely Lives', with Kachalov in the leading rôles, and by 'The Cherry Orchard' and 'Ivanov'. And when at the same time you recall the atmosphere behind the wings created by these performances, you at once remember the moods of the company, the perturbed, agitated, nervous, unhappy, irritated, confused reactions: there they want to disturb us with new problems of a political nature; here they fall into despondency, you see anxious faces, you hear rumours of the approaching end,—when you see this vast discrepancy between the moods on one side of the curtain and those on the other, you stand amazed at the colossal, miracle-working, beautiful, brilliant *lie*, woven by stage art.

Of materials for the encouragement and cheer of the company there were plenty. To begin with, we already had a permanent theatre—subject to a contract, it is true, limited to twelve years, but for the young spirits it seemed a long term. The dressing-rooms were comfortable and tastefully furnished; every actor had his own, which he arranged as he desired; everywhere were order and cleanliness. Moreover, these were the first years of the 'Association'; the artists, i.e. the chief of them, were becoming masters of the undertaking. The success of the Theatre with the public was enormous and grew as rumours spread of the collective and intelligent spirit behind the wings. The Theatre was assuming a guiding rôle; it already led the movement of so-called 'sociability', and there had begun those years concerning which, in the time yet to come, men of science and of 'free professions' would say: 'We were brought up on the Art Theatre!'

Every actor was in demand at the clubs, in the small select circles, in the salons and the drawing-rooms. And as, generally speaking, the Russian artist is not often seen unless in make-up and costume, and our artists for a long time held to this rule, they attracted increasing interest and curiosity.

The artistic success during these years was outstanding. The performance of 'Julius Caesar' outshone the fame of the celebrated German company of Meiningen, which brought out that play as its crowning spectacle. Quite apart from its purely artistic qualities, this performance revealed the organizing talent of the Art Theatre, its collectivism. Neither Stanislavsky nor I could have attained such success if the entire Theatre, in the literal sense of the word, had not done its full share of the work. There was little exaggeration in what was so often said and written of the Art Theatre: 'It is a moot question whether the Theatre owes its fame to its artistic talents or to organization.'

These years saw the writing and presentation of 'The Cherry Orchard'—Chekhov's swan-song—a play which later became the 'ace of trumps' in our scenic art. At the time of its *première* the beloved author was present for the first time. Moscow honoured him, experiencing, as it were, the presentiment that it was taking farewell of him, that in the course of several months he would be no more.

In short, there was more than one reason for feeling pleased and for courageously looking forward. The members of the company were mostly of a propitious age: there were but few elderly persons; most of them were between twenty and forty years old.

But pure joy is, evidently, sent as a rare blessing; usually there is a worm at the core. There was 'The Cherry Orchard' and Chekhov. Only many years afterwards did this play provide us with a fulsome feast; yet actually, while the play was furnishing agony to the author in the writing, it was furnishing agony to us in the expectation of it; when it arrived, it did not produce the effect we counted on; the rehearsals were disquieting; there was frequent friction with the author: Chekhov wanted to be present at all rehearsals, but soon was convinced that while the actors were still 'seeking', his presence hindered more than helped them; apart from this, some of them did not satisfy him.

The performance itself, at the beginning, was not received by the public with the same enthusiasm as 'Fyodor', 'The Sea Gull', 'An Enemy of the People', 'The Lower Depths' and 'Julius Caesar'; what was still more curious, the receipts soon began to fall off. I have already said in my chapters on Chekhov that such was the fate of all his plays: their true value became evident only in the subsequent seasons. Add to this an event which shook the Theatre: the death of Chekhov, only five months after the *première* of 'The Cherry Orchard'.

Such were the numerous motives which poisoned the atmosphere behind the scenes. But 'Julius Caesar!'

Who among an audience could have believed that this spectacle, gleaming with unbroken joy, should be one of the most difficult and agonizing behind the scenes? In such measure is this true that, notwithstanding its colossal artistic and material success, I removed it from the programme during the second year and sold it to Kiev: I sold the scenery and costumes, and I even presented the Kiev manager with my manager's copy. The public, of course, lamented the disappearance of the play from our programme. On the other hand, we behind the scenes were indifferent and even pleased.

Here we meet with the interesting activities of the theatrical 'kitchen'.

The spectacle was a very complex one in the quantity and significance of so-called 'national scenes'. We treated the whole scenic arrangement as if the tragedy were called

'Rome in the Epoch of Julius Caesar'. The chief rôle was played by the People. The chief acts were the streets of Rome, the assassination of Caesar in the Senate, the funeral of Caesar, the revolt, and the military scenes. More than two hundred persons participated in the spectacle. This was a great many for a theatre better adapted for plays of an intimate character. But the main thing was that these two hundred persons were not simple supernumeraries fulfilling their obligations for a stated fee. These were secondary actors, pupils of our school, university students, joyously seeking an opportunity to earn a little money in our theatre, and therefore called 'co-workers', who were serving by day in various ways and by night in the theatre.

While the rehearsals were in progress, while through all this throng there revealed itself the Roman tragedy in Shakespearean images, while the management was creating interesting colourful groups amongst it, awakening passions, seeking plastic forms—in a word, while the work went on and even while the first performances were being given, these our two hundred helpers, all intelligent persons, ardent admirers of art, burned with joy, with fervour, and gave all their strength. In this consisted the chief attraction of national scenes in the Art Theatre: that all who participated in them brought to the Theatre their whole imagination and their whole energy, and the same fervour with which the leading rôles were played. How often, later in life, it was my lot to meet advocates, teachers, and even men who became great writers, who said to me: 'You don't remember me? I was a student in the crowd of "Julius Caesar" . . .' or 'in the crowd of "Brand" . . .' or 'in "An Enemy of the People".' And every one inevitably added: 'If you only knew how much we learned at those rehearsals! Yes, of the psychology of the crowd and of the psychology of the individual, and in the matter of judging historical events, and, certainly, in the matter of taste. . . .'

And while complete rôles were being created in the crowd —idlers, senators, warriors, ardent patriots, conspirators, priests, conjurers, dancers, courtesans, vestals, matrons, market women—it was all a joy. And to play these parts—to make up, to dress, to step before the footlights—was very interesting.

Gradually, however, after twenty to forty performances, the emotion of novelty was dulled, the interest became exhausted, the execution of the rôles was transformed into a learned trade and began to be tedious. But the discipline continued to be exacting in its demands. The slightest negligence of any one among these two hundred was noted, and on the following day the guilty person was subjected to a reminder, a reprimand, or a penalty. The stage management of the Theatre did not permit those banal, soulless, careless, unrhythmical, unplastic crowds which are allowed in all other theatres! And that which earlier, in the ardour of novelty, went unnoticed now began to fatigue and pall: the weight of the shirts of mail, the shields, the weapons, the wild beasts' skins, the headgear, the togas whose folds it was necessary to watch, the fatigue of changing clothes, the need of constant attention, all this taking place now on the stage, now under the stage, now above the stage—this was hard, and after an hour well-nigh unbearable.

The American manager will not understand this. For him each one of these two hundred is a definite unit and nothing more. And, from his own point of view, he is right. For us, however, each is a living soul, whose interests cannot be limited to the fee received. One must be particularly careful in considering pupils. The more gifted they are, the more anxious they are to graduate from the crowd and to play rôles, while the stage management cannot deny them participation in the crowd, in which they furnish the superb 'spots' and the distinguished temperaments. Subsequently the Art Theatre avoided plays which contained too many crowd scenes; unfortunately, there were too few 'intimate' plays, such as Chekhov's or Ostrovsky's.

It was this that poisoned the atmosphere behind the scenes in 'Julius Caesar'. But not this alone.

Each performance should be a joy for the actors themselves, in which case it is sure to prove a joy for the public too. Otherwise, at best, it is merely distinguished 'art', invariably cold, unless warmed by the splendid mood of the actor. But in 'Julius Caesar' it was possible for only two actors to enact their rôles with joy: for Kachalov, who made a remarkable Caesar, and for Vishnevsky, who had a great success in Antony. The public cannot have the least idea of the torment experienced by the actors when this joy is lacking, even in a play which is having a success; all the more so since some of the colleagues reap all the laurels. In a case like this, the remarkable actress of the St. Petersburg Theatre, Savina, had refused her rôle at the second performance. With us it would have been impossible to find a substitute; if it were possible, we should have to do it during the rehearsals. For this reason the phantom of an unsuccessful rôle frightened our actors during the rehearsals far more than in other theatres.

Furthermore, imagine the assurance of the actor who believes that he is following the true artistic path, and that his public has not yet reached his taste; this, it goes without saying, happens quite often. Thus it was here with Stanislavsky.

He had conceived the image of the 'Last Roman' as something bright, burning, revolutionary, while the public wanted to see in Brutus one of the 'gentle' wavering images of Shakespeare. No matter how much he perfected his design, from performance to performance, this gap between him and the public refused to be bridged. He was in a nervous mood, and this reacted on his colleagues.

Finally, there was much perturbation behind the stage during this epoch because of events outside the Theatre. The unsuccessful war with Japan seemed like sheer folly, not justifying the enormous sacrifices. The revolution of 1905 was coming to ripeness. The atmosphere was becoming more and more openly charged with hatred. 'Most likely we've got a wretched master!' a friendly peasant once shouted to me across the village street. He had asked me, 'Well, how are affairs going there?' I had answered, 'Wretchedly!' By the word 'master' he clearly implied the head of the State. And—as you can see—he did not hesitate to express his opinion.

One gentleman told me this: he was returning in the early hours of the morning—at a time when the workers are on their way to work—from his club, with winnings from card play, in that peculiar morning mood of one who has not slept. The fine-looking droshky in which he sat was forced to stop at a crossing. At the same point, very close to the droshky, a group of workers, about to cross the street, was also held up. One of them looked intently at the man in the droshky and flung at him: 'Have you kissed enough, you

son-of-a-bitch?' It was quite another verb he used, unprint-
able here.

I was once travelling from the South. It was after dinner
on a lovely summer day when, close to the station situated
near a factory, our express train killed a woman worker
with a strange blow, merely on one of the temples. During
the long stop I went to the place where she lay on a table
—young, beautiful, half naked; the very white body had a
singular gleam. In the surrounding crowd, upon something
high, sat a large working woman, with a handsome, broad,
pure-Russian face, wet with tears; she was gnawing at sun-
flower seeds. 'Have a good look!' she said suddenly, glancing at me with malignant eyes. 'Satisfy your curiosity, until
you're undressed like that yourself. . . .'

Uneasy life cast up to the surface both simple perplexity
and all sorts of mud and trash. The tranquil idyll had
vanished.

I remember, but five or six years before, I was travelling
across the hot, unpeopled steppe, and on the way I dropped
a handsome velvet plaid scarf. This was about twenty versts
from the farm. It goes without saying I had not even
thought of looking for it. Two days later, however, a
neighbouring peasant brought it to me. 'Is this your plaid?'

And here is another incident of the same summer. I was
returning from Ekaterinoslav. At the station of Malenkoe
Sinelnikovo the train was kept standing for about twenty
minutes. It was near midnight. I was alone in the compartment. A window looked out from the side of the station
in the wake of the train. The platform, covered with white
sea mussels, was bathed in the greenish light of an invisible
electric lamp. Not a soul. A little farther on was a freight

[253]

train, with a conductor's lantern left on the steps of the carriage. I listened intently in the silence, and it seemed to me that the mussels were crackling under some one's feet. But a fortnight before I heard that a robbery had taken place near one of these stations. As I remembered this, I began to peer intently down the length of the train. No one! But scarcely had the signal bells rung and the train begun to move when from that same wall of my carriage, almost under my window, a human figure became outlined and mounted the steps of the carriage. It was followed by another. I ran into the corridor to find the conductor. He was nowhere to be seen. At the window on this side stood a passenger.

'What do you want of the conductor?'

'I have an idea that some suspicious persons have entered the carriage.'

'Well, what next! Nonsense!' he laughed.

Nevertheless, I hastened to my compartment and turned the key and put the chain on. In the course of a few moments I heard my brave neighbour doing the same.

The train was already speeding. Suddenly the handle of my door turned; the chain held the door. Then there was a loud whisper: 'It's on the chain!' The door quietly closed. Presently from the opposite end of the corridor I heard a din, two men speaking in loud voices, and the next instant—batz! batz!—one shot followed another, and the thud of falling bodies. I rushed to open the door, with every prospect of presenting my breast to a shot. At this instant the chain-brake hissed and the train stopped with a jerk. Evidently the pair jumped off. The corridor was silent. I opened the door. Two bodies and a lantern lay on the floor. I

rushed to the nearest body. Blood! . . . My brave neighbour remained hidden in his compartment. I ran to my
window. Far down on the right, along the rails, stood a
brigade of conductors in white uniforms, illumined by the
moon. The Chief Conductor was already shouting past me
to the engineer: 'Go ahead! It's nothing! . . .' I called to
them.

Investigation showed that our conductor had been killed,
and his assistant severely wounded.

CHAPTER SIXTEEN

In the evolution of the Russian actor during the fifty years of my recollections—from the strolling Nestchastlivtsev and Arkashka to the 'artist-citizen' of the Soviet Union—the Art Theatre played an important rôle. Here, more than elsewhere, the actor was drawn into the life and interests of the leading intelligentsia.

Just think: fifty years ago, when I first found myself behind the scenes of the Moscow Small Theatre, I heard its leading actor, Samarin, address 'the actor of petty rôles', the esteemed Milensky, as 'thou', while the other addressed Samarin as 'you, Ivan Vassilyevitch'. Soon there remained not a trace of this custom; nevertheless, between the brilliant leading men and secondary actors there was a perceptible gap.

The better metropolitan actors possessed excellent literary taste, knew their classics of literature well and loved them, but were remote from the new seething currents—not alone in life but also in literature. And their existence—their bonds, habits, morals. . . . To be sure, they were not cut off from society, like the actors of the provinces, where the devout inhabitants still fought shy of 'comedians'. In Moscow, in St. Petersburg, they maintained strong bonds with domestic homes, had friends among the professors of the University, were members of clubs, and generally enjoyed the esteem of others; nevertheless, they continued to take

'benefits'; at these benefits they accepted all sorts of offerings
—flowers and costly things, and silver sets and furs. Argue
as you will that these are gifts of love and sympathy; all the
same, their bestowal placed the actor in a unique position.
In the Art Theatre the conflict with the habits of life in the
old theatre was fought on all fronts. Benefits there were
none; flowers and even wreaths were sent to the actors'
dressing-rooms; the actors did not even answer curtain calls
to receive applause. Outwardly too the actors, and especially the actresses, did not show characteristics common to
the profession. All this, very likely, ensued from their art
itself; for, after all, it lays its stamp both on the diction and
manner of speaking, and on bodily movement; the more
simplicity in art, the less 'artifice' does the art show, and the
more simple is the actor in life.

Stanislavsky, I think, has already told in his book how
the woman guard of the theatre in St. Petersburg, when we
first arrived there, could scarcely believe that these most
ordinary women were the actresses of our company.
'What sort of actresses are these?' she asked with scorn,
having expected bright, loud costumes, coiffures, hats, a
special bearing, a special mirth. . . .

The pulse of sociability was felt very strongly in the Art
Theatre. The company had connections among all strata.
The sympathies of the actors were, of course, different in the
extreme. The spiritual tendencies of some of them, their
music of life, were subject to such influences as might be
called 'Chekhovian' or 'Tolstoyan'; at any rate, something
anti-revolutionary, or even quite apolitical. One of our best
actresses made no effort to conceal the fact that she never
read newspapers. But in many burning eyes it was possible

[257]

to detect, and in repressed conversations in a corner here and there it was possible to hear, that music which might be called the 'Gorkian'.

'Rights are not given, but taken!'

In the section about Morozov, I have told about his tragic infatuation for the revolution—and he our chief shareholder, a millionaire manufacturer.

If in their youth some of them were attracted by Maeterlinck, Baudelaire, D'Annunzio, Oscar Wilde, and already were dreaming of new dramatic forms, others were equally occupied with plans for people's theatres, and for the realization of these plans not a few of our actors even left us.

The coming together of Gorky and Maria Fyodorovna Andreieva created a tremendous impression behind the scenes. Perhaps the most beautiful actress in the Russian theatre, the wife of a major official of the rank of general, the devoted lover of the 'Circle of Stanislavsky', subsequently occupying the leading position in the Art Theatre, she suddenly quite 'found herself' in the seething circle round Gorky, leaving her husband and soon thereafter abandoning the stage.

Ultimately, while Gorky's next play, 'The Children of the Sun', was being staged, the atmosphere of the Theatre was by no means what it had been three years before. From the very beginning the feeling was prevalent that it would be difficult to mobilize the playgoing public. Theatre managers are well aware that in war-time the audiences increase in numbers, while during revolutionary fermentations they diminish considerably. The Russo-Japanese War had already been fought and lost; Witte had concluded the ambiguous peace of Portsmouth, for which he gained the title of Count;

in St. Petersburg we attained *bonne mine au mauvais jeu*; over all Russia threatening waves rose; crowds paraded the streets of Moscow; the police dispersed demonstrations in the squares; the square near Pushkin's monument, convenient for meetings, began to achieve historical significance. At this time 'provincial people' tried to persuade the Tsar to save the Constitution, but he still believed that of revolutionaries in all Russia there were scarcely more than one hundred and forty.

The atmosphere in the Theatre was, as one might say, ragged. We opened the season of 1905–1906 with a revival of our 'angel', 'The Sea Gull', with new scenery and a revised cast. The revival proved a failure. Everything was excellent, but the old aroma was gone. These were flowers which had lain pressed for some years in a book.

During the same season we presented: 'Sorrow From Wit', Knut Hamsun's 'The Drama of Life', and then 'The Children of the Sun'.

We began to work on the latter play. The rehearsals did not run smoothly, there was much argument, the stage management underwent changes, artistic fervour was lacking. Gorky was called upon to settle disputes. But he was little interested; he was absorbed in matters remote from the theatre.

The first performance sank in the mire of political events. The play was quite ready for presentation when suddenly, on October 17, the Constitution was proclaimed. During the first days people's thoughts were far from the theatre; all life seethed in the streets. In the theatre itself there was no inclination for acting; the corridors were filled with a din, with exclamations, news, gossip. I can recall that gifted pupil, Katya Filippova. With her broad face, beautiful eyes, and low voice, she was an exalted creature. She glided now here, now there, and rapturously told of the street demonstrations and of what happened in the square of the monument to Skobelev, where she had leaned against the leg of the general's horse. I can also recall the charming G. S. Burdzhalov, an actor of no great gifts, but a precious member of the *collective*, devoted and conscientious, never spoiling a single rôle and very liberal, extremely cautious however in his liberalism. He also flamed, as far as it was in his nature to do so. The wiser members of the company, however, held themselves in restraint or else did not trust at all the common state of exultation.

For a while we cancelled our performances and decided to wait for a time more propitious for attracting theatrical audiences. Finally, we scheduled the *première* for the 24th of October. But during these days everything had changed. To express oneself in metaphor, there suddenly arose a whirlwind, the sun became obscured by clouds, the air was filled with helpless leaves, everything grew grey and arid and cold. This happened after the famous funeral of Bauman, at which Moscow witnessed for the first time an immense Red demonstration consisting of half a million people, stretching down the boulevards for several versts, after which occurred the beating-up of the revolutionaries returning from the cemetery.

Officially nothing had changed, the dear Constitution was still there, but it became clear that the reactionaries would never reconcile themselves with it and that the so-called 'Black Hundreds' would be let loose to do their worst.

And now for the *première* of 'The Children of the Sun'.

It was one of the tragi-comic episodes in the history of the Art Theatre.

Quite early that morning rumours were already flying about town that the Black Hundreds would not permit the performance of Maxim Gorky's play. These soon developed into reports that the Art Theatre would be dispersed, as a nest of revolution. Nevertheless, the theatre was full. For the calming of the public, the administration of the Theatre established a surveillance of the street and the yard. And although nothing untoward occurred, the public found itself in a state of self-encouragement. In the interludes one heard such jests as this: 'They say that the Theatre will be dispersed this evening. Well, what of it? Misfortune shared is but half of a misfortune!' Nevertheless, during the action of the play, the auditors found it difficult wholly to yield to it, but seemed to be on the *qui vive*, listening for sounds beyond the walls of the theatre and but faintly trying to realize the merits and demerits of the piece.

In one fashion or another we managed to reach the last act without incident. In this act there is a national scene dealing with the 'cholera disorders': the crowd, with outcries, falls upon the professor; it is one of the manifestations of the fatal distrust by the ignorant crowd of the intelligentsia. I, who managed this scene, wanted on this day to flaunt a new stage-managing device: to present the national scene not according to the customary manner of the Art Theatre, i.e. in variegated style, with all the differentiated types, but in monotone. My whole crowd was an association of plasterers, all similarly attired, soiled with white lime, and provided with scrapers and small spades. The result was restrained, and definite, and quite realistic. There was nothing tragic about this scene. The working-men, flourishing their fists, advance against the professor, who, retiring before them, swings his handkerchief in their faces as a gesture of self-defence. It is true that the professor's wife runs out on the steps with a revolver, but at this time the yard porter comes on the scene and very methodically beats up the offenders by striking their heads with a board. At the dress rehearsal this scene was enacted amidst unceasing mirth, caused by the professor's handkerchief and the settling of the mutineers by the yard porter. This mirth even disconcerted us, so that we put the question to the author as to whether it violated his conception, but his only answer was: 'Let them laugh!'

Alas! The mood of an audience can mix up the cards and upset the most subtle calculations. When from behind the wings became audible the first voices of the advancing crowd —and, of course, we gave a very lifelike representation of the scene—the audience was at once on its guard. With the approaching din, it became perturbed, began to drone, to look around, to rise from their seats. And when with re-treating back, swinging a handkerchief, Kachalov appeared, followed by a group of plasterers with threatening gestures, a clamour arose and outcries. And scarcely had Germanova with an extended revolver in her hand sprung out on to the steps when hysteria broke out in the parterre, then in the upper tiers, then somewhere in the depth of the auditorium. A part of the public, thrusting out their elbows, rushed toward the exits; another section raised an outcry to per-suade the timid ones that the scene was not reality but part of the performance. Some one shouted, 'Water!' Others shouted, 'Stop the play!'—'You dare not make sport of our

nerves!' A woman's voice screamed brokenly: '*Seryozha!*
Seryozha!' A celebrated ballet dancer writhed with hysteria.
There was jostling in the corridors, some tried to fight their
way to the cloakroom, others fled as they were—with no
other thought than to save themselves. . . .

The truth is, the public took my association of plasterers
for members of the Black Hundred, who had come to break
up the Theatre and had begun with the artistic personnel.

The most diverse shrieking din filled the theatre. And
Kachalov and Germanova and my plasterers and Shadrin—
the latter was a man of the people playing the part of the
yard porter—all stopped playing and in perplexity gaped
into the auditorium. The stage-manager's assistant had the
curtain rung down.

The really remarkable thing was that the confusion continued for some time. Many who had not had time to escape
remained on being persuaded that the men on the stage were
real members of the Black Hundred and that they had entered into negotiations with the management. The auditors
imagined all sorts of things that never happened. Even such
auditors whom it was impossible to call naïve—as, for example, a certain young professor—were ready to swear that
they had seen several revolvers in the hands of the Black
Hundred intruders aimed at Kachalov.

When calm was restored the performance continued,
but the theatre had been emptied of more than half of its
audience.

Our first revolution—the December revolution of 1905—
was approaching. The public stubbornly refrained from
play-going. The capital of the Association was melting

away. Even among us behind the scenes there were hints of a strike. Some one handed me a list of demands from the 'co-workers'. 'Tsar Fyodor' was on. During the act from which they were free I went to them, presumably to have a 'chat' with them as regards the demands which were reasonable and those which were not. After half an hour of talk I said that I would consult with the Management. Some one then said: 'Only try and give us an answer during the next intermission.'

'But I can't collect the management at once.'

'That's your business.'

I began to understand. 'You mean you'll stop the play?'

'That's our business.'

Experienced in having my own way and not at all experienced in strikes, I flared up and quite firmly announced that I could not possibly give an answer before to-morrow; moreover, that I did not want them to fall into the error of expecting my own answer to such demands to be anything but in the negative.

I then left them, bearing away with me a memory of their diverse facial expressions and poses. Half-naked, made-up; some stood with their hands behind them, others sat in the chairs near the shelves which held mirrors and paints; the faces of the novices, especially of the students, were provocative, but the old fellow-workers awkwardly refrained from meeting my glance. Only one of them, our oldest, esteemed by the whole company, in a sixteenth-century coat, in soft high green boots, with a large glued-on grey beard, cast angry glances. It was clear that he was an opponent of the strike and was ready to fight it.

The performance continued without a break. The leaders

of this small movement were political débutants. With particular vividness there has remained in my memory the chief of them, the *esdek* (Social Democrat), a handsome, ardent fellow, with whom I afterwards often had real 'chats'. At the height of the street conflicts he helped M. F. Andreieva to arrange a shelter in the corridors of the theatre.

When the December events came we were rehearsing 'Sorrow from Wit'—the third act, in which the whole company was engaged. Gorky did not come, but Andreieva brought some fragmentary news of the approaching happenings, without telling all she knew. At one such rehearsal she went up to the stage-manager's table, at which Stanislavsky and I sat, and, speaking for herself and Gorky, expressed extreme perplexity that in such days as these we could think of engaging in rehearsals. We had worked out a rule: when political happenings interrupted the normal life of the Theatre, to allow any person full freedom of action according to his or her conviction; but to demand from those who did not actively participate in any activity outside the Theatre double and even treble work. You cannot awaken creative self-consciousness in yourself, but there always will be found a purely technical polishing of rôles and of the performance.

On December 11 we were still rehearsing the same third act of 'Sorrow from Wit', the ball at the Famusovs, and made the most incredible exertions neither to hear nor give heed to the reports of occurrences in the Square of Triumph we went on rehearsing until shots were heard under the very windows of the theatre and the theatre yard was invaded. The same Katya Filippova, who had but two months before exulted, now writhed in an hysterical fit in the upper foyer.

[265]

But scarcely had our street grown silent, and scarcely had we all found ourselves cut off from our living quarters, when hammocks were strung up in the corridors, while Stanislavsky was already sitting at the stage-manager's table and explaining to the tailor Dellos, from the artist's drawings, details of the costumes of Chatsky, Famusov. . . .

In the course of another twelve years, this question—what the actor ought to do in the heat of revolution—would become still sharper. . . .

Then began the long gloomy days of the siege of Presny.[1] There was martial law; it was forbidden to appear in the streets after nine o'clock in the evening. We arranged our theatrical conferences, with a night's lodging, now in this house, now in that, mostly in the large suite of apartments occupied by Stanislavsky. In all of us there ripened a strong reluctance to continue our performances, even if we should receive the permits. The 'pacification' of Moscow was assigned to Rear-Admiral Dubasov. He soon demanded that the theatres resume their performances, even if beginning only with matinées—for we know that the smooth running of theatres is an indication of tranquillity.

The Art Theatre was silent.

There came the tempting thought of going abroad for the whole second half of the season. But how realize it? To begin with, we needed money for this, yet we had already spent our entire capital. Our material position at this time was sufficiently hopeless. Quite apart from our loss of capital, we were heavily in debt. From whom could we expect support? As regards the shareholders who had personal means—Stanislavsky had only lately paid heavily for his

[1] Factory quarter in Moscow, where the mutineers erected barricades.

effort to establish a studio of new forms, Morozov was experiencing the sharpest moment of his tragic fate in connection with his immense factory; we did not even know where he was. The rest were so frightened by events that they decided to take no more risks on the Theatre. I remember a noteworthy instance of their caution. I had a project for the erection of a new theatre on the very spot where the Art Theatre stood; to be more precise, for an addition at one side of another theatre, more spacious and accessible, with an exit on the Stoleshnikov Lane (the street opposite). The landlord of the Art Theatre, Lianozov, was willing to accept for this property with its immense square the sum of 900,000 rubles. Our wealthy shareholders had already agreed to the purchase, but after the December events they would not hear of it. And when after two years, with the assistance of a bank, I again raised the question of the project, Lianozov was already demanding 1,200,000 rubles for half the land.

But the Art Theatre 'had fortune on its side'. Often was it said of it: 'The little old woman has it under her wing.'

During these years there functioned in Moscow, with great success, the Literary-Artistic Circle. Under its auspices took place the most interesting disputes in Moscow, balls and jubilee celebrations. Its chairman was also its founder, the favourite of Moscow, Prince Yuzhin-Sumbatov, whose name is so often recalled in this book. This institution came to our rescue: it gave us the necessary means for going abroad.

I want to add here that in the course of the following seasons the Art Theatre paid its debts, restored its lost capital, and consolidated its material position. It is true, we were also helped by the 'Berlin fairy tale'—the accession to our shareholders of N. L. Tarassov and N. F. Baliev,[1]—but if it had not been for our journey, there would not have been any 'fairy tale'. In general, the financial history of the Art Theatre abounds in interesting details.

As soon as it was clear that the revolution would be crushed in Moscow, Gorky and Andreieva were assisted in their departure for St. Petersburg by railway engine.

Gorky has remained in my memory as he was during one of the rehearsals of 'The Children of the Sun'—irritable, with not the slightest interest in the performance, and attending it only out of a feeling of responsibility; and, generally speaking, absorbed in other interests.

Even earlier he had a trait—it is difficult to define it— shall I call it self-assurance? Yes, if one is not to understand by this, arrogance. It was a great faith in something leading him, in words and deeds; this man doubted nothing. For us who at every step ask ourselves the questions, 'This way or that way?'—'Is this good or bad?' this trait was an enviable one. Now it had become even more marked in him and harsher; and it embarrassed us.

Almost simultaneously with the Theatre Company, Gorky left for abroad, with Andreieva. They definitely emigrated. The bonds between them and the Theatre were broken.

Gorky wrote several more plays after this, but we did not produce them, nor did he offer them to us; apparently he himself did not think them worthy of that enormous exertion of all the creative forces of the Theatre with which we worked.

[1] See chapter on Tarassov and the foreign tour of the Art Theatre.

Our dream of creating our own playwrights was not realized—playwrights close to the problems of our Theatre, like Chekhov and Gorky. Naidenov, Chirikov, and Yushkevitch flashed by; a considerable success fell to the lot of a single play by Sergutchev; but none of these did the public accept as masters of the repertory of the Art Theatre. Best of all fared Leonid Andreiev, a very gifted and original playwright, irrepressible and mutinous in temperament. The Theatre presented four of his plays, but only one of these had an exceptional success—'Anathema'. But there was an insurmountable difference in the tastes of the Theatre and Andreiev, in the very conception of a 'living human being' on the stage.

There were also efforts to dramatize some of Chekhov's and Gorky's stories. This created a type of 'miniature' which was afterwards introduced in some of the other small theatres. To this day our intimate performances include 'Strasti-Mordasti', 'Chelkash', and 'Mother'; while in the past 'Malva', 'On a Raft', and 'Cain and Artyom' had seen presentation.

But these miniatures could not create a 'great' spectacle. The Theatre had grown up, attained manhood; for the actor's mastery, for the stage-manager's imagination, and for a wealth of technical skill the Theatre demanded big 'canvases'. It decisively directed its course toward the classics.

Then followed a series of the most brilliant seasons for the Art Theatre—the creation of lofty spiritual values, the radiance of artistic truth, the tremor of perennial youth in the classic repertory. Griboyedov, Gogol, Pushkin, Turgenev, again Turgenev, Leo Tolstoy, Ostrovsky, Shakespeare, Molière, Goldoni.

The Theatre felt, as it were, crowded. Its art had a desire to burst asunder the frames of established 'stage possibilities'. Is it so important that a play should be divided into acts and scenes? That an act should last from thirty to forty minutes? And that all this should take place in a single evening? Well, we decided to present 'The Brothers Karamazov' in the course of two evenings, and not three—only because the Censorship would not permit us to use the scenes involving Father Zossima. One scene 'in Mokroe' would last an hour and a half and the public would not feel that it had lasted that long; while another would last but ten minutes and the public would not feel that it had been so short. This sort of thing does not depend on time but on the force and logic of lived experience. Powerfully to impress the public, is it necessary to present popular scenes, in the full glare of the footlights. But there Ivan Karamazov and Smerdiakov or Shatov and Stavrogin would hold their conversations in the light of a single little lamp for a full forty minutes and the public would be absorbed in the scene every instant; while Kachalov in the stupefying scene of the 'Nightmare' would appear quite alone, and remain alone on the stage for thirty-two minutes!

We felt that Dostoievsky was, in essence, a very great dramatist, although he had never written for the stage. Marvellous psychologist that he was, he was to prove profoundly, organically close to the actor's art. Finally, he was plastic and inexhaustible in wealth of language, in cascades of living speech. One has but to begin to speak of him to find it necessary to use superlative expressions: greatest, most powerful, etc.

I have already told in the first chapters of this book how

in youth I found myself under the hypnosis of Dostoievsky, and how later I felt shaken by his famous speech at the unveiling of the Pushkin monument—shaken by the firm, powerful logic, at once wise and inspired.

How is one to determine when, under what circumstances, was born the idea to dramatize his novel? It was born from our active love for the theatre and from seed which had lain fallow in the experiences of youth.

And how the whole Theatre flamed when we stepped to our work. It was all so unanticipated. We should have begun the season of 1910–1911 with 'Hamlet', which was being prepared by Stanislavsky and Gordon Craig. Quite suddenly, just before the beginning of our autumn labours, Stanislavsky, who was sojourning on the Caucasian waters, fell ill with typhoid. His illness was a prolonged one; it was necessary to rearrange the whole schedule.

And I called upon the Theatre to perform 'The Brothers Karamazov'. I called upon the whole Theatre. There was a repetition of what happened during the preparation of 'Julius Caesar': every one was seized with an unforgettable fervour, with an even more intense mood of exaltation than in 'Julius Caesar', because the material was deeper, more native, and because its stage problems were bolder, and newer, and harder.

The result exceeded all expectations. Dostoievsky created a new epoch in the life of the Art Theatre. The first Russian tragedy. The most 'acting' spectacle of the Art Theatre. A spectacle-mystery. During the performance, the mood behind the scenes could not be described otherwise than as religious.

I emphasize all this, in order to make clearer to the reader the collision which occurred on this ground between the Art Theatre and Gorky. This happened before the presentation of another Dostoievsky novel, *The Possessed*, of which our dramatized version was called 'Nikolai Stavrogin'. Gorky lived in Italy at the time, on Capri, and he wrote from there. In one of the most widely read newspapers, *Russkoye Slovo*, there appeared his open letter warmly protesting against the presentation of this play and calling upon the Russian public to join in the protest.

This created the impression of an exploding bomb. The whole Theatre was in a state of perturbation. It was necessary to reply. As Gorky's accusation was aimed at me, not only as the chief guide of the repertory, but also in a personal sense, I stepped aside—let the Theatre speak for itself! Large general gatherings were organized; cautious in such responsible situations, Stanislavsky asked Alexander Nikolaievitch Benois to come from St. Petersburg. This artist, whom I regard as tremendous in the broadest sense of the word, a theatrical worker of exceptional universality and catholic taste, loved our Theatre, knew it well, and had written a remarkable essay in connection with the production of 'The Brothers Karamazov'. With his collaboration an open letter was written in reply to Gorky.

The Theatre relied for its justification on the 'higher probings of the soul'.

Gorky's attack called forth a storm in the Press and in society. With insignificant exceptions, few in number, the newspapers fell upon him with long articles and *feuilletons* in defence of the 'free' Theatre and Dostoievsky.

Gorky published still another open letter in the Press, in the course of which he said:

[272]

I know the frailty of the Russian character, I know the compassionate wavering of the Russian soul and its tendency, in its torment, weariness and despair, toward all contagions. . . . Not Stavrogins should be shown it now, but something quite different. It should be exhorted to boldness, spiritual health, activity, and not introspection; it should be exhorted to return to the source of energy—to democracy, to the people, to sociableness and to science.

But we, idol-worshippers of Art, had joined it, this art, to science and sociability, and we regarded it as the source of energy for healthy activity: the frail soul of 'Uncle Vanya', and the introspection of Hamlet, and the 'Symphonie Pathétique' of Tchaikovsky—it all depended on how it was done.

The question of the repertory of a theatre has never within my memory, despite fifty years' intimacy with the theatre, been a settled one. It has always aroused argument and conflict. Within another four years the greatest revolution would come to pass, and this question would become more acute, more angry, more pitiless. That which made the substance of the answer to Gorky would be repeated in heated skirmishes, in disputes, in official reports, in lectures. The most important theatres of the Soviet Union would transform the 'higher probings of the soul' into a symbol of faith, and would make use of it as a defence against the intrusion of politics into art. Between the ideology of the old theatre and revolutionary politics there would ensue a ceaseless conflict, to continue for many years.

Then, later, along the whole theatrical front, through the strained exertions of both sides, guiding synthetic formulas would be worked out. Both sides would conscientiously abandon their extreme positions: the revolutionaries from the fear that in this conflict they might lose the cultural values of the past, the theatres from the fear that these much-vaunted 'probings of the soul' might actually become transformed into idle rhetoric.

And only in consequence of heated frays in discussions, lectures, passionate articles, in such tenseness of noble thought as theatrical ideology has not known in all the ages of its existence, there would become crystallized the unshakable formula that art, by its very nature, cannot be apolitical. Then would come to pass new meetings of the Theatre with Gorky. . . .

PART IV

THE FIRST TOUR ABROAD

CHAPTER SEVENTEEN

Only Allah knows whence came our courage: to gather up the cumbersome apparatus—eighty-seven human beings and seven freight-wagons of scenery and properties —and go on tour abroad. To a foreign land! And only in the eighth year of the Theatre's existence! 'Aren't you afraid that to return you'll have to walk along the rails?' we were warned. What was it? Youth? Arrogance? Sagacity? Blind faith?

It is true, we knew that rumours about us, 'tempestuous, sectarians', had penetrated abroad. But whom could they interest? The fringes of theatrical circles? This could give no assurance to the box-office.

And everything at our own risk! It was not quite the same thing as when fifteen years later we were to be transported by the celebrated Morris Gest, no, not into a neighbouring country—a journey of a mere twenty-four hours or so—but beyond an ocean, and our whole tour guaranteed. No one gave a thought to us, and had we come to a bad end no one would have been sorry for us, but every one would have said that it served us right.

Our first problem was to find a vacant theatre in Berlin: no joke, at the height of the season! It was in January. We sent A. L. Vishnevsky on ahead. Even before the existence of the Art Theatre he used to arrange tours in Russia; he had the necessary experience. He found the 'Berliner Theatre' in

Charlottenstrasse. Its proprietor was the well-known actor, Bonn, whose affairs were going none too well and who was willing to let us have the theatre for a month and a half. His demands were exorbitant, but we had no choice.

We made the most minute inventory of our properties, in order to avoid paying customs on our return.

We were provided with letters of recommendation to representatives of the Russian authorities, which, I must add, were of little use to us.

We sent the artists on ahead. We decided that it was more convenient to prepare some of our scenery on the spot rather than take those we already had.

We held a whole series of conferences with the company in order to work out the rules for our conduct abroad, not only during the performances but outside the theatre. In our own fashion we had worked out ten commandments, which all were obliged to sign. Every one was under promise to cherish the reputation of the Theatre, the reputation of the Russian actor, to hold himself under strong discipline, not alone while performing his duties but also at home—in the *pension* or in the hotel—and in the street, the restaurant, and the alien theatre.

Besides the actors, there came with us all co-workers, *costumiers*, make-up assistants, property men, and the more important of the stage hands. Only a few spoke German; hence the company was broken up into groups, and each group was reinforced by an individual who spoke German. At the beginning he was called a 'guide', but later he came to be known as 'Makar', because of the proverb, 'There's not a misfortune that misses poor Makar.' He was torn into bits, he was called upon now to translate, now to

[278]

explain the most delicate matters; he was blamed for every mishap.

We took five plays with us: 'Tsar Fyodor', 'Uncle Vanya', 'The Three Sisters', 'The Lower Depths', and 'An Enemy of the People'. This point of view was established: the Russian Theatre should present Russian plays. We were afterwards asked in Berlin why we did not bring with us one of our best performances—'Lonely Lives', by Hauptmann, the favourite of Germany. But we considered it an impertinence to show Germans how to act their own plays. Our only foreign play was 'An Enemy of the People', an exception we made in order to allow Stanislavsky to appear in the leading rôle.

It was essential to preserve in our performances the tremor wholly peculiar to Russian literature, that which Turgenev approximately defined as 'Slavonic melancholy' and which so enchanted the foreign critics.

The German writer Scholtz was invited to acquaint the German public with our Theatre. He had a fair knowledge of Russian, had translated a great deal into German, had connections with the theatrical and journalistic world, and enjoyed a considerable reputation. He collaborated with us in issuing booklets in which the history of the Theatre was outlined, with suitable photographs.

Moscow was filled with reactionary excitement. Every passer-by was subjected to the suspicious surveillance of the police. It was painful to go out in the evening. There is the unforgettable memory of a nocturnal incident. The white snow was illumined by a chain of street-lamps and the clear moon; the street was utterly desolate. Amidst the complete silence, two quick shots were heard. Then, suddenly, there

[279]

became audible a woman's desperate outcry, fast coming nearer—it seems to me I had never in life heard so desperate an outcry; a sled came fiercely dashing by; two policemen in it were holding a girl; the cry quickly died away.

The nerves of all were on edge from the events of the past month and from ignorance of the future; hence the arrival in the calm, cultured capital of Germany was impressive. Moreover, we had left winter behind and enjoyed almost spring-like weather. Finally, the majority of the company had never been abroad before; everything that was new attracted attention: the clean German houses, factories, villas and roads. Our spirits rose; and immediately disputes began as to which was better—this dry, hard pedantry of established order or the Russian disorderly breadth: Russian culture, bourgeoisie, little curtains, flowers, depth of spirit, anarchism, the filth of the Russian village; Goethe, Schiller, and Beethoven or Tolstoy and Dostoievsky; and so on.

The theatre was engaged for ten days before the first performance. In these ten days it was necessary to make it convenient, comfortable. We had the rule: if you are to demand from the actor not merely conscientiousness but also fervour, then you must create for him a favourable atmosphere.

The stage of Bonn's theatre barely accommodated the complex technical apparatus of the Art Theatre. The stage-managers and administration began their assiduous labours, further complicated by ignorance or scanty knowledge of the German tongue. The German working-men, as always when labouring at something in which they were unsuccessful, were in this Theatre careless, undisciplined and at the same time incredulous that a genuine art could come to them out of Russia; they worked either indifferently or with open hostility, and mocked our mutilation of German words. Often there were sharp collisions. We could attain the slightest thing only by continuous tipping, but even this they considered as their legal right: to fleece the foreign barbarians was quite natural. 'Russische Schwein' (Russian swine) was a common expression with the man of the street in Berlin. Our own working-men, with the splendid Ivan Titov at their head, quickly learned the German back-stage terms, and made every effort to secure the friendly co-operation of their colleagues; but they did not succeed in this until the first performance. To make up for this, it was impossible to recognize the native workers on the morning following the performance. The transformation was almost comic; they walked about quietly, cautiously, as if with gaping mouths. It was not that they were overcome by our art, for they saw it at the rehearsals; no, they were completely shaken by our triumphant reception.

While the more technical matters were being attended to, the actors were becoming acquainted with the city, visiting the museums and the German theatres. Then they rehearsed the mob scenes. For these we could not bring our own men from Moscow, so we reinforced our crowds with Russian students residing in Berlin.

Parallel with our purely theatrical labours, publications were being prepared for the printer. Again, involuntarily, I recall the great master in this field, Mr. Morris Gest. We had with us for this purpose only the modest and even timorous Scholtz. But justice must be done to the fairness of the German Press; we did not have to spend a single mark for advertisement. That which I later encountered in Paris was wholly absent here. It was necessary for Scholtz to explain the Art Theatre in detail in every important newspaper office. And the notices which these newspapers published were consistent with their whole-hearted confidence or expectation; there was no necessity for puffs.

We turned to the Russian Embassy. Stanislavsky and I were even given an audience by the Count Osten-Sacken himself, but we met with a reception so restrained in character that it could not have been worse. In any case, we were given a great deal of advice, but it all breathed such an effort to curry favour with the Berlin authorities and bankers that we failed to avail ourselves of it.

Ah, these officials! How often one recalls the difficulties met with by theatres, owing to them! Everywhere—both abroad and at home, where the authorities ruled. And in what a servile position they placed the theatres and the actors!

And then, at last, the opening night. The tension behind the scenes was extreme; it was as if before a new conquest. It was possible to compare the perturbation and the spirit of the company only with the original opening of the Theatre in Moscow. The attitude towards Russians was at this time wholly negative, and little was known of Russian stage art. Of the ensemble, the scenic art of the Russian theatre, there was little conception. The negative attitude towards Russians was only intensified by the recent political movements in Russia.

'Tsar Fyodor' was abbreviated to such limits as were customary to the German playgoing public. The decorations were simplified, to facilitate rapid changes of scene.

MORRIS GEST AND NEMIROVITCH-DANTCHENKO
Vienna, 1925

p. 282]

The German theatres allow one, at the most two, so-called pauses—as it were, interludes—during which the Germans sup, munching sausages, eating bread and butter, and drinking beer.

Thanks to the absence of a censorship, it was possible to restore to the tragedy the figures of the Metropolitan Dionysus and the Archbishop Job in costumes contemporary to the epoch, in sumptuous lilac-coloured vestments, in mitres. It was very picturesque.

Moskvin, of course, appeared in the leading rôle. Savitskaya played the part of the Tsaritsa. The remaining rôles were, as always, left to Vishnevsky, Luzhsky, Artem, etc.

We succeeded in having an imposing audience.

Not without certain stratagems, the theatre was filled. At all events, from morning the box-office bore the legend '*Ausverkauft*' (Sold Out), before which Bonn respectfully removed his hat. The auditorium was full of representatives of theatres and newspapers; the celebrities were pointed out to us. Our embassy was also present, as were the bigwigs of German finance, and very many Russians.

The first interlude amply demonstrated our tremendous success. Those who participated in the performance remember to this day the unanimous outburst of applause from the vast audience. Both men and women stood up and continued their applause.

Notwithstanding the alien tongue, the performance, it was quite evident, stood out in such relief that the lines of the tragedy reached the public with immediate force and overwhelmed it. The power of the actors' temperaments and the graphic character of the groups helped to bring this about. It must be confessed that such a success came as a perfect surprise. Nor did this success diminish, but rather increased with each succeeding scene. The performance ended in a complete triumph, and when on the following day there appeared in the Press the extensive, serious, excited articles of the German dramatic critics, there could no longer be any doubt of the victory of Russian art in Germany. Here are some extracts:

From an article by Alfred Kerr:

That which I have seen at this performance is first-class—indisputably first-class. You do not possess the slightest knowledge of the Russian language, you have no understanding of the separate details of the interpretation, but within two minutes you already know: this is first-class.

In all its lustre, there is the spirit of clarity here, of simplicity, of an inwardly fortified repose, which the excellent art of Reinhardt has not yet reached. At a time when I, contemplating the recent productions of Reinhardt, am impelled to consider how strong, how disciplined has been the stage management which organized them, I cannot get away from the thought in the passages which most perturb one: forty rehearsals. Forty? Forty-three! Forty-five rehearsals! Forty-five! In his strong passages Reinhardt somehow forces you to consider the labour. On the other hand, in the case of the Muscovites I see something which makes me wholly forget the preparatory exertions. And in this is the whole difference.

It is all so casual, so even, this masterly craft so assimilated in itself, so clear, so silent as to what is locked within. There is nothing which shouts, nothing which proclaims the freshly varnished article. It is something—I can scarcely express it—something brilliant,—no, something brilliantly scintillating. Moreover, you feel that the performance given is by no means the strongest which they have. . . .

One question still remains an open one: it may be that this repose, this clarity, this restraint, are possible only in these Russian productions, in which Russian types are represented and the Russian steppe glides by; in which play is almost apathetic, and something like dullness resides in the race; a kind of blunting of the sufferings depicted; in which there is no outcry, and pathos itself almost soundless, and apparitions hover in sunlit silence, their contours, as it were, softened by remoteness . . . in which made-up women imitate, as if unconsciously, the images of the Madonna with her glance, permeated with Russian Christianity, to us unknown . . . in which men both slavishly and in human fraternity bow down to fate and surrender to earth their destiny. Here happiness and suffering are dimmed, remote; one feels the East.

From other newspapers:

To the impression created by the Muscovites, it is possible to juxtapose only the very best that we have known to date in the art of representing human beings and in the craft of directing all means of the stage.

We have seen the art of another nation, having its own rhythm, its own forms, but offering in its marvellously worked-out æsthetic detail an exquisite pleasure to the connoisseur of the stage.

Such feeling of style, such self-revelation in content, I have not seen before. . . . And what should one say of the individual artists? . . . Magnificent masks and complete reincarnation in play. Heavens, but why do these actors speak in Russian? Why couldn't we entice them to us for the renewal of our theatres? . . .

Hats off to you, Muscovites! You have grown up in the soil of modernity and in the soil of the historic past, but there is something in you which belongs to to-morrow and the day after, and the future.

These are but brief extracts from a whole stream of articles, all of the same tenour.

[285]

It was now that our 'Makars' won esteem: they were much sought after; they were implored to translate the notices, while the rooms in which Stanislavsky and I lived with our families—also Lilina, Knipper, and Vishnevsky—were filled from early morning with other actors, and the duties of translation fell upon two women who knew the German tongue well; they were Knipper and my wife—the latter, by the way, was known among us as the 'mascot of the Art Theatre'.

The moral triumph was complete, but what was our astonishment when, notwithstanding such a Press, which in Russia would have brought us a whole series of packed houses, we found the auditorium scarcely half filled! This was as true of the second day as of the third; and so it went. Suddenly it became entirely clear that performances in an alien tongue could not attract large audiences, notwithstanding the best recommendations of dramatic critics.

It is difficult to convey how disheartening this was. Bound wings, a fettered spirit—with what else can one compare this feeling? The conviction that art has reached its summit, the faith that it is universal—but no! If a German is ignorant of Russian, he is not interested in Russian dramatic art—cannot be interested! But the same thing happened to the company from Meiningen in Moscow. They were able to present a play three or four times at the most, while during their second tour they played to empty houses. But behind the Meiningen company was a duke, while behind us was no one; in Moscow we had only debts. And our expenses increased during this period. As always happens, the list of 'unforeseen' items grew. The audiences, it is true, were sufficiently large to obviate any loss, but there could be no thought of putting anything aside. Out of sheer caution, I put away a certain sum to assure our 'return home'.

Our second production was 'Uncle Vanya'. Local theatrical men tried to persuade us to produce 'The Lower Depths', which under the title of 'Nachtasyl' ('A Night's Lodging') had been presented in Berlin hundreds of times, while 'Uncle Vanya' had some years before been produced in a German translation in Berlin and had had no success whatsoever. But we had our own artistic plan; we were obliged to bear witness with our art to Chekhov. And we were not mistaken. 'Uncle Vanya' had a success almost greater than 'Tsar Fyodor'. The essence of Chekhov's poetry and the new rhythm of this production were excellently understood, and proved exciting. Again we had a brilliant Press. By now it was established that the Moscow Art Theatre had been called to sound an alarum in the stage art of Germany.

At one of the performances of 'Uncle Vanya' the Theatre made the acquaintance of Hauptmann. His enchanting presence—a high forehead, large, grey, pensive eyes, an energetic and at the same time soft line of the mouth, the charm which he always instilled into our theatre, experienced by us in 'The Sunken Bell', 'Hannele', 'Lonely Lives',—all this was made known by his attendance as our most precious guest in Berlin. Particularly did he grow close to us after his agitation during a performance of 'Uncle Vanya'; in the course of the four acts he never ceased wiping his tears. Even more comprehensible became his gravitation toward Russian literature, and the reason for Chekhov's tender love for Hauptmann's works, which was the cause of their kinship.

Several meetings with him, each lasting from two to three

hours, were devoted to the most exciting talks on art. Hauptmann lived outside Berlin, though he maintained in the city a small permanent flat; he was nearly always inaccessible, and received few visitors. He spoke no language but German, but our 'mascot' managed so deftly to follow Hauptmann with her Russian translation and me with a German rendering that there was the sense of our speaking in a common tongue.

This association with Hauptmann was one of our highest compensations for all the exertions we had expended in the eight-year life of the Theatre. Every one knows what a joy it is for the actor, artist or writer to be understood and appreciated to the full depth of his intention. And when the person thus able to understand you is himself a great artist and possesses sound judgment, upon which you may count, the compensation derived from his approval becomes a very real, rare happiness. And when we understand one another to the last syllable, we find ourselves in a continuous exaltation of thought, than which nothing is more precious, nothing more noble, more disinterested.

Thus it was between us and the great German writer Hauptmann. Within eight years of these meetings the War began, patriotic passions were aflame, the German writers came forward with a bitter, angry declaration against the 'Russian barbarians', and Hauptmann's name was among the first. And in my study, from the bookshelves along which rested portraits of writers, some one of my friends, apparently in a similar fit of patriotic indignation, extracted the portrait of Hauptmann and destroyed it. To this day there gleams the empty white oval frame over the section devoted to his works.

[288]

It was Maupassant who said: 'Patriotism is the seed of war.'

After a week's stay of the Art Theatre in Berlin its success in the literary and theatrical world was so firmly established that with remarkable rapidity the Theatre entered into relations with the best representatives of literature and the drama. 'The Lower Depths' added nothing new, all the more as Reinhardt's production was practically a copy of ours. The triumphant mood of the company did not by any means abandon it in later performances; nevertheless, the Germans were not generous in their patronage of our theatre.

Then Fate suddenly sent us a marvellous advertisement.

This is how it happened: one Monday we had scheduled the last *première* — 'An Enemy of the People.' On the evening before, we were sitting in the office, my secretary and I. The telephone rang; the secretary picked up the receiver; with wide eyes he turned to me and, after covering the transmitter with one hand, whispered: 'The Emperor would like to see "Tsar Fyodor" to-morrow!'

'What are you saying? The Emperor himself is speaking on the telephone?' The frightened face of Maximilian Schick gave one that impression.

'No. It's from the palace. They say that the Emperor would like to come to-morrow, Monday, and see "Tsar Fyodor"!'

'But it's difficult to change to-morrow's programme. To-day is Sunday, all printing shops are closed. That means that announcements of a change can't be printed until to-morrow morning. The posters can't appear until the afternoon. On the one hand, those who have tickets for 'An Enemy of the People' will be informed too late; on the

[289]

other, it's almost impossible to sell the tickets for another production at such short notice!'

'Good. That's what we'll report to the Emperor.'

Nevertheless, in the course of another half-hour the telephone again rang. The Emperor persisted in asking that Tsar Fyodor' be shown the following day.

We called on Bonn for assistance. He began to persuade us to forget our Russian ways and accept this request as a command. Announcements of the change were posted Monday noon. In red letters, athwart the announcement, according to the custom of German theatres, was printed: 'By the request of His Majesty.' And by three o'clock there was not a ticket for the evening left at the box-office! That was the first authentic 'full house'.

Wilhelm came with the Empress and the Crown Prince. The Empress had already seen 'Tsar Fyodor' at a previous performance. 'The Empress speaks so often of your Theatre that I said: "I also want to see it!" '

The Emperor was attired in a Russian military uniform. It goes without saying that the whole Russian Embassy was present at the performance. At its conclusion, Wilhelm expressed—to do him justice—some extraordinarily exact observations on Russian stage art: 'Art without gestures.'— 'I had no idea that it was possible to speak so simply on the stage.'—'I had never supposed that the theatre could so brilliantly offer me several volumes of history.'—'Never shall I forget the eyes of the Tsaritsa!' (Savitskaya had truly the remarkable eyes of a Madonna.)—'And the beggar on the church porch!' (Burdzhalov)—'Could there be anything more touching than this will-less Tsar? But he has real wisdom!' (The conversation was carried on in French.)

[290]

A smile of joy lighted up the face of the Empress. 'It was I who brought him here,' she whispered.

'It was I who brought him here,' whispered the representative of the Russian Embassy, this time heartily pressing our hands.

'It was I who brought him here,' said General T., a Russian who was close to Wilhelm, as he invited us afterwards to a café.

'It was I who arranged this,' said the happy landlord of the theatre, Bonn.

It was as if at the waving of a magic wand not only had the attitude of the Russian Embassy to our theatre wholly changed, but also that of the entire German public. From this day on we played almost uninterruptedly to full houses. It was a pity that only six or seven performances remained.

During the most difficult periods of the Theatre's existence the whole company and stockholders, with Stanislavsky at the head, showed the greatest trust in me; as a result, I bore the brunt of the practical responsibilities of the tour. Sometimes I took counsel, sometimes I was consulted, but as a rule everything was left to me.

The situation was a difficult one. In order to leave Berlin for other cities, it was necessary beforehand to secure local theatres, and agree on terms; while in order to agree on terms it was necessary to have the assurance that there would be enough funds for the tour.

I had already been to Dresden and Prague, in order to see the theatres and interview their managers. I also started negotiations with Paris, and awaited the arrival from there of a representative for the drawing up of a contract. But whether we would go there or retrace our steps home I did not know for certain; and I agonizingly tried to gauge the future, in order to estimate the extent of the risk.

In the meanwhile our actors were zealously taking advantage of their presence in Berlin. At that time Greater Berlin did not yet exist, the city did not go beyond the Tiergarten, the streets Kurfürstendamm and Tauentzien had not as yet squeezed out the Friedrichstrasse and Unter den Linden: but of theatres, shops, restaurants, cafés and diversions there were plenty to answer all demands, great and small. In Berlin, as in St. Petersburg, as later in Dresden, in Leipzig, throughout all Europe, and in America, there were always to be found local theatrical enthusiasts who derived tremendous pleasure from boasting of local attractions, among which not the least rôle was played by the excellent cabarets, famous taverns, and special dishes and wines. Moskvin, Knipper, Kachalov, Vishnevsky, Luzhsky, Gribunin and Alexandrov were especially able to appreciate this; and indeed they were particularly in demand.

One day Moskvin and Vishnevsky told me that two young Muscovites wanted to make my acquaintance—wealthy bachelors, fervent admirers of the Art Theatre. When rumours were current in Moscow that the Art Theatre was planning a tour abroad, they said to themselves: 'We will follow them. Where the Art Theatre goes, there we go also!' They had not even a single acquaintance in the company; they first met some of our actors only in Berlin. They were Tarassov and Baliev, two friends whom death alone could succeed in parting.

It was hard to imagine a more finished type of exquisite, charming, half-modest and half-audacious dandy than Tarassov. He was not to be classified under the heroes of Oscar Wilde; yet you could not avoid thinking of them. In general, he was not to be classified under any particular type; he was quite himself: simple, candid, tender,—yes, even tender—but bold; he approached everything with taste, giving the impression that there was nothing he feared so much as vulgarity.

Every one knows his friend Baliev under the name of 'Nikita Baliev'. At that time he had not begun to reveal himself; he was merely 'gathering honey'; he observed, sharpened his wits, collected materials for future creation.

Baliev came to see me alone the first time. And when he perceived that an acquaintance had been established, he very cautiously approached the subject of the material conditions of our tour. I quite frankly told him that notwithstanding the tremendous success and alluring prospects, there was the sad chance of returning home prematurely.

'How much is necessary for the Theatre to continue its tour undisturbed?'

'In order that the Theatre, in the event of failure, may not find itself in a distressing situation, 30,000 rubles!'

'And if this money were offered you? By Tarassov and me?'

This was so wholly unexpected, sounding like a fairy tale, that I didn't reply at once.

'On what conditions?'

'None.'

'As a debt, without interest?'

'Of course not! Let's not talk of interest! Nor of a debt. If you lose it, no matter. If not, let it remain in the business.'

'That is, you'll become one of our stockholders?'

'As you like. Arrange it in any way most convenient to yourself.'

Surely, the little old woman had the Theatre under her wing!

When on meeting Tarassov I began to thank him, he with delicate embarrassment would not allow me to go on.

Twenty-five years have passed since this meeting in the office of the Berliner Theater in Charlottenstrasse. Tarassov has long since finished accounts with his short life of a 'will-o'-the-wisp'; Baliev has long been a celebrity and is already bewailing fatigue; the Art Theatre has passed through all the stages of revolution, is already forging a new repertory and a new life; for the Theatre these two lounging rich Muscovites are now, for all their charm, class enemies; nevertheless, it is impossible to forget that feeling of buoyancy and cheer which seized upon us all then, in the days of the youth of the Art Theatre.

This money remained unspent. The rest of the tour paid all expenses and allowed us to return to Moscow; moreover, we now had money to continue our work.

All theatrical people in Berlin now tried to persuade us to remain another month. But in the first place, we were already contracted for in other cities; in the second place, we considered it more important to show our art in as many cities as possible than to make money out of it, even at a period so crucial for us. We gave thirty performances in Berlin. The last proved to be a complete triumph for the Theatre; every seat was sold out two days before the performance; there were continuous ovations all evening, and speeches were made. On the following day an immense crowd accompanied the company to the station, where again there were wreath-offerings and speeches. The visit to Berlin had been also marked by several dinners given for the company, the warmest recollection of which remained from the dinner arranged by Hauptmann.

Among the memories of this month-and-a-half visit to Berlin of a large theatrical family, increasingly friendly with each new day that it remained torn from its native land, are a multitude of diverse little pictures, some of them joyous, some perturbing, some comic, some sad. Gratified, triumph-ant ambition came into collision with the need of practising economy, of denying oneself in many ways. The 'cultural attainments' of Germany gave pleasures, but many among us had left their families in Moscow and were homesick. The oldest member of our company and common favourite, Artem, did not want to perceive anything, and contended that the Germans were pretending out of mere chauvinism not to understand Russian; and he yearned for the Russian samovar. One of our actors, who bore an unusually heavy load of care, was in a state of great nervousness while waiting for news from Moscow, and played in a particularly exult-ant mood on the evening that he received a telegram from his wife: 'I have borne thee a healthy son.'

In the meantime, there still remained before us many cities, new impressions, and exertions for new conquests, and the unknown, the unknown. . . .

Travelling from Berlin, one feeling possessed us all: Whither were we going? Whither into the distance were we being borne by the express train? But this feeling was one of courage, and was permeated with faith, because it was young and single-minded.

CHAPTER EIGHTEEN

Already during the first half of our stay in Berlin, when the success of the Theatre was clearly defined, we began to receive proposals from other cities. It became obvious that this business of touring required a special knowledge, and that it was impossible to manage without some sort of experienced impresario. I made arrangements with Stein, now no longer among the living.

He was by no means the usual type of theatrical agent one meets with abroad. A small office all covered with variegated posters and announcements, a pile of prepared contracts, connections with the agencies of European centres, an unceasing telephoning to all the cities of Germany and Austria, railway offices, etc. The chief field of activity: *cafés chantants* of the whole world. The clients: all 'directors' of the 'Apollo', 'Alhambra', etc., and all manner of entertainers, jugglers, gymnasts, and the like. Stein was proud of having conducted Duse and Sarah Bernhardt through Germany.

On his own initiative he offered us his services. He was captivated by the Art Theatre, and displayed an enthusiasm which might have awakened suspicion were it not for the fact that he demonstrated his sincerity by his dealings. When he spoke of what charmed him in our art, when he became acquainted with one or another of our artists, he showed great heartiness, as if in his work for us he found a cleansing of his sins. About forty years old, flaxen-haired, gentle-mannered, always quiet and obliging, he did not give at all the impression of controlling an extensive *café chantant* clientele. He abandoned his own office, and never quitted ours. At the beginning he proposed merely to arrange the technical part of our tours, but later decided to accompany us. 'You can't go on like this. You're undertaking the work of six men,' he said.

The honorarium he asked scarcely covered his personal expenses. But he refused the increase offered him. 'Don't you worry about me! You Russians are always looking for something to worry about. The transporting of your Theatre will be an advertisement. It will bring me business!'

Even before Stein joined us we had concluded terms with Dresden and Prague.

The director of the Dresden Royal Theatre was Count Zeibach, while its 'dramatist' was Meyer. Attached to every German and Austrian theatre is a so-called 'dramatist of the theatre'. He conducts the repertory and sometimes does stage-managing.

Count Zeibach, one of the most elegant of men, was strongly reminiscent of the director of our Imperial theatres, Vsevolozhsky, a court type and an amateur of the theatre. It goes without saying that he spoke French well, and it was possible to conclude terms with him without the aid of an interpreter. He proposed that the Theatre should present only two performances, 'Tsar Fyodor' and 'The Lower Depths'; but we told him that the Theatre would not come without 'Uncle Vanya'. The Count rejected 'Uncle Vanya'; we insisted. Then he proposed three performances.

As practical men, every stage-manager would have called us, of course, fools and wasters. . . . Usually the journeys of actors are arranged thus: they arrive in the morning; in the evening the performance is given. In our own case, we arrived in Dresden and found it necessary to give the entire company three free days, to afford them an opportunity to see the famous Dresden Gallery with Raphael's Madonna, the Saxon Museum, the old city, and anything else they might find interesting.

It was much easier to establish ourselves in the new theatre than in the one in Berlin. It was a great joy to enter the handsome theatre with its superbly arranged stage.

As I recall the multitude of European theatres in which we had quickly to establish ourselves, the Dresden theatre is remembered with especial gratitude. It is perhaps the only theatre in which as much thought was given to the comfort of the actors as to that of the public; there was a sufficient number of dressing-rooms, excellent accommodation for costumes and properties, and a stage which allowed ample room for every one. Everywhere else the architects give more thought to the decorations of the auditorium and the foyer than to conveniences behind the scenes. One of them explained this to me: 'When an architect undertakes to build a theatre, he provides himself with an advertisement. You must agree; with whom must he reckon in his quest of advertisement: the tens of actors and stage-managers, or the thousands and tens of thousands of the public?'

When I consider the growth of the actor's personality at home, I recall how we erred in thinking that in Germany, Austria, France and America the behaviour of the directors toward their actors was distinguished for refinement. In the overwhelmingly large majority there is the execrable tone which one expects in a shopkeeper. The best dressing-room goes to the *prima donna*, the best men's room to the leading man—here are to be found rugs, and mirrors, and opulent furniture; the large and luxurious study is for the director. But here all solicitude ends. The rest of the company find shelter in desolate corridors, while the supernumeraries are provided with large, cold, barn-like stalls—badly in need of repairs—with mean little mirrors. The caprice of a *prima donna* or of a hero causes every one to walk on tiptoe, while the protest of secondary and lesser personages is likely to be answered—well, if you please, with the loss of the protester's job.

Dresden left in my memory another curious fact. When the stage-hands of the theatre, forty in number, were promised gratuities, they rejected them. 'We know when real art arrives, and we know from whom we ought to receive extra compensation.' We thought that this was only a pretty phrase. But when on finishing our performances we offered gratuities, they were definitely and unanimously rejected. Moreover, these workers daily entertained our stage-hands and showed them about town. We had no alternative but to contribute a certain sum to a mutual aid fund.

The words 'Moskauer Künstler Theater' did their work: the three Dresden performances were played to almost full houses. To the astonishment of Count Zeibach—he himself admitted it—the greatest artistic success fell to the lot of 'Uncle Vanya'.

In the hour of revelation criticism is silent. It has nothing more to seek or demand; there is nothing for it to do. It can only rejoice and take pride in the fact that it has been witness to this evening of artistic, sacred rapture. We shall remember this evening as one remembers a great, strange, rare human being, who

[299]

came to us with large, clear, childlike eyes and pressed our hands, and whom we comprehended at once, for he had found a harmonious response in our yearning. . . .

Actors and critics, decorators and stage directors, artists and the public, all have been able to learn something in these Russian productions. . . . Unquestionably they have taught us at least one important thing: that the force of realism on the stage is far from becoming extinguished. . . .

For the spectator there will always remain the powerful and never-to-be-forgotten impressions of an art which presents equally the highest inner and the highest outer truth. . . .

Leipzig. . . . Great numbers of Russian youth . . . extraordinarily noisy . . . very fervent. . . . Only two performances, both to full houses. . . . At the conclusion of the second performance, five hundred demonstrators led our actors along the dark streets, the demonstration ending at the famous Goethe tavern. . . .

In Prague, those of us who left our own kin behind us in Moscow suddenly breathed freely. In the course of the preceding two months these members of our company had conscientiously carried out their duties, were pleased with the successes, surrendered to impressions of novelty; but it was as if some spiritual valve were tightly shut within them. The feeling that they were not at home had never left them. And this feeling had hindered our labours and, as it were, rendered arid the joys of success and of impressions. But in Prague there appeared the illusion of our native land. . . .

The Czech national theatre is called *Narodny divadlo*. This is a big, sumptuous structure, with a large stage—a theatre proud of the fact that it had been built on funds contributed by the people, who made sacrifices. With pride they emphasized the fact that Franz Josef had contributed to the capital a 'mere' 25,000 kroner (10,000 rubles).

In the oppressed condition in which the Austro-Hungarian Czechs found themselves, the theatre concentrated in itself almost their whole national life. It was perhaps the only institution in which the national tongue was freely spoken. Here, as in a club, all the national forces became united.

The theatre was managed by a Committee. The administrators at the time were the director Schmorantz and the dramatist of the theatre, Kvapil. His wife enjoyed the rôle of the leading actress, by right of her real gifts. The prices of admission were low, and the Committee was hostile to any proposal for raising them.

Our preliminary conversation a month before brought us to no conclusion. There was not the least possibility of transporting our company to a place where full houses could never bring us even a half of our expenses. And the Committee refused to authorize the raising of prices.

While still in Berlin I received a wire from Schmorantz, requesting a reservation of three places for one of our last performances there. He arrived with Kvapil and his wife that they might see our performances. We played 'The Three Sisters'. Even before the conclusion of the performance the telephone with Prague became busy, and finally the question was settled: the raising of prices was authorized.

Speaking for ourselves, we had a strong desire to make this journey; a political aftertaste got mixed in with the performances; it was sweet, the feeling that we might safely taunt some one guilty of injustice.

An effective reception was arranged for the Art Theatre. If some snapshots had not been preserved, it would be difficult to believe it. A crowd of several thousand gathered in the street and at the station, greeting us with flowers, outcries, and the waving of handkerchiefs. We arrived at eleven o'clock in the morning. At one o'clock the chief personages of the company received visits, while at five every one was invited to a rout. Here were gathered the representatives of Czech society: sumptuous toilets, flowers, generous and sincere cordiality—and a Russian samovar! Artem, yearning incredibly for Moscow, stood silently eyeing this samovar, first one minute, then another, and, never removing his gaze, wept silently.

The Czechs cherish their old historic monuments, and made intent efforts to acquaint us with them. For this purpose the members of the company were divided into several groups, and each group was provided with a young scholar or professor.

Stanislavsky and I were entrusted to the care of Professor Ierzhabek. Thirty-six years old, he impressed us with his deep eyes, pensive air, and almost emotional devotion to science and his native land. Two days were devoted to an examination of the city and an acquaintance with its history; afterwards we spent some hours each morning in sight-seeing. Ierzhabek infected us with affection towards everything he showed us; he drew our attention to every detail. For half an hour he would hold us before some example of 'genuine Baroque', would tell us a detailed history of every street, every palace, every monument; he would conduct us within the most ancient, tiny, doll-like, four-story houses, and with tremors in his voice would tell us of the prison

holes into which they used to throw living human beings.
. . . And we would grow sad from his agitated voice, from
his unconcealed feeling of being a son of a subjugated
country.

Besides the *Narodny divadlo*, Prague had a German theatre,
subsidized by the Austrian Government. As if with the intention of creating opposition to the performances of the Art
Theatre, or perhaps in order to divert German playgoers,
this theatre presented, parallel to our own performances, a
series of plays by Kainz, the idol of the Austrian Germans. In
any case, it did not look as though any places would be left
for Germans at our performances. We gave in all five performances, and not only all the seats but all the aisles were
filled.

It was possible, however, to make some sort of calculation
as to the number of Germans present. Our Berlin *Text-
bücher* were translated and published in the Czech tongue;
the box office sold both versions. From the final figures of
Czech and German copies sold, it was evident that the ratio
was 95 to 5.

On the second evening after our arrival a gala performance was arranged at the *Narodny divadlo*, 'in honour of the
arrived Slavonic guests'.

The national opera, Smetana's 'Prodana Nevesta' ('The
Bartered Bride') was given; the best members of the opera
and ballet participated. It was an excellent production,
which impressed one as much by its gifted execution as by
its beautiful aspiration to please the Slavonic brothers. And
on the stage, by day, every one exerted himself to help in our
technical labours.

The final scene of 'Tsar Fyodor' (the requiem for Ivan the

Terrible, at the Archangel Cathedral) was never executed by us with such fervour as at Prague, because the choir, taking advantage of the absence of censorship, sang what it should at the requiem, and not a strange imitation. A passionate lover of sacred chants, Moskvin energetically worked over them, while the singers executed their parts with touching devotion.

Only on the third day after our arrival did we begin our performances, which had a colossal success.

How often during these days did we think of the sad dependence of art on economics! At the sight of the inspired faces of these auditors, the overwhelming majority of whom were in straitened circumstances, there arose the desire to perform especially for them. This was no accidental audience, no mere gathering of two thousand persons moved this day by a common desire to see a theatrical performance, and, above all, a foreign performance. These two thousand persons were united by one deep, repressed dream of freedom—freedom which could be attained only at the price of a cruel war. It was these thousands who were seeing the performance, sent hither from 'Mother Russia'.

The Art Theatre, of course, did not have a clearly defined political aspect; and how could it be otherwise? To-day in Prague, we were playing before the Czechs; a few days hence, in Vienna, before their conquerors. But the tendencies of the Theatre were very evident; apart from that, revolt against the oppressors always met with tremendous sympathy in the soul of the Russian actor.

Kramarzh, the representative of the national unification of the Czechs, had a definite halo in our eyes. He, it goes without saying, came to us; he made a special journey from

Vienna. On the very eve of his arrival, Director Schmorantz
was conjecturing—he would come, he would not come, he
must come—and on that same evening he entered the study
reserved for me, fervent with triumph: he had come! During an interlude he visited the actors on the stage and saw
Stanislavsky; he was friendly and smiling.

He was with his wife. I had met him a long time before in
Moscow, in her salon, when she was still Abrikosova. She
was born a Khludov—the Khludovs were multimillionaires
—and had married the manufacturer Abrikosov. Both she
and her husband belonged to that part of the Moscow merchant class who were drawn to the sciences, the arts, politics,
had studied abroad in London, and spoke French and English. Of the wild sprees of their fathers and grandfathers,
with their breaking of mirrors in restaurants, there remained
not a trace.

Abrikosov, a confection manufacturer, was engaged in the
publication of a periodical of philosophy and psychology,
while his beautiful wife had her salon. Here it was possible
to meet chosen writers, artists, scholars. In her dimly lighted
drawing-room was heard the laughter of Vladimir Solov-
yov, then the idol of philosophical circles—laughter truly
remarkable for its crystal-like quality; it was as if there
sounded in it his clear, pure world-contemplation. In a
corner of the divan it was possible to see this spirited handsome fellow with long hair and long beard—how many
Russian actors had made use of his photograph when they
had a part to play of a charming scholar!

It happened one day that there appeared in this salon
Kramarzh, the brilliant young politician from Prague. The
visiting orator, energetic, conscious of his success, spoke on

the theme of which was better: to have many tiny bells ringing, or to fuse all these tiny bells into one mighty bell?

My memory has never retained the details of the romantic stories over which so much ado was made in Moscow. Hence I cannot gratify the curiosity of my women readers with the tale of how this brother-Slav enticed away the handsome mistress of the Moscow salon, of how she married him and exchanged Moscow for 'Golden Prague'. In any case, I think, they passed the summer on her estate in Crimea.

A triumphal reception was arranged for the company in the Town Hall, a banquet in the club 'Slava', and a brilliant supper at the house of the Chairman of the Committee of the Theatre, Shimaczek.

Spring was in full bloom; it was hot. By day our energies were expended in seeing the city and studying its history, interest in both of which was maintained by the professors; in the evening there was the performance. At the same time, before us lay the prospect of a conquest of Vienna.

In the foyer of the theatre in Moscow hangs a gift brought from here, a picture, 'Zlata Praga' (Golden Prague), a view of old Prague. There also are to be found souvenir gifts from individuals, among them one from the mayor of the city. Modest, somewhat sentimental in their friendliness, our admirers timorously brought us each what he could: a picture of one's own painting, a chain made from a whole stick, and other things.

We left Prague at nine in the morning. The crowd at the station was so large that many of us could scarcely make our way to our carriages just before the departure of the train. It was at the station that Ierzhabek said: 'Do make some arrangement to preserve the costumes and ornaments of your

[306]

different nationalities. Ten or fifteen years will pass, and you'll no longer find them anywhere, and they will perish for history!'

Dear Ierzhabek! Dear Prague!

The Vienna we visited was the older city of which contemporary tourists have not the slightest idea: Vienna the smartly dressed, the elegant, the gay; with the then-reigning Viennese operetta everywhere squeezing out the French; with 'The Merry Widow' of Lehar, 'The Swing', sung the whole world over; Vienna of the unforgettable Strauss waltzes, of the actors Zonnenthal and Kainz, of the remarkable edifice of the Royal Theatre, of the splendid Vienna equipages; Vienna the capital of the 'crazy-quilt' kingdom, of gay political scandals, of beautiful women with the sparkling eyes of men upon them; Vienna, disputing the right of Berlin to grant the diploma of world celebrity.

Rumours of the Art Theatre's success had of course already reached the city, but the newspapers met us with extreme caution; each line proclaimed that Berlin tastes were not at all acceptable to them.

It was essential for us to conquer Vienna; our European success must be unanimous. Only then could we return victors to Moscow and recoup our losses at home, even though we should have to recoup them on that same 'Tsar Fyodor', which had long since ceased to attract audiences at home.

Well, shall I tell you now? In the following season in Moscow 'Tsar Fyodor' made the permanent billboards. Astonishing, isn't it? What a flock of sheep, after all, is the theatrical public!

From Berlin we brought only three plays: 'Fyodor', 'The Lower Depths', and 'Uncle Vanya'. The rest of our properties we sent to Russia. We had seven wagons and a hundred men; as there was little time to collect local helpers in new cities and have them rehearse with us, we had brought along some Berliners; the transportation was always by express train. On the advice of Stein we sold all the performances in Vienna to a Viennese manager; this guaranteed us against loss.

We played in the new Bürger Theater. We should have been happy to have got the Bürger Theater; with envy we examined its remarkably arranged stage, with its wealth of technical devices, of which, it appeared, the managers made little use. But to secure this theatre seemed at first not even remotely possible. The Volks-Theater would have pleased us even more. Here we were received with a cool affability, and were informed of the constitution of the theatre, according to which 'no other tongue except the German may sound on this stage'. Let us remember this.

We were offered an old popular theatre, in which operettas were given, but it proved unbearably inconvenient for us. The Bürger Theater, on the other hand, was quite new, and only recently erected.

The first performance was spoiled by an unexpected circumstance. The police discovered that our decorations were not impregnated with a fireproof fluid. Hitherto we had not been warned anywhere of a similar demand. But there had been a tremendous fire in Vienna ten years before, which had had many victims; hence the police maintained a rigorous watchfulness in this regard.

The alternatives were either to cancel the performance, or

permit the police commission to impregnate the decorations during the performance. We agreed to the latter, and the especially engaged manager assured us that everything would pass easily and smoothly. But immediately we had to pay for having sold our independence; we should of course have cancelled the performance and not believed the manager. There were long fatiguing interludes and, quite apart from that, there was such a strong odour of ammonia on the stage that many of the actors developed headaches.

And the theatre was far from full. All this had the result that the first scenes, while meeting with a good reception, did not by any means arouse the same fervour as in Berlin, Dresden, Leipzig, and Prague, where the tremendous success became patent at once. But as the action of the tragedy developed, the auditorium became increasingly stirred. Success grew with every succeeding scene, the militant mood of the actors became intensified, and the performance ended in a triumph, in the full sense of the word.

From an article by the chief critic, Ludwig Bauer:

. . . Toward loud, big words one is apt to be sceptical, but what of big, loud deeds? . . . (Therefore, we venture to proclaim: this evening should create an epoch in the history of our theatre! Since yesterday we have the clear, firm knowledge: the illusion of fervent dreams has become realized; perfection on the stage has been actually realized! . . . the indelible impression left by this clear, sparkling evening, that feeling of ruthlessness toward all mediocrity, which it has awakened in us. This means that it is *possible* to attain everything; it follows that it is *essential* to attain it. For in art that which is not *everything*, not perfection, is trifling! . . . It is possible that everything which we saw last evening is merely the result of hard work and taste. Be that as it may; all the same there is genius in this; there is genius in being able to labour thus and to possess such taste.

Neue Freie Presse:

... The play of this ensemble reminds one of the play of a brilliantly rehearsed and conducted orchestra: not for an instant do we pause to consider who plays on each separate instrument; we absorb into ourselves the harmony of the whole, we are captivated in listening, and we forget the existence of each separate performer. This is another tremendous step forward in the art of the theatrical ensemble. No other company has so closely attained this end as the Moscow company. Hence, in speaking of them, it is possible to speak of the new art of the theatre, of new summits. It is possible to speak of the *perfection* of the Muscovites. By what paths was this perfection achieved? That is the secret of the Russians, which interests us so much. ... The chief secret is the disinterested, self-abnegating love they feel toward art, which is what makes the artist.

Wiener Allgemeine Zeitung:

... The Western-European actor always argues: 'I can play the rôle *thus* or *differently*, or even *in another way*.' He then tries the whole three ways and compares them: this is good, this is better, this is still better, and naturally he chooses the one which is 'still better'. The Russian approaches his rôle in quite another fashion: he puts the problem to himself: *How should I* play this rôle? And then he begins to seek, to try, to learn, to examine, in order that in the end, with the true instinct of a human being, seeking the nearest, most natural, most simple way, the only way, he may come to the conclusion: I will play the rôle *thus*, because thus only *should I* play it. ... When Kainz holds us, when Novelli captivates us, when Zacconi astounds us, when even Duse herself, with the depth of grief or the conquering softness of her art, subjugates us, then we always feel: 'They might have approached our soul by different paths and equally conquered it; we should have followed them even if they had not brought us *these same* gifts of their soul. But the play of the Muscovites could never give birth to such thoughts. Here reigns the unshakable conviction: *Thus must it be, because thus men are, thus life is.*

Of Moskvin:

Better forget the names of fifty celebrities; but remember the name of Moskvin.

The criticisms in the Press did their work, and the performances in Vienna were attended by splendid audiences. But our triumph came after the third performance, when the administration of the Volks-Theater, which had earlier refused us their building, proposed that we give several extra performances. Unfortunately, it was too late, as we had already made arrangements for extra performances with our manager.

As in Berlin, so in Vienna, the local dramatic artists proved to be the most grateful auditors. As there Barnai, so here Kainz and Zonnenthal were regular visitors and fervent admirers of the Theatre. Kainz went so far as to cancel his own performances during the Art Theatre's stay in Vienna, in order not to miss a single one of ours.

Either because Vienna was more scattered than Berlin, or because we had more time in Berlin, our Viennese literary and theatrical recollections are poorer than those of Berlin. They are limited to Viennese dramatic artists and Russian correspondents. In general, our productions bore the usual character of those to which celebrated European names are attached. A fact perhaps contributing to this was that in the Art Theatre there was a total absence of self-advertisement, which helps artists to create a clamour around their names.

[311]

At this time reports came from Russia of the first State Duma, and avidly we snatched at this and discussed the precious news.

To conclude about Vienna, I am going to relate a characteristic incident from our life behind the scenes.

As you know, during the tour the company was broken up into groups, and to each was attached a guide, 'Makar'. We always sent on a man ahead to procure living-quarters for the members of the company. He used to meet the company at the station of every new city and gave each member the address of his or her room, if only a temporary one.

We had with us two very talented girl pupils. They now have considerable fame in their chosen art. One of these, Koreneva, you know from a whole series of rôles from Dostoievsky and Turgenev in the Moscow Art Theatre; the other, Koonen, has played the rôle of leading actress of Tairov's Kamerny Theatre, in 'Phèdre', 'Adrienne Lecouvreur', 'Giroflé-Girofla'. They were then mere beginners, seventeen-year-old young ladies, inseparable companions. Whether they were dissatisfied with the rooms to which they had been previously assigned, or simply became bold, on reaching Vienna they decided to act independently: they abruptly refused the address given them, indeed all services, and even drove away the young actor attached to them. As they explained later, they were tired of his tutorial tone. They left their things at the station and went to seek quarters for themselves.

It was seven o'clock in the evening. Spring, blithe air, lovely weather, a new city, the Danube—no one to bother them, no one to instruct them. They look in upon one *pension*; it doesn't please them; another is too expensive; a third, the landlady is a hag. They decide to go to a café, gay, carefree.

The twilight passes into night, and after ten o'clock in the evening they are no longer admitted anywhere and are regarded suspiciously. When they call themselves actresses and, moreover, of some unheard-of Moscow Theatre, they are merely laughed at and are apparently taken for street-walkers. At this point they stumblingly assert that they do not even know the theatre in which we are going to play. And when they find the announcement on a column, it is already too late.

Even such a beginning to this misadventure finds them gay. Little by little, however, their courage fails them; they feel distressed, and cold, and hungry.

It ended in their spending the night now on the boule-vards, now at the railway station; it was not until morning that they found the Bürger Theater with some difficulty and appeared before us with tear-stained faces, like two lost children.

These silent tears passed into sobbing, when Stanislavsky insisted—and I supported him—that they immediately, accompanied by a responsible person, be returned to Russia, so we would not have to answer to their parents. And we recalled our decision only after they gave their word of honour that they would refrain in the future from such independent adventures, and our eldest actress, Rayevskaya, said she would vouch for them.

Our Vienna manager and agent exchanged glances and shrugged their shoulders. The young pretty actresses behind

[313]

the scenes! Instead of something piquant, they were talking of papas and mamas! . . .

We worked out this plan: Vienna, then a single performance in Düsseldorf *en route* to Paris, then Paris. The performances had been planned to take place in the Théâtre Sarah Bernhardt. The contract had been drawn up while we were still in Berlin, where an authorized representative of that theatre journeyed to see us for this purpose.

Lugné-Poë, the head of the theatrical firm 'L'Œuvre', and the permanent impresario of Eleonora Duse, had agreed to arrange the performances. Duse had visited the Art Theatre in Moscow, and while we were in Berlin, too, and she recommended Lugné-Poë to us.

While yet in Prague I began to receive disconcerting reports from Paris, and in Vienna I received a telegram from Lugné-Poë asking me to come immediately, as no preparations were being made in Paris and our tour might be compromised.

It took but little time after my arrival in Paris to learn that either we should play to empty houses or our success would cost us a pretty penny; in short, in one or the other instance we would risk losing even what we gained by the Berlin 'fairy tale'.

The President of the Comédie Française, Claretie, had already promised us co-operation in a letter to Berlin. He was not to be found in Paris; he had left for a long sojourn in the country.

Through some Moscow University friends I had some connection with Melchior de Vogue, scholar and author, who incidentally spoke Russian well. Sadly, but categorically, he informed me that without extensive advertising our

[314]

venture would come to nothing. 'And even with advertising it is a question whether you'll succeed in mobilizing *le gros du public*.'

The important theatrical journalist, Alexander Brisson, showed me a whole bundle of articles in prominent places, illustrated with photographs, prepared for the most widely circulated journal—I hardly know if I ought to name it. Brisson graphically illustrated how the editor of this journal laid the bundle on the palm of his right hand and—as it were, weighing it—considered how much should be paid for it.

As for the Germans and the Czechs, we prepared special libretti in French. They were very well executed by Professor Persky, of the Sorbonne. But the newspapers which he ventured to approach refused to publish any information about the Theatre unless they were paid. Lugné-Poë, it was evident, knew more than Persky of the ways of editors, and no sooner did he begin operations than all the newspapers published the first notices about the Theatre, consisting of a few lines, gratuitously. But when, several days later, he sent them a second notice containing new information about the success in Germany, only three newspapers published it. He sent out and personally distributed long, preliminary articles, but not one newspaper published them. He again tried some short items to the effect that the Theatre, in its triumphant tour, was approaching Paris, but everything found its way into the waste-basket.

Lugné-Poë and the management of the Théâtre Sarah Bernhardt recommended to me, first, without fail to arrange a patronage, and second, to entrust the so-called *publicité* to the experienced editor of the theatrical section of the

[315]

newspaper. I hardly know if I ought to name this, either; it was one of the most widely circulated newspapers.

Monsieur B: 'What does patronage mean? It means that the first performance must be dedicated to some charitable purpose under the protection of some generally esteemed lady of the higher circles.'

'The wife of our Ambassador Nelidov—is that sufficiently authoritative?'

'Yes, of course, fully.'

And she, and the Ambassador himself, always distinguished for his exquisite courtesy, met the representative of the Moscow Theatre in a friendly way, and promised co-operation. Madame Nelidova eagerly undertook the patronage, but for this, she said, more time was necessary than we supposed. Then began the conferences, lasting two days, with Monsieur B.

These conferences took place in the presence of the authorized representative of the Théâtre Sarah Bernhardt. I must confess that for a long time I could not reconcile myself to the tone in which the proposals were made. And the matter was really very simple: it was necessary to pay. According to the reckoning of Monsieur B., the advertising should cost, approximately, from 20,000 to 25,000 francs! More than 9,000 rubles, according to the exchange then. For the concentrating of the public's attention on the Moscow Art Theatre it was necessary to make daily use of three or four newspapers; as for the rest, it was advisable to insert an occasional short note. Monsieur B., with masterly detail, described how this should be done.

It was evident that I was beyond my depth, because all the suggestions aroused in me a scarcely concealed irritation.

'What do you expect?' asked Monsieur B., shrugging his shoulders and by no means offended at my tone. '*In no circumstances whatsoever* can you count on accomplishing anything without loss. Consider Duse. When she came to Paris the first time, she had to go through with this (I cannot remember the figure he named). On her second visit she played without loss. To make up for it, no matter how often she comes now, she always receives a huge profit.'

'But the Art Theatre, with its seven wagons and a company of a hundred, does not contemplate coming a second and a third time. And it would be quite satisfied if it covered its expenses!'

'It's impossible! In any case, I wouldn't count on it.'

A year later, back in Moscow, some one told me that in a certain cinema house a picture was being shown depicting the street life of Paris and that one picture exhibited me. I went to look at myself, and remembered that on leaving the Théâtre Sarah Bernhardt, after the conference with Monsieur B., I had remained standing a long time on the pavement, smoking a cigarette and surveying the seething movement of the Parisian street; I had thought to myself: 'Well, what's an Art Theatre to these? By what forces can I divert the attention of this human stream and direct it to a handful of actors newly arrived from Russia?' As it happened, at this very moment an omnibus was standing at no great distance from me, and I saw a host of passengers clambering into it rapidly. Then I thought: 'What grimacing bipeds these Frenchmen are! Here they are, clambering into that omnibus quite like a lot of poor supernumeraries.' Subsequently it proved that they actually were supernumeraries; and a film apparatus was revolving, and I was caught on it,

[317]

too, with a cigarette in my hand, sadly following the movement of the Parisian street.

After I had questioned every one whom I could find, I decided that I had no right to subject the Art Theatre to such a financial risk. On the following day I brought to the Théâtre Sarah Bernhardt a forfeit and tore up the contract. And so the tour to Paris did not take place.

It is worthy of note that twenty years later, when the Art Theatre gained world fame and, *en route* to America, gave some performances in Paris, the audiences far from covered expenses. There is no public in the world more chauvinistic than the Parisian one.

'Why have you brought us here?' we asked Stein in Karlsruhe.

'But, my friends, isn't it on the way? All companies stop here!'

He had a regular routine. And for all his enthusiasm for our art, he could not understand that it was not worth while for a single performance to erect our complex mechanism on the stage, and for a single performance to compel human beings to labour under high pressure. This Karlsruhe recalled only Bismarck. It was a dim spectacle, the theatre was far from full. We presented 'Uncle Vanya'. We received several excellent responses in the provincial papers. A part of the company, which had not participated in the production, was despatched direct to Frankfurt.

Since the Paris project had been abandoned, we decided to play in Warsaw on the return journey. Before reaching Warsaw, we gave two performances in Frankfurt, one in Wiesbaden, one in Düsseldorf, and two in Hannover. Warsaw alone presented some interest for us; there, it seemed to us, we had a special mission. But for our actors—especially those not too busily engaged—the visit to these astonishingly clean, well-ordered towns, with beautiful gardens, especially in the spring, helped to overcome a natural weariness.

The fame of the Theatre everywhere preceded the performances. The order of life entered a monotonous, somewhat tedious, but not particularly fatiguing rut. There was the arrangement of the performances according to a worked-out routine; the rapid repair of the decorations damaged *en route*; the distribution of the dressing-rooms; the short hour-and-a-half rehearsal; the theatrical press; the very friendly conduct towards the company of the local artists; and the bustle of transportation to another town, the renting of living-quarters by our advance man, etc. In those towns which had the larger Russian populations we had also the larger external success. Our stage-hands had already got used to arranging a performance in a single day. The costumiers and the make-up men had also learned to orientate themselves quickly in every new theatre. Our workers manifested an astonishing combination of intelligence, speed of action and self-possession. Our 'elder' Titov was showered everywhere with praise. On one occasion, at a railway junction, the wagon containing the properties was attached by mistake to a train going in the direction of Switzerland. On another, it proved impossible to load the scenery in time; but never was there the least confusion, and always an excellent way out was found!

At this time the future of the Art Theatre became clear, materially secure. Our imaginations already aspired to new labours in Moscow—to Griboyedov's 'Sorrow from Wit'

[319]

and Ibsen's 'Brand'. In Frankfurt, in Düsseldorf, in Hannover, we were already holding technical and administrative conferences.

It is not always easy to contend with that triviality which finds a nest in every theatre where commercial considerations have the first place. In this connection, there was the distressing episode in Düsseldorf.

This city has a municipal theatre, but our impresario, Stein, found it too small for our purpose and hired a private theatre—the Apollo. The name—what's in a name? What difference did it make if the company of the Art Theatre played in the Apollo Theatre? Stein argued so warmly that it was hard not to believe him. It was precisely in this theatre, he said, that Duse, Sarah Bernhardt, Kainz, and other famous artists always played.

We arrived at Düsseldorf in the morning. I walked up to the theatre; near the box-office were suspended red and yellow announcements of incredible size, with immense index-fingers pointing to extracts from various German newspapers. I felt disgusted. I went to examine the interior ; the parterre was crowded with tiny tables as in a vaudeville theatre; the stage smelt of wild beasts. It was explained to me that this was due to a sensational number in the programme in which elephants appeared. I called Stein and asked him if he realized the sort of place to which he had brought us. Stein continued to persuade us that all this was in order and that celebrities always played here. He gave his word of honour and swore by all that was holy. On the stage our hands were being ordered about by some sort of little stage-manager in a grey frock-coat and high hat, the most impossible sort of man for the tone of the Art Theatre.

[320]

Titov's eyes followed him with the greatest pity. Some one sat in the parterre, drinking beer and smoking a cigar. Members of our company began to gather here. One of our girl pupils turned to the little manager with a question. Quite likely, from the habit of dealing with his *café chantant* chorus girls, he answered her with a coarse, ribald jest. This was the last straw.

Inevitably, again and again, one was driven to fierce exasperation. Such an atmosphere of nervous, burning tension provides moments in which the most restrained person can lose his self-possession. I began by driving this little stage-manager from the stage; I announced, raising my voice to a high pitch, that the performance would not take place at all unless immediate energetic measures were taken to put the stage and the auditorium in proper order. I called the director of the theatre and Stein. I no longer requested, I gave sharp orders, furiously insisting on my rights.

I demanded that their stage-manager refrain from entering the theatre for a whole day; that not only the paraphernalia of the vaudeville programme be removed from behind the scenes, but that all the elephants be removed; that everywhere there should be placed the most rigorous guards to maintain order, on the stage as well as in the auditorium; that placards should be immediately ordered and displayed, informing the public that during the performance the drinking of beer and smoking would be absolutely forbidden, etc. etc.

Either my manner was impressive, or else—which is the more likely—influence was exercised by the fact that at Wiesbaden, just before our arrival in Düsseldorf, Emperor Wilhelm had conferred gifts and orders on us; but the Herr

Director and poor Stein, both pale, silently listened to all the demands, and in half an hour the inhabitants were able to enjoy the spectacle of a peaceful procession of elephants emerging from the 'Apollo Theatre'. I have no idea where they were secreted, but in the end the performance was given in such tremulous silence as we had never managed to obtain for 'Tsar Fyodor', even in better-arranged theatres.

The most brilliant spectacle between Vienna and Warsaw proved to be the performance at Wiesbaden, thanks to the presence of Wilhelm and the Empress. Wiesbaden, I think, is about thirty kilometres from Hamburg, and was the summer residence of the Kaiser. On learning that the Art Theatre on its return journey from Vienna intended playing at Wiesbaden, he informed us of his purpose to witness the performance. I do not know whether Stein had foreseen this, or whether he had counted on the opulent resort public; in any case, he put tremendous prices on the seats. We played to a full house. The public had to appear in evening dress; no male auditor was permitted to enter the parterre without a frock-coat.

The first interlude dragged for forty-five minutes. In reply to the questions of the stage-managers, the director of the Wiesbaden theatre said that the Emperor was holding a reception in the foyer and that it would be necessary to hold back the performance. At the conclusion of the performance, Wilhelm invited us to his box and conferred on Stanislavsky and myself the Order of the Red Eagle, and presented the chief artists with gifts.

'A souvenir—for your buttonhole!' he said, thrusting the order into my hand.

Subsequently the newspapers of Berlin reproached the

Emperor for not manifesting similar appreciation of *his own* artists. . . .

There has also remained in my memory the conclusion to this evening. Directly after the performance we had to transport ourselves to Frankfurt. It takes forty minutes from Wiesbaden to Frankfurt by direct train, but this train went shortly after eleven o'clock. When the Emperor prolonged the interlude, it became evident that we would never catch the direct train. It was necessary to take a later one by way of Mayence, where there was a stop of a full hour; the scenery of 'Tsar Fyodor' we had to send by horse transport. We turned to Stein: was it possible by telephone to order a supper for the company at Mayence? At the conclusion of the performance, the actors waited for the stage-hands to collect all the properties, and in one big crowd we trudged to the station. Here, occupying several carriages of the third class, the company sang in chorus and solos, and thus cheerfully reached Mayence. A modest supper for a hundred persons was awaiting them at the station in Mayence. Before every plate of soup was a tankard of beer. We reached Frankfurt at three in the morning and parted from one another with that light, joyous and comradely feeling which really only a friendly family, bound together by one purpose, can feel.

It was strange, of course, to consider Warsaw as a part of our tour abroad. For Warsaw was a city within the Russian Empire. On the other hand, it was impossible to dismiss the feeling that we were abroad; and the reputation we made in Berlin was greater than our reputation in Moscow. Be that as it may, when I was driving at seven o'clock along the street toward the theatre, I heard a discharge fifty or a hundred paces behind me. Judging from the picture which met my eyes, of people running in all directions, it was easy to guess that a bomb had been thrown. Aha! That meant we were at home!

The Warsaw performances had their mission. Poles never went to Russian plays, and we desired that they should come to those of the Art Theatre. We desired the reunion of irreconcilable nationalities under the standard of art.

The behaviour toward the Poles of those directing the Russian governmental theatres was, if I may say so, quite absurd. Controlling three immense companies of Polish artists, the Russian officials bore in their souls an implacable hostility towards them. They could neither deny the considerable talents among the Polish actors nor the high culture of their art, but some kind of cowardice prevented them from openly acknowledging this and from showing them deserved deference. For, surely, it was cowardice, or a fear of reproof from St. Petersburg. But how was it possible to be a good director if you did not love those whom you directed?

'No, you may rest assured, the Poles will not come to you. The scamps!' said the director.

After several performances it became evident that, relatively, a good many Poles visited the theatre.

'So some Poles have actually come to the theatre! What scamps!'

We realized that by announcements alone we should never attain 'unification under the flag of art', and we entered into conversation with the best Polish journalists. But all our arguments met with a rebuff.

[324]

'Perhaps logic's on your side—perhaps! But quite apart from logic, there's psychology—and that's, surely, on our side. You must know that the theatre is the only institution in which Polish speech flows freely. That is why we cling so tenaciously to this and fight against the Russian drama. And if we visit your performances, then the authorities will make use of this precedent gradually to squeeze out the Polish drama. No, don't say anything! A burned child dreads the fire. Our interest in your art will be turned into a weapon against us!'

The result was a situation similar to that of Prague, only reversed. We felt uneasy. 'Unification under the flag of art' —for realistic politicians it evidently seemed only a pretty phrase, perhaps even a dangerous one.

As a result we began our performances with such an original press as, it appeared to me, no other theatre in the world ever had. At the opening of our theatre, all the newspapers published articles of praise, acknowledging our tremendous services to art, but with the proposal—and, in some newspapers, with the *demand—not to visit our performances!* 'But we will accept this art with open arms when it shall come to us, free, from a free Russia.'

Nevertheless, about twenty per cent. of our audiences were Poles, while Polish artists visited our performances in great numbers; the unification with them was complete.

The Art Theatre returned to Moscow. Four months of fervour and intensified labour had been experienced since the company's departure. During this time, in the Berlin and Vienna newspapers, we had more than once met with the admission that the tour of the Art Theatre had won a great battle. This always happened when, speaking of Russian art, the newspapers recalled the recent failures of Russia. It was but the year before that Russia had engaged in the Japanese War. The great German public considered Russia, as it were, uncrowned. Our first meeting with the German workers in Bonn's theatre, when they openly laughed at us, was characteristic and seemed deserved. All the members of the company understood the responsibility of the tour: artistic failure could only have further lowered the wavering prestige of the Russians. Our Berlin and Vienna Embassies were positively ashamed of us. They acted as if they feared we would compromise the Russian representatives.

All the more proud were we in our feeling of triumph when we returned to our native country.

Artistic ambition is insatiable. It gives the appearance of having found full satisfaction in the labour itself; but actually it also seeks visible tokens of acknowledgment. On approaching Moscow, the company of the Theatre awaited some sort of particular, triumphant welcome. Something like the welcome it had met at Prague, perhaps. But, lo! At the station there were but a few close kinsmen of the artists. To be sure, a few stations before Moscow we were handed a telegram of greeting from the mayor of Moscow. But that was all.

Turgenev has a phrase: 'Traces of human life fade very quickly.'

PART V

THE TOLSTOYAN ELEMENTS IN THE ART THEATRE

CHAPTER NINETEEN

One day there walked into the office of the periodical, *Russkaya Misl* ('Russian Thought'), an old man attired in a sheepskin coat and fur cap. He brought a manuscript. The secretary took it from him; it was a story written by a peasant named Semenov. The secretary asked the old man to return for an answer in two weeks. Precisely in two weeks the old man returned. The secretary asked him to wait, indicating a wooden seat, and went into the editor's study. At this time a very animated conversation was going on in the study between two editors and the publisher. The occasion was a generously festive one; indeed, the company was indulging in red wine. The secretary announced that some one was waiting for an answer about the story by the peasant Semenov. The *belles-lettres* department was in charge of Remizov, a tall fair-haired man with a bifurcated beard, wearing spectacles.

'Yes, yes. I've read it. Let him wait. I'll see him presently.'

It was impossible, however, to interrupt the animated conversation, and much time went by, an hour and a half or so. Once more the secretary appeared on the threshold of the study.

'Mitrophan Nilovitch! The old man's still waiting out there.'

'Yes, yes. I'll see him immediately.'

[329]

Again, much time went by, and the secretary felt impelled to appear for the third time. Finally, Remizov sought out the manuscript and went to the waiting-room.'

'Where is the old fellow?'

The old man in the sheepskin coat rose from the wooden seat. Remizov went toward him.

'Was it you who brought the story by Semenov? I've read the story . . .'

Remizov raised his eyes to the old man. He did not finish his sentence, he grew mute: before him was Tolstoy himself! It was Leo Nikolaievitch Tolstoy who had been quietly sitting for over two hours, waiting for the editor to receive him. And he was very anxious to see the publication of the story written by an unknown peasant by the name of Semenov; he wanted to recommend the work, which he considered gifted and deserving of attention.

The position of the editor was desperate. And it was rather awkward to conduct the old man into his study promptly, because the bottles had not yet been removed.

'Don't give it a thought. It's nothing. I was resting here,' said Tolstoy, evidently having sincere pity for the distraught respectable *littérateur*; perhaps even blaming himself for unintentionally forcing a human being into a state of consternation.

I cannot remember precisely why for a long time I did not seek a personal acquaintance with Tolstoy. It was possibly because he was always surrounded by many persons; it seemed to me that he would not necessarily be in an amiable mood to meet any stranger who introduced himself and wanted to talk with him.

Actually, Chekhov himself behaved in the same way with

respect to Tolstoy. When one day I asked him why he did not seek an acquaintance with Tolstoy, all the more as the latter had highly praised him as a writer, Anton Pavlovitch replied: 'I don't want to be introduced through S.'

This S. had been a schoolfellow of Chekhov's in the Taganrog *gymnasium* and was intimate with the whole Tolstoy household. Notwithstanding the fact that he generally conducted himself very correctly, he conveyed the impression that he capitalized this intimacy, used it to bolster up his own self-esteem, not of course with any object of material profit, but only with the idea of increasing his prestige. And S. behaved as a priest of Tolstoyan ideas: his tone was a didactic-humble-sermonizing one, he spoke in a low voice, and he tried to look at you with a deep intentness. And the morality which he made some effort to cultivate was suspiciously altruistic, flavoured with pharisaic wisdom.

For example, when I once told him the episode of my train journey in the Ekaterinoslav province, when bandits tried to rob me (I have told of this episode in the chapter on Gorky), S. began to reproach me. He said that if the bandits wanted to get at me in my train compartment I should have opened the door to them and given them everything they demanded of me, instead of locking myself in and waiting for them to be caught in the corridor. It can be understood why Chekhov did not want to be introduced to Tolstoy through this schoolfellow of his.

I was taken to see Tolstoy by the young professor of philosophy, Grot, who was also intimate with the household. This was in Moscow, some years before the founding of the Art Theatre, in the evening. There was a reading going on in the reception-room, and the whole family was there. Sofya Andreievna was engaged in some handiwork. Here also sat Tatyana, the daughter of Leo Nikolaievitch; his favourite daughter, Alexandra Lvovna, was also present, I think. Herzen's *My Past and Thoughts* was being read by Marya Lvovna.

Leo Nikolaievitch interrupted the reading, and took me to his downstairs study, where we remained for half an hour. Then we went upstairs again. He asked me to read, and I eagerly accepted the invitation. As every approval on the part of the great remains in the memory, so I well remember how pleased he was with my reading. This impression was confirmed several months afterward. He had just finished writing *Hajji Murad*, and for some concert or other he was asked permission to have a chapter read from this new work. Sofya Andreievna herself came to me with the announcement that Leo Nikolaievitch granted permission provided I did the reading.

Very little remains in my memory of this first meeting. Well, of course, there were his famous eagle eyes, almost rapacious in their searching gaze—his most astonishing feature. They were eyes which instilled into you the thought that no matter how much of a virtuoso you might be in the art of lying, you would still fail to deceive their owner. They penetrated into the very depth of the soul. At the same time in their very fixity and sharpness there was a spontaneity which nothing held in check. This was not the sharpsightedness of shrewd calculation; on the contrary, it was, in the best sense of the word, the artlessness of a being who had nothing to hide and who was always ready with the most spontaneous receptiveness.

I should be in danger of fabrication if I tried to tell what I experienced when at last I saw before me features made familiar to me by numerous portraits. My memory retains but two moments from our conversation. The first was when I asked him if I might smoke. He appeared astonished and asked: 'Have you read my pamphlet on the harm of tobacco?' I confessed that I hadn't. He became very expansive on the matter, and was even perturbed. He made me promise that I would without fail read the pamphlet.

The other moment occurred during our conversation on Ibsen. Tolstoy did not at all consider him a remarkable writer. At that time I was very much interested in Ibsen, and I proceeded to defend him. Finally, I said that I would bring Tolstoy a copy of 'An Enemy of the People', which he had not read.

Later I brought him the Ibsen play, and after a lapse of time Tolstoy came to me. What a joyful surprise! He returned 'An Enemy of the People' and said that he didn't like it. 'This Doctor Stockman is by far too conceited.' Stubbornly he again asked me if I had stopped smoking. I said that I had read his pamphlet, but was continuing to smoke as before.

Tolstoy asked a good many questions about writers with whom I was more or less on intimate terms. He greatly praised Chekhov.

Tolstoy's influence on the writers of my generation was tremendous. Perhaps Chekhov alone did not yield to this influence, because he himself was a brilliant, original figure. It goes without saying that every new work of Tolstoy was pounced upon by us with such avidity as no other writer in the world aroused in us. It was Tolstoy the artist who conquered us. Toward Tolstoy the preacher we behaved with coolness; but the artist staggered us. His astonishing *simplicity* was a lure to imitation. However fine Turgenev was, he nevertheless, from our point of view, added touches of adornment in colour and line. However profound and trenchant Gogol was, we nevertheless found him to be an astounding 'author'. Dostoievsky, too, is staggeringly simple, but the baring of the nerves and the wrought-up images tended toward melodrama and theatricality. It was necessary to possess a mighty temperament, an immense heart, in order to dominate such a severe form as Dostoievsky's.

For us Tolstoy was simple, profoundly realistic, an extraordinary master of character, and so near to us that it seemed as if with a slight exertion on our part we ourselves could become Tolstoys. At every step, in reading his work, the thought flashed: Ah, how extraordinary, and yet how simple! Precisely as I myself have thought! Yet actually nothing of this had come into my head, neither these images, nor these situations, nor these definite colours, nor these clear, simple words! . . .

It is impossible to forget the stupefying impression created upon us by the tiny book, the popular edition of 'The Power of Darkness'. Without exaggeration it is possible to say that I trembled with artistic ecstasy from the astonishing delineation of images and the richness of the language. Or take the stories, *Master and Man, How Men Live*; or consider the terrific impression made upon us by *The Kreutzer Sonata*, etc., *ad infinitum*.

Leo Nikolaievitch came to see a performance of 'Uncle Vanya'. He stubbornly refused to acknowledge Chekhov as a dramatist; his biography and diaries are full of negative responses on this score. Here he noted down that 'it is impossible to understand anything of this'; there he called the play simply 'nonsense'; elsewhere he reproached the author for an unnecessary tendency to autobiography in 'The Sea Gull'. During the performance of 'Uncle Vanya' we furtively kept our eyes on him. It seemed to us that the performance drew him into its atmosphere, that his attention was held, that in spots he was moved. But either we were mistaken, or else he banished his own simple, spontaneous receptivity, because during the intermissions, as I remember, he did not praise anything. It is true, he did not censure anything; it was as if he was waiting to see how it would end. At the conclusion of the performance he said:

'What else does he want—Astrov? It is warm, the guitar is playing, the cricket sings beautifully. And at the beginning he wanted to take some one else's wife, now he's dreaming about something . . .' And disapprovingly he shook his head.

I have already said that his comedy, 'The Fruits of Enlightenment', had been played in Moscow by the Circle of Alekseiev-Stanislavsky. The reader, of course, knows that the play was written by Tolstoy for performance at home. Many young people visited Tolstoy's estate in Yasnaya Polyana, and Leo Nikolaievitch wrote the play for them. The rehearsals, it seems to me, were the most interesting part of the performance. Every one was infected with gaiety, with a desire to show off his talents. It was during the Christmas holidays. Tolstoy kept pages of the play he had begun. Its theme was how the servants in the kitchen talked about their masters. The rehearsals went on not only at Yasnaya Polyana, but also in Tula, the capital of the province, at the house of a Moscow member of the Court of Justice, Davidov, a friend of Leo Nikolaievitch, the same Davidov who gave him subjects out of his legal practice both for 'The Power of Darkness' and *The Living Corpse*.

While the rehearsals were going on, Tolstoy was all the while engaged in rewriting the play, and would have continued had not Davidov dissuaded him.

Tatyana Lvovna played the part of Tanya.

Later the performance was repeated in Tula, in the big reception-room of the Hall of Nobles, with several changes of rôles. Thus, Tatyana Lvovna this time played the part of Betsy. With my friend Yuzhin-Sumbatov, I made the journey to see this performance at Tula. The amateurs played superbly; the impression was one of animated brilliance. The entire family of Leo Nikolaievitch was present; he alone was absent. It was only then that I made the acquaintance of Sofya Andreievna. She said that Leo Nikolaievitch had escorted them to Tula, and from there had gone back to his estate on foot, a matter of approximately fifteen kilometres.

Afterwards Alekseiev-Stanislavsky gave a performance of the play in his Circle in Moscow, the rôle of Betsy being played by the subsequently famous Vera Komisarjevskaya.

Several times we were prepared to produce this play in the Art Theatre. Each time, for various reasons, we gave up the idea. This fact is all the more remarkable because no theatre in the world had such a superb company of actors for the performance of the play. It might have been one of the Art Theatre's best productions. Some purely technical reasons, or reasons of a petty nature, robbed the Art Theatre of this pleasure.

'The Power of Darkness', however, was staged in the Art Theatre. This play served to open our new theatre, i.e. our new building. Something did not go quite right with this performance. Except for the remarkable Anisya (Butova), not a single character has remained in my memory. The staging was ultra-realistic. Stanislavsky, who produced it, was still in the power of objects, pauses, sounds. A journey was made to a Tula village, where the realities were studied and songs copied; from there a native woman, a peasant, was brought to act in the rôle of consultant during the production. Our actors, however, did not know how to act peasant rôles, and they missed something essential in the dramatic nerve of this play.

Subsequently, when I met Tolstoy, he said that he had been told of this production and that he was very much dissatisfied because of various natural sounds reproduced on the stage. With all the amiability and humility I could muster I had to explain to him that he himself had such directions in his play as 'The neighing of a horse becomes audible', and 'The closing of the gate is heard', etc.

CHAPTER TWENTY

We heard reports that Tolstoy was writing a new play. Quite naturally, we wanted to get hold of it before it was published and accessible to all the theatres. I telegraphed to Yasnaya Polyana, asking permission to pay a visit; Sofya Andreievna promptly replied, naming a day.

In order to avoid staying overnight—which in fact was suggested to me in the telegram—I left on an early morning train. When I arrived from the station in some sort of two-wheeled cart at Yasnaya Polyana, it must have been between ten and eleven in the morning. I was told that Leo Nikolaie-vitch was at work, and of course when he was working he was not even informed of the arrival of a visitor. I was conducted to his library, a smallish room on the ground floor. It contained a divan, a table in the middle, shelves with books, etc. The furniture was of the simplest,—of ash, if I remember correctly.

On the table was the latest issue of *Russkaya Misl* ('Russian Thought'). The periodical was open at the pages containing my article on Ibsen's play, 'When We Dead Awaken', which I was on the eve of producing in the Art Theatre, and preliminary to which I had written this interpretive essay.

As I left Moscow very early, it was suggested to me that I might rest, and I lay down on the divan. Scarcely twenty minutes passed, when I noticed a figure pass by the window. It peered into the room, then vanished; it was Leo Nikolaievitch himself. Later I learned that he had left on horseback. When he returned, we met.

I spent the entire day with him. The play, it appeared, had been merely sketched in. Moreover, he tried to discourage me by saying the play would need a revolving stage, as it contained a whole series of brief scenes; I told him that we would have such a stage. Then we again discussed Ibsen, and again he abused him; he said he had read 'When We Dead Awaken', and he didn't like it. 'If it were really such a play as you describe, and had the contents you attribute to it in your article, it would then be a very good play.'

Of course, Leo Nikolaievitch ate no meat at dinner. After dinner, we played chess. We played two games; I lost both. He played with remarkable spontaneity.

He was greatly perturbed when I told him that before the season opened there was a *Te Deum* service in our theatre, and that even the ikon of the Iberian Virgin was brought to it. Yes, he was greatly perturbed. 'Why do you find it necessary?' I justified our young theatre by saying that the theatre workers, the various merchants who were relatives of Alekseiev, and the owner of the theatre, the merchant Stchukin, wanted it. We went on playing chess. Then he once more interrupted the game and persisted: 'No, I can't understand it. Why did you have to bring the ikon and have a *Te Deum* service? A young theatre! I simply don't understand it!'

During this visit I received an unhappy impression from Sofya Andreievna. While we were playing chess, she sat near-by in the room doing some handiwork. As our play was constantly interrupted by snatches of conversation, Sofya Andreievna joined in the talk.

[339]

Leo Nikolaievitch happened to be saying that he had had a visit from the woman editor of a children's periodical who asked for an article; and he added, with evident incautiousness: 'I promised.' Sofya Andreievna laid her work on her knees, flashed her eyes on Leo Nikolaievitch, and sharply asked: 'What! You promised an article to that monkey-face?'[1] I particularly well remember this precise expression and the sharp, one might almost say petty-bourgeois, tone she assumed.

Leo Nikolaievitch growled: 'Yes, I promised.' Sofya Andreievna shrugged her shoulders and rapidly, hysterically, resumed her work. Then she said: 'I don't understand it at all. That false specimen, that hypocrite! And you are going to give her an article!'

I was dumbfounded. How dare any one, how dare a woman, even though she happen to be the wife, the most intimate companion, of this great man, how dare she maintain towards him this vulgar commanding tone?

We, writers of that epoch, were generally speaking inclined to misogyny. We were moved to vexation by those intelligent women of our circle who attempted to play in our lives a greater rôle than our love of freedom would allow. There were many such women who tried to seize the summits of those interests to which their husbands devoted themselves, and who considered it their right not only to meddle in all the reciprocal relations of their husbands, but even to dictate their conduct.

It would be impossible to say that our relation to such women passed into a definite hatred of women, made suffi-

[1] An actual translation of this word is impossible. 'Monkey-face' is only approximate.—*Translator*.

ciently modish at the time by the skilful pen of the Swedish writer Strindberg. None the less, all of us, at one time or another, in the various characters of our literary productions, took turns at poking fun at this type of woman. Chekhov, too, once had a monologue in his 'The Three Sisters' which attempted to define a wife. At first the monologue was a long one; but later, apparently concluding that the theme had already been sufficiently worked out in literature, he cut the monologue down to a single phrase: 'A wife is a wife.' What was one to think of this, that near the greatest man of that epoch there should have been such a 'wife', a new image of Xantippe?

Stories and discussions concerning the intimate relations of Sofya Andreievna and Leo Nikolaievitch, which were so profoundly dramatic, infinitely more complex than one could gather at the first glance, relations eventually leading to a tragic finale—these tales engaged the attention of the whole of Russian cultured society of the time. Numerous persons tried to penetrate them, to examine the details and arrive at some solution. It was difficult, however, to arrive at any conclusion. There were the children here; and the necessity of the wife to look after everything in the house; and there was the jealousy of Leo Nikolaeivitch, which became inflamed even after he was no longer young—evidently there was a fastidious regard for trivialities, accepted as jealousy; and there were the diverse characters of the children, some more devoted to the father, others more devoted to the mother; and there was the announcement by Leo Nikolaievitch granting the free publication rights of his works to all—limited, to be sure, at the insistence of Sofya Andreievna, to works published before 1885; and the most essential, the most tremendous, the most agonizing thing for Leo Nikolaievitch was the discord between his entire surroundings and his own teachings. In his Diary he expresses distress at the manner in which they 'devour' pancakes in his house during Shrovetide, at the way the servants run about, slavishly serving their masters. His whole being longs to simplify his life, to make it like a peasant's, while his wife and the whole family are leading the most ordinary, the most trivial bourgeois existence.

In his *Diary for Myself Alone*, Tolstoy, not very long before his flight from home, has this entry:

'20th of Aug. I have just thought, in recalling my marriage, that this was something fated. I have never even been in love. But I couldn't help marrying.'

To analyse all this from the outside was, of course, much easier. The great majority of people attacked Sofya Andreievna. Americans are well acquainted with this from the book of recollections by Tolstoy's favourite daughter, Alexandra Lvovna. Yet she also had her defenders. Later there appeared amongst them such a man as Gorky. With a wisdom scarcely less profound than that of Tolstoy, Maxim Gorky invited human beings to consider the incredible difficulties which fell to the lot of Sofya Andreievna, both as the mistress of the house who had to think of its physical welfare and as the wife who, more than anyone else, had to endure all her husband's extravagant demands from human beings and from life.

CHAPTER TWENTY-ONE

About the time I visited Tolstoy in Yasnaya Polyana, he had lost all interest in going on with his new play; after his death a few lines were found in his Diary to that effect. That is why he showed little eagerness in speaking to me about the play. I had not insisted, of course, had not urged him to finish it, as I had done in the case of every other author, even Chekhov.

This play, indeed, we received much later, after the death of Leo Nikolaievitch. This is how it happened. As you know, Leo Nikolaievitch had willed the disposition of his materials to his daughter, Alexandra Lvovna. I made haste to turn to her, fearing that the theatrical snatchers would seize this play and publish it in great haste, in order to diminish interest in it. Alexandra Lvovna told me that Chertkov, Leo Nikolaievitch's devoted friend and disciple, was now engaged on all the manuscripts. He was a remarkable man: an officer of the Guards, handsome, an aristocrat, who, attracted to Tolstoy's teachings, abandoned everything, became intimate with Leo Nikolaievitch, and arranged his life in complete dependence on this intimacy. In consequence of this relationship, he became for Sofya Andreievna, from her point of view, her worst enemy; it goes without saying that in all her differences with Leo Nikolaievitch, Chertkov always sided with his great teacher.

I shall digress here to say that even after Tolstoy's death

[343]

Chertkov dedicated his whole activity, all his labours, and all his time to matters connected with the manuscripts of Leo Nikolaievitch and their publication, and with the Tolstoy Museum, etc.

Chertkov lived in Tolstoyan fashion. On arriving at his house in the village of Telyatinki to see him about the play, I had to enter a circle of life quite new to me, who was used to a bourgeois existence. I had to dine and sup at a large table, without tablecloth; every one served himself, and all sat together—the masters, the servants, and the visitors. As a mark of especial amiability, they all helped me to a plate of thin barley gruel, some peas and some sort of vegetables and fruit. Of course it was a strictly vegetarian table.

Notwithstanding the alien environment, it was filled with friendliness. Wholly banished was that feeling of unease before attendants and working-men, a feeling which the writers of my generation could not altogether dismiss; we were inoculated with it from youth, by our acquaintance with the better writers and sociological books; this feeling was enhanced by the teaching of Tolstoy, no matter what restraint we exercised toward it. Yet this feeling, which once oppressed and embarrassed us, was completely transformed here, perhaps changing into some sort of humility before the very same people.

Everything in this house was extraordinarily simple. The only conspicuous thing was the absence of Chertkov's wife, which was explained by the fact that she was ill. Of course, Alexandra Lvovna, with generous healthy features, unusually reminiscent of her father, was present here on an equality with the others.

Chertkov told me that the play was almost finished and

was due for publication in the summer, and that, by the request of Tolstoy, all his works were to be accessible, free of cost, to all who wished to publish them. To this I responded with the question: had Tolstoy any kind of material desires, which were now hard to realize because his works were to be published without compensation?

And I received an answer which I considered propitious. Yes, Tolstoy had made a promise to carry out a certain project for the benefit of the peasants at Yasnaya Polyana, for which a sum of several tens of thousands of rubles was necessary. He added that this problem would become the concern of himself and Alexandra Lvovna. Where were they to get the money?

I came forward with the proposal: 'Why not hold back the publication of the play until say about the middle of September and give me the rights to make the first production, after which all the other theatres would have the right to produce "The Living Corpse" without compensation? For this privilege I will pay, to start with, ten thousand rubles, and, after that, a permanent royalty of ten per cent, no matter how many performances the Art Theatre may give.'

When later my proposed conditions became known, many at first called me a squanderer. What? For the sake of producing the play somewhat earlier, to pay tens of thousands of rubles?

But I went yet further. The Small Theatre, through its representative, Yuzhin, announced a protest, to the effect that the oldest Russian theatre could not be treated like this in the matter of 'The Living Corpse', that it had the same right as we to work over the play. I acknowledged this right, with one reservation: that I would give the Small Theatre a copy of the play only a month before our *première*, which, by agreement with Chertkov, I scheduled for September 23. The month's grace allowed the Small Theatre was quite sufficient; I merely wished to prevent it producing the play before we did.

The Art Theatre, however, was so popular at this time, at such a height of its endeavour, that all possibility of a successful rivalry was excluded; hence the Small Theatre itself decided against the production. As the matter ended, after the Art Theatre's production in Moscow no other theatre ventured to put on 'The Living Corpse'.

My advantage did not cease here. It was a fine advertisement for us, you understand, because all the American newspapers published a despatch stating that there was a manuscript of a new, nearly finished play by Tolstoy, that it was in the hands of the Moscow Art Theatre, which had the sole right to produce it.

Finally, I arranged on the same conditions of ten per cent royalty for the production of the play in St. Petersburg. I went to St. Petersburg myself, and read the play to the directorate and the actors. In the summer I went to Paris, to arrange for a paid translation of the play into French, and possibly for its subsequent production.

The performance of 'The Living Corpse' was one of the most remarkable in the Art Theatre. It was by no means an exaggeration when a critic said that 'about this performance it would be necessary to write with a golden pen'.

This performance revealed that Tolstoyan element which was hidden in the organism of the Art Theatre. It is possible unmistakably to assert that this organic quality of the *col-*

lective of the Art Theatre reflected the passion of the famous Russian literature of the nineteenth century,—even including Dostoievsky, who later was so brilliantly revealed in our production of 'The Brothers Karamazov'. It was as if Dostoievsky were for the theatre a keener, more nervously wrought Tolstoy. The 'deposits' of the Tolstoyan world-perception were in the very womb of the training of our actors' *collective*. Even when the performance of 'The Three Sisters' was given, the production perhaps revealed a sense of Tolstoy more than of Chekhov. The spirit of the house of the Rostovs, Karenins, Volkonskys, Stcherbatskys, and Oblonskys seemed to have penetrated even here. The Tolstoyan nobility was brilliantly Great-Russian, Muscovite. And we knew it: the Sologubs, the Stcherbatovs, the Dolgorukys, the Stakhovitches. The spirit of 'Anna Karenina' and 'War and Peace' infected our artistic relation to it. 'Resurrection' made it clearer and enriched it, but accomplished nothing revolutionary.

The idealism of Tolstoy, his tender relation to the human being, his creative affection for many of his own characters, even for those toward whom he did not have a wholly positive attitude, his deep faith that in every human being there is, when all is said and done, something 'divine', his purely pagan love of existence—all this is evident; and there were also the quite elusive qualities of his genius which made the celebrated charm of Tolstoy, a charm that enveloped the whole world created by him with a peculiarly joyous light and warmth. It was here that the essential creative tastes of our theatre were formed. This helped us to accept Chekhov; at the same time it served to make the actor hostile to Strindberg, and left him in the end equally

[347]

cold to Ibsen, in spite of my great effort to graft that Northern giant on our theatre.

The rôle of Protasov, in which Moissi distinguished himself in both Europe and America, was played by Moskvin. His gifts did not very much accord with the type of the society Man; to compensate for this, he marvellously sensed the other aspect of the rôle: the gypsy spirit. Through the enchanting gypsy song, now poignantly amorous, now charged with the soul of the broad steppe; through the dissolute vagabondage; through the temperamental whirlwinds of happiness and sorrow, he immersed reality in tears and dreamed of a splendid freedom, which disrupted all the conditions of social existence, of dismal legality, of slavish order, of hypocrisy. Moskvin, as the phrase goes, bathed in the atmosphere of gypsy life and brought into it the 'delicacy' of the Tolstoyan relation to human beings.

Another brilliant interpreter of the Tolstoyan point of view was Germanova in the rôle of Liza. Even externally she was already extraordinarily attuned to the Tolystoyan conception of women. Her figure, eyes, tone, her whole manner, suggested Anna Karenina.

Behind the figure of Stanislavsky it was possible to recognize a whole series of Muscovite nobles, who, without the least conceit, preserved the spirit of aristocracy in all their relations, in simplicity, delicacy and . . . inertia—human beings noble-minded, charming, but incapable of human combat.

A splendid type of the same order, but of a much younger generation was Kachalov (Karenin). The Tolstoyan elements were well served by all the subordinate characters.

In general, it was a performance on a par with 'Tsar Fyodor', the plays of Chekhov, 'The Brothers Karamazov', 'Enough Stupidity in Every Wise Man'—which brings us the thought that the highest in art issues only from the womb of intense nationalism.

The actor has, at the hands of the author, assumed a character based on two main currents: living and theatrical. The living current may descend to 'everydayness', to petty, banal, naturalistic truth; and it may rise to synthesis, to great truth. A new current has broken into the actor's receptive centres—the socialistic current. The contemporary stage image is created out of a synthesis of these three elements——living, socialistic and theatrical.

On the threshold of new currents in the theatre, on the threshold of new social problems, in the transition to the creation of new images forming in the life of the Soviet Union, there is an increasing realization of the rupture between the Tolstoyan world-perception which I have described and the problems which inspire the actor of to-day.

INDEX

ABRAMOVA, dramatic company of, 35

Abrikosov, 305

Alekseiev-Stanislavsky. *See* Stanislavsky, Constantin Sergeievitch

Aleksey, Veselovsky-, 41

Alexander III, Emperor, 14; death of, 48, 49, 98, 99; commends 'New Undertaking', 40

Alexandrinsky Theatre, and Chekhov, 195

Alexandrov, in Berlin, 292

Alexandrovitch, Grand Duke Sergey, Governor-General of Moscow, 124–127; and Morozov, 131, 132; and 'Hannele', 178

'Anathema' (Andreiev), Art Theatre production of, 179–181

Andreiev, Leonid, and Nemirovitch-Dantchenko, 157, 158; his 'Anathema', 179–181; quoted, 205; his tastes unlike those of Art Theatre, 269

Andreieva, Maria Fyodorovna, 265; and Gorky, 258, 268

Art, Russian, stationary, 30, 31

Art-Accessible Theatre. *See* Moscow Art Theatre

Artem, in Berlin, 283, 295; in Prague, 302

Art Theatre. *See* Moscow Art Theatre

BALIEV, N. F., benefactor of Art Theatre, 268, 292–294

Baranov, in 'Smug Citizens', 240

Barnai, in Vienna, 311

Bauer, Ludwig, Viennese critic, on the Art Theatre, 309, 310

Bauman, funeral of, 260

'Bear, The' (Chekhov), 11

Bellgard, and 'Anathema', 179, 180

Benois, Alexander Nikolaievitch, 272

Black Hundreds, 261, 263

Blaramberg, composer, 170

Blaramberg-Chernova, Minna, wife of Skirmunt, 242

Boborikin, Piotr Dmitrievitch, his opinion of Chekhov, 5; his stagecraft, 101, 102; and Goreva, 116

Brisson, Alexander, 315

'Brothers Karamazov, The' (Dostoievsky), 270–272

Budilnik, 7

Burdzhalov, G. S., 260; in Berlin, 290

CHALIAPIN, 80; and Gorky, 234, 235

'Chekhonte.' *See* Chekhov, Anton

Chekhov, Anton, and Nemirovitch-Dantchenko, 3, 4; 'the man of great promise', 4, 5; his literary gifts acknowledged, 5, 6; the playwright, 6, 7; his opinion of Goltzev, 8; description of, 9, 10; his 'Ivanov', 10, 11, 14; his family, 15, 16; his early poverty, 16–18; 'champion of freedom', 18; his attitude toward the drama, 18–23; on young writers, 32; a physician, 32, 33; his social relations, 33, 34; success with women, 34; his 'Wood Demon', 35; and Society of Playwrights controversy, 50, 51; and Yuzhin, 53, 54; and the *Russkaya Misl*, 60–61; and Suvorin, 61–65; moves to

A CHRONOLOGY OF THE LIFE OF
VLADIMIR NEMIROVITCH-DANTCHENKO

1858   Born December 11 in the Caucasus, near Poti. His father was a Ukrainian in the Russian army, his mother was Armenian.

1863   After the death of his father, he lived with his mother, three brothers and a sister, near Tiflis. His older brother was to become a well known writer. One brother and his sister went on the stage. The third brother died.

1867   At the age of nine he lived opposite the Tiflis summer theatre then being built. "All my games were centered there." Watched actors through scaffolding; played "rehearsal"; read voraciously.

1871   Wrote a play of five acts, also a vaudeville sketch and a drama in verse.

1873   Wrote an historical novel which was published in the Tiflis school magazine which he edited.

1874   With his mother went frequently to concerts and the local opera; in summer was tutor in the household of a stage director where he met actors; was allowed to go backstage, witnessed rehearsals.

1876   Graduated from Tiflis Gymnasium, writing a final paper on Pushkin and Gogol; entered Moscow University.

1877   Met Turgenev at a literary society; during his summer holidays he returned to Tiflis where he acted; later was active with an amateur group in Moscow; published article entitled *"Our Provincial Theatres"*; after which constantly wrote drama criticism, and also general articles about the theatre.

1882   A play by Nemirovitch-Dantchenko was produced at the Maly Theatre in Moscow in October and a second (*Our*

Americans) two months later. This was the beginning of frequent productions of his plays in Moscow and elsewhere in Russia.

1886   Married in August to Baroness Ekaterina Korf, daughter of a distinguished scholar; began publishing novels and short stories; continued to write plays.

1888   Met and soon became a close friend of Anton Chekhov.

1891   Met Tchaikovsky and was asked by him to write the libretto for an opera; began to teach acting at the Philharmonic Institute.

1892   Stanislavsky, with actors from the Maly Theatre, acted in *The Lucky Man* by Nemirovitch-Dantchenko; N.-M. witnessed a performance by Sergey Rakhmaninov's *Aleko* for which he had written the libretto.

1897   Continued to teach at the Philharmonic Institute, where his best pupils included Olga Knipper, Maria Savitskaya, Ivan Moskvin, and Vsevolod Meyerhold, all of whom were later to be members of the Moscow Art Theatre Company. Nemirovitch-Dantchenko held the famous eighteen-hour conversation with Stanislavsky in the Slavyansky Bazaar Restaurant which resulted in their founding the Moscow Art Theatre together.

1898   On October 28th the first production of the Moscow Art Theatre opened. It was *Tsar Fyodor* by A. Tolstoy and was followed eight weeks later by the successful production of Chekhov's *The Sea Gull*.

1899   Chekhov's *Uncle Vanya* staged by Stanislavsky and V. V. Luzhsky.

1900   Nemirovitch-Dantchenko and Stanislavsky took the Moscow Art Theatre to the Crimea to play for Chekhov who was too ill to come to Moscow. Nemirovitch-Dantchenko directed Ibsen's *When We Dead Awaken*.

1901   Nemirovitch-Dantchenko took over from Stanislavsky the last three weeks of rehearsals of *The Three Sisters* which opened January 31.

1902   *The Lower Depths* of Maxim Gorky was jointly directed by Nemirovitch-Dantchenko and Stanislavsky.

1903   Nemirovitch-Dantchenko directed Ibsen's *Pillars of Society*, and Shakespeare's *Julius Caesar*. His determination despite all opposition to found a Moscow Art Theatre School was vindicated by the success of a student production. Now he had 140 applicants for six places in the school.

1904   Directed Chekhov's *The Cherry Orchard* jointly with Stanislavsky; Chekhov died in July in Germany. Break with Gorky. Nemirovitch-Dantchenko directed *Ivanov*.

1905   The breach with Gorky was healed by the Moscow Art Theatre production of his *Children of the Sun*, which was planned by Stanislavsky and directed by Nemirovitch-Dantchenko; but Gorky continued to disapprove of many of the Art Theatre projects, particularly the Dostoievsky ones.

1906   On tour with the Art Theatre; Nemirovitch-Dantchenko met all the leading writers and theatre people in Berlin, Prague, etc. He directed, with Stanislavsky, Griboyedov's *Sorrow from Wit* and directed Ibsen's *Brand* with V. V. Luzhsky as his assistant.

1907   Directed (with V. V. Luzhsky) Pushkin's *Boris Godunov*.

1908   Directed Ibsen's *Rosmersholm*; helped Stanislavsky with rehearsals of *The Blue Bird* of Maeterlinck. This play opened in late September, and was followed by Gogol's *Inspector General*, jointly directed by the two heads of the Moscow Art Theatre.

1909   Unanimously elected president of All Russia Congress of Stage Directors; directed Knut Hamsun's *At the Gates of the Kingdom*; directed Leonid Andreiev's *Anathema*; cut Turgenev's play *A Month in the Country* at Stanislavsky's request for production by the Art Theatre; it opened in December.

1910   Began work on dramatizing scenes from Dostoievsky's *The Brothers Karamazov*, to be acted by the Art Theatre; expressed great enthusiasm for Yushkevitch's *Miserere:* "It has the enchantment of talent. It is original, elegaic, and beautiful . . . a great lyric quality." He directed it late in the year, just a little over two months after *The Brothers Karamazov* had opened. In writing to Madame

Lilina, Stanislavsky's wife, he said: "I believe that the way I am working on the Karamazov play brings the actors very close to Stanislavsky's theories. . . . This I am doing with conviction and in all sincerity." After the performance of the second half of the play Stanislavsky wrote him: "I salute your directorial genius, your Napoleonic ingenuity and energy. I admire, am proud of, and love you with all my heart." When *Miserere* opened, it was received by many as a "dramatized funeral for the revolution of 1905." Death of Leo Tolstoy; a non-religious memorial service held in the Art Theatre.

1911   As soon as Knut Hamsun's *In the Claws of Life* opened in late February, preparations were started for the production of Leo Tolstoy's *The Living Corpse* which opened in late September under the direction of both Stanislavsky and Nemirovitch-Dantchenko. The next production was *Hamlet* with the scenery of Gordon Craig. The major part of the directing was in the hands of Stanislavsky, assisted by Sulerdzhitsky, but Nemirovitch-Dantchenko also participated.

1912   Two Turgenev plays were followed by Ibsen's *Peer Gynt*, of which Nemirovitch-Dantchenko was the principal director. He also directed a drama by Leonid Andreiev, *Ekaterina Ivanovna*.

1913   Except for a one-act Molière play (as a curtain raiser for *The Imaginary Invalid* directed by Stanislavsky) Nemirovitch-Dantchenko did not direct any plays until October when he did *Nikolai Stavrogin* based on *The Possessed* of Dostoievsky.

1914-   The outbreak of World War I disrupted the repertory
1915   and personnel of the Art Theatre. At this time Nemirovitch-Dantchenko felt "much younger" than his actual age. He wrote to his wife of "being carried away" by his enthusiasms, by his idealization of events and people. Gorky writes that despite disagreements with Nemirovitch-Dantchenko he respects him, to which Nemirovitch-Dantchenko responded with characteristic cordiality.

1918-   With the confusion arising from the Bolshevik seizing
1920   of power the Art Theatre marked time, played old pro-

ductions like *The Blue Bird* and *The Three Sisters* to full houses despite the fact that street fighting caused occasional delays. Nemirovitch-Dantchenko staged operas at The Bolshoy Theatre. Half of the principal actors of the Art Theatre were stranded "abroad" when their touring company was cut off by Denikin's White Army in the Ukraine. Since a number of the younger remaining actors sang well, Nemirovitch-Dantchenko conceived the daring and original idea of a Musical Studio, in which trained actors from the Art Theatre could bring new qualities and methods to light opera. The first given by the Musical Studio was *The Daughter of Madame Angot*.

1922-
1924   The main company of the Art Theatre left for a tour of Europe and America which was to keep them away from Moscow for two seasons. In their absence Nemirovitch-Dantchenko produced *La Perichole* of Offenbach and *Lysistrata* of Aristophanes with music by Glière, and began work on his version of *Carmen* which was renamed *Carmencita and the Soldier*. He remained in close touch with all the Studios of the Art Theatre. He wrote: "There are not enough hours in a day. I must do with less sleep." His *Carmencita* opened to enormous acclaim in June 1924.

1925   The next important production directed by Nemirovitch-Dantchenko was an historical play by Trenev about Pugatchov and the peasant uprising he led in the eighteenth century. According to some reviews this was a turning point in the history of the Art Theatre bringing it into closer touch with contemporary life in Soviet Russia.

1926   Nemirovitch-Dantchenko brought his Musical Studio to New York in December; it was received with great enthusiasm. At the end of the season he decided to spend a year in America studying the technique of making moving pictures. As always his wife was with him.

1928-
1929   When he returned to Moscow his Musical Studio gave a concert in his honor; and he made the unequivocal statement that only in the Art Theatre could he do creative work. The first production he took an active part in was *The Squaring of the Circle* by Katayev; this was

followed by a contemporary play, *The Blockade* by V. Ivanov, and *Uncle's Dream* based on a story by Dostoievsky. Nemirovitch-Dantchenko was deeply disturbed by Stanislavsky's heart attack during the celebrations of the thirtieth anniversary of the Art Theatre; he wrote him a long and warmly affectionate letter of encouragement and reassurance.

1931   His production of *Resurrection*, a series of scenes based on Tolstoy's novel, was greeted as an entirely new form of theatre. He also supervised *Chicago* by M. Watkins and staged *Three Fat Men* by Olesha.

1931-   Illness; travel abroad for health reasons; preoccupation
1934   with writing *My Life in the Russian Theatre*. While in Italy he was much gratified by a very warm reception of his play *The Price of Life*. Duse had told him that the Italians would never tolerate the pauses, the tempo of Russian plays. "How wrong she was!" said he, after the noisy ovation he received in Turin. On his return he supervised the production of Gorky's *Egor Bulitchov*. At the end of 1934 he directed Ostrovsky's *The Storm*.

1935-   After staging (with M. Kedrov) Gorky's play *Enemies*,
1936   he began work on a dramatization of *Anna Karenina* which he had had in mind for a long time. He took a hand in rehearsing Bulgakov's play *Molière*, and he directed a contemporary play together with Sudakov which had its premiere at the very end of 1936. It was called *Lyubov Yarovaya*.

1937   The much-acclaimed opening of *Anna Karenina* jointly directed by Nemirovitch-Dantchenko and V. Sakhnovsky was in April, while concurrently he was rehearsing Offenbach's *La Belle Hélène* in his Musical Studio. He regretted that he no longer wrote plays: "All that had seemed infinitely complicated and endlessly tangled forty years ago now seems so clear, so simple and above all so possible of realization."

1938   After the death of his wife, Nemirovitch-Dantchenko was ill and remained absent from the theatre for months. He went abroad for his health in July but returned at the time of Stanislavsky's death in early August. In speaking

[364]

at the grave of Stanislavsky he said: "My memory is so full of all we went through together during the 41 years of our association . . . that this is no time for oratory. . . . There is only one thing I would ask of you here, my comrades in the Art Theatre, that you will vow you will maintain the attitude towards the Theatre, the profound sense of self-sacrifice, that was Stanislavsky's." He plunged again into the work on *Sorrow from Wit*, saying he had received such an overwhelming number of wishes for his recovery that he felt he was perhaps still needed. Leonidov wrote: "He wept when he spoke to the company about beginning the season without Stanislavsky. But he gave a buoyant speech and said; 'Looking at you, I can feel that the Theatre is still alive.'"

1940-1942 Nemirovitch-Dantchenko was preoccupied with restaging old plays in the repertory but, as Kachalov wrote to his son: "He has all kinds of new plans." He discussed a production of *King Lear*, one of *Antony and Cleopatra*. When he was too ill to come to the Theatre, the actors rehearsed in his home. He also continued work with his Musical Studio which was merged, in 1941, with Stanislavsky's Opera Theatre.

1943 He was well enough to conduct rehearsals of *The Last Days*, a play which interested him much, about the death of Pushkin in which the poet never appears. On April 18 he appeared to be in pain, but on recalling a rehearsal earlier that day he became elated and exclaimed, "How good to be alive! Just that; it's so good to be alive." After attending a performance of *Swan Lake* at the Bolshoy Theatre on April 20, he had a heart attack and was taken to the Kremlin Hospital where he died five days later, on April 25.

Elizabeth Reynolds Hapgood.
1967

4